THE

Sealed Book of Daniel opened.

"Take the little book which is open in the hand of the angel, and eat it up."—REV. x. 8, 9.

For the word of God is "the joy and rejoicing of the heart."—JER. xv. 16.

God's sacred book is opened now,
Hear it, O Earth, and humbly bow.
The seals are loosed, its truths disclosed.
It triumphs now above its foes.
It points to an immortal day,
And guides us on the heavenly way.
Were all the gems of earth our own,
We'd part with all for this alone.
Thus, leaving transient things so vain,—
Yes, leaving all our home to gain,—
We'll take this volume for our guide
And firmly by its truths abide.
For by its holy, solemn awe,
By its divine, celestial law,
The word of God, we know it now,
Of him who bled on Calvary's brow;
Of him who, in the jubilee,
Will come to set his captives free.
In that great year of his release,
We'll soar above to dwell in peace.

OUR

Bible Chronology Established.

THE

SEALED BOOK OF DANIEL OPENED;

OR,

A BOOK OF REFERENCE

FOR

THOSE WHO WISH TO EXAMINE

THE

"SURE WORD OF PROPHECY."

BY

WILLIAM C. THURMAN.

"Understand, O son of man: for at the time . . . appointed the end shall be."—DAN. viii. 17, 19.

"Write the vision, and make it plain upon tables, that he may run that readeth it; . . because it will surely come, it will not tarry."—HAB. ii. 2, 3.

PUBLISHED BY JOHN GOODYEAR,
N.W. CORNER OF SEVENTEENTH AND PINE STREETS,
PHILADELPHIA.
1864.

TO THE READER.

In obedience to the precept of Heaven, that we "consider the vision" (Dan. ix. 23), the author, having for seven years been searching the Scriptures, prying into the chronological order of the holy oracles of God, and making astronomical calculations extending through more than six thousand years, to ascertain the truth, can, with confidence, offer this work to the public as worthy of the most serious and prayerful attention of every lover of truth; for, though we may differ in opinion as to prophetic dates and the time of the second coming of our blessed Lord, every intelligent man, who will take the trouble to examine for himself, must admit that if those dates, as found in our Hebrew Bible, can be credited, we have at least settled the long-disputed question as to the age of our world, and ESTABLISHED THE CORRECT CHRONOLOGY of our Bible. This alone claims for this work a place in every library. But that which appears unto the author, at least, to make this work of so much real worth, and worthy of the strictest investigation, is that he can by his own experience with confidence say that no man with a well-balanced mind, open to conviction,—no, not even the most confirmed infidel, atheist, or deist,—can make himself master of its contents without being compelled to admit that Jesus is the Christ, the Son of the living God; and those who in sincerity and truth really "love the appearing" of our Lord, are taught with holy, solemn awe to listen to the admonition of Christ: "Look up and lift up your heads;" yea, rejoice; "for your redemption draweth nigh." (Luke xxi. 28.)

PREFACE.

HAVING, through the light of astronomy, examined those unerring records of God's celestial calendar, as given "For a declaration of times and a sign of the world" (Ecclesiasticus xliii. 6), and thus discovered the truth as to the correct chronology of our Bible, which removes the seal and opens the book of Daniel, my object in this work is to "Write the vision and make it plain upon tables" (Hab. ii. 2); to disclose that portion of the "sure word of prophecy" (2 Pet. i. 19) which was "shut up and sealed till the time of the end" (Dan. xii. 4, 9); and prepare a book of reference for the convenience of those who, calling no man "father upon earth" (Matt. xxiii. 9), wish to act the more noble part in that they examine for themselves and "search the scriptures daily as to whether those things are so." (Acts xvii. 11.)

Those who will take the trouble to notice the connection in which each reference is found, and so ponder the subject at issue as to have an understanding of the matter, will find the Bible a new book,—or a new and rich theme issuing from its exhaustless fount on which the soul delights to feast.

In that "book" which, being "shut up," was handed down to us both "closed up and sealed" (Dan. xii. 4, 9), we now read that which is truly sublime; for its sacred truths are now unfurled, and "THE WISE SHALL UNDERSTAND." (Dan. xii. 10.)

Upon the page of this newly-opened book we discover a new internal evidence of the divine inspiration of our Bible,—a clear and positive demonstration of its heavenly origin, which, having been concealed under the heavy seal that closed the book of Daniel, had never before been seen. But the truth-testing powers of astronomy having removed the seal and opened the book, that all important question,—"Is the Bible the book of God?" is ANSWERED NOW; or, at least, the author, who was not only a deist, but even doubted the existence of a God, can now truly say—not that "I believe," but—"I KNOW that my Redeemer liveth, and that he shall stand at the latter day upon the earth." (Job xix. 25.)

If, ceasing to be drifted on with the current of popular opinion, man would only suffer wisdom—the more noble faculty of the soul—to speak; would let reason and the weight of evidence govern and control the mind, then—as darkness is dispelled by the rising sun—infidelity would vanish, and the earth be lighted up by those brilliant rays now beaming forth from the sacred page of this newly-opened book; the church renouncing the doctrine and traditions of men, would put on her celestial robe of righteousness,—even that of obedience to Christ; and thus mirror forth the loveliness of the gospel plan of salvation.

But, alas! the prejudice even of the deist is not so impervious to the light of truth, as that of those whose god is the custom of the age in which they live, and whose faith is but an assent to the religion of their fathers. But since those newly developed truths, which have not yet appeared to the world, have already been instrumental in the salvation of one for whom Christ died, may we not be encouraged to raise the light, to send the newly-opened book to earth's remotest bound; for, though none of the wicked shall understand, the authorities of heaven declare "THE WISE SHALL UNDERSTAND."

INTRODUCTION.

THOSE who wish to understand the book of Daniel must bear in mind the two prominent points as presented in that book:—

First. That it was to be sealed up until the time of the end.

Second. At the time of the end "THE WISE SHALL UNDERSTAND."

From the first declaration, we learn that, until the time of the end, this book cannot be understood. Who can read a letter until the seal is broken? If "no man in heaven, nor in earth, neither under the earth, was able to open the book" before the seals were loosed (Rev. v. 3), we cannot expect to gather information concerning the vision of Daniel from the writings of those who lived before the time of the end. Indeed, what they have written concerning the matter, has only vailed in obscurity those rich and sublime truths as found in the book of Daniel. For example:

The Jews commenced the seventy weeks of Daniel (ix. 24) with the ruin of the first temple by Nebuchadnezzar, and extended them to the destruction of the second by Titus. The "seven weeks," they say, is forty-nine years, commencing at the going forth of the commandment by Cyrus, and reaching to the second year of Darius; and by the expression, "anoint the Most Holy," they understand that the King of Persia should become great so as to build Jerusalem.

A. C. McLaughlin extends the seventy weeks to the year A.D. 87, which is seventeen years after the destruction of Jerusalem.

Though Daniel informs us that the sixty-nine weeks are to be commenced at the going forth of the commandment to restore and build Jerusalem (Dan. ix. 25), the learned Bishop Usher commences them at the twentieth of Artaxerxes. Had Daniel not informed us that these things were sealed up and closed until the time of the end, we would feel truly astonished at the bishop—who has exhibited so much learning on other subjects—thus commencing them eighty-three years after the commandment to restore and build Jerusalem had gone forth, and many years after Jerusalem had been built (Ezra iv. 12), and at a time when there was no commandment given to build it, but merely a favor granted Nehemiah (ii. 4),—which was the privilege of building the wall that enclosed Jerusalem; and, so far from Nehemiah having been commanded by the king to do this, it seems to have been with fear and trembling that he made his desire known. (Neh. ii. 2.)

Scalinger commences these sixty-nine weeks at the second year of Darius Northus. This makes Ezra, who went up in the seventh of Artaxerxes, not less than two hundred and eight years old at the seventh of the next Artaxerxes: for we are told that he was the son of Seraiah (Ezra vii. 1), who was slain at the destruction of Jerusalem. (2 Kings xxv. 18.)

As merely to mention the above views sufficiently exposes their absurdity, we will not intrude upon the patience of the reader by going into an examination of them. But the most popular opinion, or that most generally received, is that of Prideaux, who commences them at the seventh of Artaxerxes.

The reader is already aware that the sixty-nine weeks are to be commenced "from the going forth of the commandment to restore and to build Jerusalem." Now, turn to the seventh chapter of Ezra, and you will find that no commandment was given at that time to build Jerusalem. By referring to Chap. iv. 12, you will see that Jerusalem was builded by virtue of the commandment given by Cyrus; then turn to Haggai i. 4, and it will be found that the Jews were dwelling in "ceiled houses" as early as the second year of Darius. But Prideaux admits, both that there was no commandment given in the seventh of Artaxerxes to build Jerusalem, and that the commandment which was given by Cyrus was properly the literal one to restore and build Jerusalem; and the only objection that either he or any one else has to commencing them with the commandment in the first year of Cyrus, is, that according to the chronology as established by Ptolemy, they will not, if commenced there, reach the nativity of Christ. So he is not willingly, but unavoidably driven to the necessity of taking the expression "restore and build Jerusalem," in a figurative sense. But all that is necessary to rescue this from his hands, and show that it can be commenced nowhere else but at the first of Cyrus, is to show that it cannot be taken in a figurative sense. To do this, let us first call to mind that the Jews were really in possession of a city, which they called Jerusalem. This city was literally destroyed by Nebuchadnezzar, and the Jews carried to Babylon. Jeremiah had prophesied that they were to remain there, subject to the king, seventy years; at the end of which time they were to return to their own land, and build Jerusalem again.

Near the end of this seventy years, Daniel was engaged in prayer,—not only for his people, but also for the literal city of Jerusalem, which was then lying waste (Dan. ix. 16); and, while thus pouring forth his soul in prayer, he was informed that Jerusalem was not only to be built again, but to be destroyed the second time (ix. 27)—which all admit to be a literal destruction—by Titus. "From the going forth of the commandment to restore and to build" this same Jerusalem, Daniel was informed that the sixty-nine weeks were to be commenced (ix. 25); and, as if to make it impossible to be taken in a figurative sense, the angel even mentioned the streets, and the wall that surrounds it. (ix. 25.) If this can be taken in a figurative sense, we may as well say the whole Bible is to be taken thus, and that there is nothing literal in it.

But, for the sake of argument, suppose we depart from the universal rule for explaining not only the Bible, but all other books; and admit that, instead of commencing the sixty-nine weeks at the going forth of the proper edict to restore and build Jerusalem, they may be commenced at the building up, or, as Isaac Newton has it, from the time they "again became a people after their captivity."

Now, we ask, What constituted them a people? Was it not the full privilege of observing their own laws in their own land? and, if so, did they not properly become a people again when, in the seventh month, in the second year of Cyrus, they commenced observing all things according to the law of Moses? (Ezra iii. 1–7.) And if the sixty-nine weeks are to be commenced at the time the Jews again became a people, does not reason say they ought to be commenced from the first period at which they, after the seventy years captivity, again became a people, and was not their restoration under Cyrus the first and most noted period of their becoming a people?

There is nothing in the seventh chapter of Ezra that does so clearly show that they did then become a people; but, even if it was yet more clear that they became a people in the seventh year of Artaxerxes than in the second of Cyrus, what right have we to commence the sixty-nine weeks seventy-nine years after they had properly become a people? Jeremiah informs us that the captivity was to continue seventy years (Jer. xxix. 10); but if the Jews did not become a people till the seventh of Artaxerxes, then the captivity continued one hundred and forty-nine years. If the angel had in so many words said, "The sixty-nine weeks are to be commenced at the seventh of Artaxerxes," they could not be commenced there so as to make sense: for it is said that they were to reach the coming of "the Messiah—the Prince,"—"which to be interpreted is the Christ" (John i. 49); and yet, if commenced at the seventh year of Artaxerxes, they overshoot the date of his appearance on earth by thirty years. To obviate this difficulty, it has been supposed that they ought to reach the time of his baptism,—making this the time at which the Messiah came,—forgetting that Paul had said, "When the fullness of the time was come, God sent forth his Son, made of a woman" (Gal. iv. 4),—not of water.

For Christ to become the complete and perfect Messiah, so as to fulfill the whole law, it was not only necessary for him to come into the world and die; but he must be made under the law. What placed him under the law,—his baptism, or his birth? It was also necessary for him to have a corporeal body. (Heb. x. 5.) Which gave him this body,—his baptism, or his birth?

Had the angel informed Daniel that the sixty-nine weeks were to reach unto his baptism, we would extend them there. But since he says, emphatically, to "the Messiah the Prince," it would be a violation of all rules for understanding the meaning of authors to say they ought to reach thirty years beyond the time of his actual coming,—at which time he was declared to be the Saviour, the Christ, the Lord. (Luke ii. 11.) The prophets, in speaking of his coming, always point to his birth, thus: "Unto us a child is born, unto us a son is given." (Isa. ix. 6.) The next period of time, as given by the angel to Daniel, was the sixty-two weeks, at the end of which the Messiah was to be cut off. By reference to Daniel ix. 26., it will be observed that the sixty-two weeks are not to be commenced with the sixty-nine, at the going forth of the commandment, but "after" the completion of the walls. Now, turn to Nehemiah vi. 15, and you will find the particular time at which the walls were completed,—from which completion the sixty-two weeks are to be dated; and this being in the thirty-second year (Neh. xiii. 6) of the same king in whose seventh year Ezra went up, it is only twenty-five years later than the first date. Now, add twenty-five to the sixty-two weeks, or four hundred and thirty-four years, and we have four hundred and fifty-nine; then subtract this from the sixty-nine weeks, or four hundred and eighty-three years, and we have twenty-four. Thus, it places the date at which the Messiah was to be "cut off" twenty-four years before the time of his appearing on earth.

To obviate this difficulty, Prideaux goes back to the twenty-fifth verse, and takes out the seven weeks which he has already used once, and, as regardless of the testimony both of Nehemiah and Josephus, supposes that Ezra and Nehemiah were forty-nine years from the seventh of Artaxerxes in reforming the Jewish State. Since this would make Ezra at least one hundred and eighty years old at that time, he rejects the reading in Ezra vii. 1, where he is said to be the son of Seraiah, or at least supposes that it might be so construed as to mean only a descendant in the line of Seraiah. But, after all this straining of points and contradicting of authors, the difficulty is not in the least removed; for the angel did not say that the sixty-two weeks were to be commenced from the complete restoration of the Jewish polity: but "after" the completion of the walls, which were to be built in troublesome times. So, even if history had testified to the fact that Ezra and Nehemiah were forty-nine years employed in reforming the Jewish State, we would yet, by the express language of the angel to Daniel, be restricted to the completion of the walls for the commencement of the sixty-two weeks. But suppose the angel had said the sixty-two weeks were to be commenced at the end of forty-nine years: it would not make sense; for it would cut the Messiah off the same day he appeared on earth. To avoid this difficulty, the date of his coming is extended to his baptism instead of his birth. Even then they cut him off the same day of his baptism,—leaving no time for his ministry; and, to obviate this, Prideaux slips down to ver. 27, and borrows the one-week covenant which was to be confirmed by the prince, whose people was to come and destroy the city. This one week he places at the end of the sixty-two weeks; and then, in spite of the testimony both of the fathers and of the chronology as given in the gospel of John, makes the ministry of Christ seven years. Instead of borrowing the seven years from the Prince of Rome, and placing it here for the ministry of Christ, why not go to the Mosaic law and get the four days in which the lamb was to be kept up (Ex. xii. 6), and place that here, making his ministry four years,—for it would be much more plausible. Prideaux observes that the angel did not say that the Messiah was to be cut off the very day, but only says that he should be cut off after sixty-two weeks, which expression he thinks will admit of a time seven years after. Unreasonable as this appears to be, it is the only point in his whole scheme that has even the appearance of plausibility. Others, observing that the ministry of Christ could not have continued as long as seven years, split the one week in half, making the ministry of Christ three years and a-half; and prove it by the expression, "in the midst of the week the sacrifice and oblation shall cease;" and as this draws the sixty-two weeks within three years and a-half of the time of the cutting off of the Messiah, it appears more plausible than for them to fall short by seven years. But what is the meaning of the words "sacrifice and oblation?"—the death of a person, or the sacrifice of the Jews under the Mosaic dispensation? And will any one familiar with the history of the Jews, pretend to say that their sacrifices and oblations ceased before the commencement of the seven-years war, in which the city was destroyed?

But it is urged that the Jewish sacrifices typified Christ, and that in this sense they ceased at his death. This would appear plausible but for the fact that Daniel does not say so. He says nothing about the Jewish types and shadows reaching their antitype, but emphatically "the sacrifice and oblation shall cease." Neither is the one-week covenant placed at the time of the cutting off of the Messiah, but down at the time of the war in ver. 27.

In order to settle this question, if the reader will examine ver. 26, he will observe that the particular personage who was to cause the sacrifice and oblation to cease, was the prince whose people should come and destroy the city,—which was the prince of Rome, or antichrist, for it was the Romans that did destroy this city: and that this prince did cause the sacrifice to cease, history declares to be a matter of fact. (See Josephus.)

The definitive adjective "the" shows that Daniel already knew that this prince was to come. Had he not been before informed of this, instead of the angel's using the article "the," he ought to have said, a prince that shall come: and by reference to Chap. viii. we learn what prince it was of whose coming Daniel had before been informed. In this chapter we observe that three different kingdoms were to exercise power over the Jews: 1, Persia; 2, Greece; but since God in his wisdom thought proper to seal up the book of Daniel until the time of the end, the name of the third is not given. Therefore the angel, in explaining to Daniel who it was that should destroy the city, and cause the sacrifice and oblation to cease, called him by no other name than "the prince that shall come."

The expression "the covenant," supposes a particular covenant already existing; and that particular covenant made with the Jews through the mediation of Moses was this;—a blessing if they obeyed the commandment of the Lord their God: but a curse if they did not obey. (Deut. xi. 26.) The blessing was proclaimed upon Mount Gerizim, and the curse upon Mount Ebal. (Deut. xi. 29.) This covenant being signed and sealed by God, who cannot lie, on the one part (Ezek. xvi. 8), and all of the Jewish nation on the other (Deut. xxvii. 26), the God of heaven, through virtue of this covenant, was as solemnly and firmly bound to pour out a curse upon them if they did not obey, as he was to bestow a blessing if they did obey. So all that is necessary to decide the question as to what this covenant was,—whether the threatened curse, or the promised blessing,—is to ascertain the fact as to whether they did obey. As the man Gabriel tells us that only seventy weeks were allotted them for their existence as a people, the natural inference is that they had transgressed. But, says Daniel, they had transgressed; "yea, all Israel have transgressed." (Daniel ix. 11.) This settles the question. And now observe, that while God is bound, by virtue of this covenant, either to bestow on them a blessing, or pour out upon them a curse,—he swears, in his wrath, they shall not enter into his rest. (Heb. iii. 11.) So it is now clear, that by the expression, "confirm the covenant," we are here to understand the outpouring of a curse, and not a blessing; and this is the way that Daniel understood it, for he says, in ver. 11, "Therefore the curse is poured out upon us, and the oath that is written in the law of Moses, the servant of God, because we have sinned against him." And in ver. 12 he uses almost the same words that the angel does in ver. 27. Let us compare them. *Daniel:* "And he hath confirmed his words." *Angel:* "And he" (antichrist) "shall confirm the covenant."

As the King of Babylon was the minister of God in "confirming his word" at the time to which Daniel had reference, so at the time to which the man Gabriel had reference the prince of Rome was "the minister of God, a revenger, to execute wrath upon" those who had broken the holy covenant. (Rom. xiii. 4.) So the word of God, which he spoke through Moses, saying, "I will bring a sword upon you that shall avenge the quarrel of my covenant," "and will punish you yet seven times for your sins" (Levit. xxvi. 24, 25), was accomplished during the seven years' war at Jerusalem.

If it yet be urged that Christ was to confirm this covenant, we ask, in the name of all that is reasonable, *First,* What covenant did he confirm? *Second,* How could he confirm any covenant seven years, if, as our divines tell us, he was cut off in the midst of the week? It could not have been the Mosaic; for those who contend that the Messiah confirmed this covenant, say that ending at his death is what we are to understand by the expression, "the sacrifice and oblation" should cease. Surely, it could not have been the new covenant of the gospel dispensation, if that did not commence until the Day of Pentecost; for this was fifty days after the crucifixion and eight days after Christ had left the world.

That the new covenant of the gospel dispensation did not commence until the Day of Pentecost, observe that the law was to go forth from Zion or Jerusalem (Isa. ii. 3), while the ministry of Christ commenced in Galilee. (Acts x. 37.) The blessing of the new covenant was this: "I will put my laws in their minds, and write them in their hearts." (Heb. viii. 10.) "Not by might nor power, but by my Spirit, saith the Lord of hosts;" and yet the Holy Spirit was not poured out until the Day of Pentecost. (John xvi. 7.) So if, as we are told, Christ was cut off in the midst of the week, we are not only compelled to blend two covenants into one to make out the full week, but have to leave one half of it to be confirmed either by the apostles or some one else. It is generally believed by our divines that the apostles accomplished the confirmation of the latter half; but as all admit that their ministry continued over three years and a half, we are unable to see how they can make any sense of it.

Some split the week in half, and say that Christ only confirmed one-half of it, and that the other half was confirmed by the Romans, at the destruction of Jerusalem forty years after. According to this view of it, one-half of it was to be a covenant of grace, confirmed by the Son of God; and the other half a covenant of wrath, poured out upon the Jews: and these two halves put together make up what Daniel calls, THE covenant which THE prince was to confirm.

If this be the right construction of it, we will no more blame those who say that prophecy is unintelligible until fulfilled; for we are sure we never would have thought of this idea until after it was proven by history to be what the prophet meant. But of all the gross absurdities ever written on this subject, that of Dr. Hales takes the lead. He, commencing the sixty-nine weeks in the year B.C. 420, ends them at the time the Roman army entered Jerusalem, in the year A. D. 65,—as if by the expressions "Messiah, the Prince," "the man Gabriel" meant the Roman army. And yet he admits that where the same heavenly messenger did, at the same time, in the twenty-fourth verse of the same chapter, use the same expression, he means the Christ. And reckoning the sixty-two weeks from the same epoch, he ends them in the year A.D. 14, which wants seventeen years to reach the year A.D. 31, at which time he says the Messiah was cut off. Dr. Clarke has displayed more wisdom in a few words on this subject than any other writer we have examined. He says: "The reason why these prophecies are at present so imperfectly understood, is that God has sealed them up: we must wait till the time of the end." (See on Dan. xii. 9, 10.)

The fact that our learned divines—who, possessing gigantic minds, have displayed so much wisdom and learning on other subjects—fall into such gross absurdities whenever they meddle with the book of Daniel, is an additional evidence to us of the truthfulness of our religion: for it confirms and establishes the fact that the book of Daniel was a sealed book. But it is supposed to be "perfect foolishness" to say a book was sealed up which the Church has been reading for more than two thousand years. To this we reply: "God has chosen the foolish things of this world to confound the wise." (1 Cor. i. 27.)

We will now examine the second proposition, which is this: At the time of the end this book is to be understood. In Daniel x. 14, it is expressly said, "I am come to make thee understand what shall befall thy people in the latter days: for yet the vision is for many days." What language do we want more expressive than this? Now turn to Daniel xii. 4, and, after observing that these things were to be sealed up until the time of the end, ask yourselves,—If these things be not understood when that time shall have arrived, how can this portion at least of the book of Daniel ever be of any worth? And yet you dare not say that any portion of God's word has been given in vain. We will now read vers. 8, 9, 10: "And I heard, but I understood not: then said I, O my Lord, what shall be the end of these things? And he said, Go thy way, Daniel, for the words are closed up and sealed till the time of the end. Many shall be purified, and made white, and tried; but the wicked shall do wickedly: and none of the wicked shall understand; BUT THE WISE SHALL UNDERSTAND." Therefore, all that remains to decide whether this book can now be understood, is to settle the point as to whether the time of the end has yet come; and, to do so, it now becomes necessary to examine the signs of the times. If we are not living in the time of the end, it is useless to meddle with the book of Daniel; for, as sure as it is the book of God, it cannot be understood "until the time of the end."

SIGNS OF THE TIMES.

We are told that there should be signs in the sun, and in the moon, and in the stars; and upon the earth distress of nations, with perplexity; the sea and the waves roaring; men's hearts failing them for fear, and for looking after those things which are coming on the earth. (Luke xxi. 26.) Here we are most clearly informed, not only that there should be signs, but that they should be such as to cause fear in the hearts of the people. We are also taught by the oracles of God to believe that they will be so clear a demonstration of the immediate coming and kingdom of Christ, that we can know his coming is at hand just as we know that summer is nigh when the trees begin to put forth leaves. (Luke xxi. 30; Mark xiii. 28; Matt. xxiv. 32.) We are not only taught to believe that we can know it, but we are as positively commanded to know it as we are to believe that Jesus is the Son of God. (See Matt. xxiv. 33; Mark xiii. 29; Luke xxi. 28, 31.) And why should this not be a commandment,—since the evidence of his second coming is given in the same way in which the evidence of his being the Son of God is received? And since one of God's holy prophets has declared that the wise SHALL UNDERSTAND, is it not as much to the glory of God that his people understand as to believe on his Son,—for not only the word of his prophet, but that of his Son (Matt. v. 18) also, must fall if we do not understand?

As the promise of the remission of sins is only to those who believe Jesus to be the Son of God, so it is only unto "them who look for him" that he has promised to "appear the second time without sin unto salvation." (Heb. ix. 28.) As it is said he has become the author of eternal salvation to those who obey him, so it is said there is a crown of righteousness laid up for all those who "LOVE HIS APPEARING." (2 Tim. iv. 8.) And if religion be faith, hope, and love, how is it possible for us to be Christians, and yet love not his appearing.

It is frequently and sneeringly remarked, by both the so-called saint and sinner, that we can know nothing about the time; and they say this with as much confidence and assured "safety" (1 Thess. v. 3) as if our not knowing the time satisfied them that Christ can never come.

It is true, "none of the wicked shall understand;" but it is equally true "THE WISE SHALL UNDERSTAND." (Dan. xii. 10.)

It is true our Lord said to his disciples, "It is not for you to know;" for at that time the vision of Daniel was "closed up and sealed;" but it is equally true that he promised, saying, "Ye shall receive power after that the Holy Spirit is come upon you" (Acts i. 8); for at the time of the end the "WISE SHALL UNDERSTAND."

It is true "that the day of the Lord so cometh as a thief in the night;" but it is equally true that "ye brethren are not in darkness that that day should overtake you as a thief" (1 Thess. v. 3, 4); for his coming as a thief is only on the condition that we do not watch. (Rev. iii. 3.)

It is true that while the book of Daniel was "closed up and sealed," our Lord could say unto his disciples, "of that day and hour knoweth no man;" but it is equally true that he did positively command them to know, after the necessary signs shall have appeared. (Matt. xxiv. 33.)

It is nowhere said in the Bible that we are to know nothing as to the time of the coming of Christ. But in the expression, "As ye see the day approaching" (Heb. x. 25), we are taught that we are to know.

Those who "have taken away the key of knowledge" (Acts xi. 52), having taught the millenial interval of a thousand years before the coming of Christ, makes it true to the letter,—"In such an hour as ye think not the Son of man cometh;" for through the newly-opened book we now discover that his coming *will be* at a time we thought not.

If those who boast of the Lord's coming "as a thief in the night," would only take the trouble to notice who it is to whom Christ will "come as a thief" (Rev. iii. 3),—"and in a day when he looketh not for him" (Luke xii. 46; Matt. xxiv. 50; Mark xiii. 36), —surely they will glory no more in the idea of knowing nothing about it. "When ye see a cloud rise out of the west, straightway ye say there cometh a shower: and so it is. And when ye see the south wind blow, ye say, There will be heat: and it cometh to pass. Ye hypocrites! ye can discern the face of the sky and the earth; but how is it that ye do not discern this time?" (Luke xii. 54–56.) "A wise man's heart discerneth both time and judgment" (Eccl. viii. 5): therefore though "none of the wicked shall understand," yet, as true as the Bible is the book of God, "THE WISE SHALL UNDERSTAND" (Dan. xii. 10): for though they have slumbered and slept, they shall trim their lamps. (Matt. xxv. 7; Ps. cxix. 105.)

They shall run to and fro over the word of God, and knowledge shall be increased. (Dan. xii. 4.) For "they that wait upon the Lord shall renew their strength; they shall mount up with wings as eagles; they shall run and not be weary; they shall walk and not faint." (Isa. xl. 31.) For their path is as the burning "light that shineth more and more unto the perfect day." (Prov. iv. 18.) Therefore Paul could safely say, "But ye, brethren, are not in darkness, that that day should overtake you as a thief." (1 Thess. v. 4.)

In Matthew xxiv. we are told that after our Saviour had been speaking of the ruin of the temple, his disciples inquired of him, saying, "Tell us, when shall these things be? and what shall be the signs of thy coming, and of the end of the world?"

To understand this chapter the reader must observe that it is an unbroken chain of history, commencing from the time at which the apostles proposed these questions, and continuing to the second coming of Christ "in the clouds of heaven, with power and great glory."

This most sublime history gives its own dates as it passes on through coming time. Verses 4 to 20 reach from the time these words were delivered, in the year A.D. 30, to the commencement of the war at Jerusalem, or the year A.D. 65; and from ver. 21 to 28, we have the history from the commencement of this war at Jerusalem to about the year 1780. The whole history of this period is given in a few words,—it should be a time of "great tribulation:" and those who have read the record, know it to be true. Modern historians cover the same time with about the same number of words: they call it the "Dark Age." From ver. 24, the history is continued from the year 1780 to the coming of Christ "in the clouds of heaven."

There is one apparent difficulty in this chapter, which is this: some tell us that by the expression "end," in ver. 14, we are to understand "end of the world." If so, then there is a mystery in this chapter which no man can unravel.

But how they can make this appear is by no means clear; for the first clause of ver. 15—which reads thus, "When ye therefore shall see"—shows conclusively that the end there spoken of was something which was to be brought about by the Roman army. (Compare Matt. xxiv. 15 with Luke xxi. 20 and Dan. ix. 26, 27.) They are disposed to think this means the end of the world, because the end spoken of here was something which was to follow the preaching of the gospel: while it is generally admitted that the gospel had not been preached in all the world as early as the time of the destruction of Jerusalem.

But by the expression, "all the world," I understand our Lord to mean all the Jewish world (Acts ii. 5); for the adjective "this" restricts his allusion to that particular gospel which he and his apostles were at that time preaching—not to the Gentile world, but—"unto the lost sheep of Israel." (Matt. xv. 24.) This, at least, is what the apostles understood him to mean: for he had forbidden their preaching to the Gentile world (Matt. x. 5); and it was about seven years after this time before they knew that the gospel was to be preached to any "but Jews only." (Acts xi. 18, 19.) If we are willing to understand him as the apostles did, then all is plain; for, a short time before the destruction of Jerusalem, Paul informed the Colossians that the gospel had then been preached "in all the world." (Col. i. 6, 23.)

We are now brought to consider whether the signs have yet appeared,—which we shall do briefly.

The first question asked by the apostles was, "When shall these things be?"—that is, When shall Jerusalem be destroyed?

First. When the "gospel" shall have been "preached in all the world." (Ver. 14.)

Second. "When ye see Jerusalem compassed with armies." (Luke xxi. 20.)

"And what shall be the sign of thy coming, and of the end of the world?"

First. "The sun shall be darkened."

Second. "The moon shall not give her light."

Third. "The stars shall fall."

And now, as the first Christians knew that the destruction of Jerusalem was at hand when the designated signs appeared, so we are taught to know that the second coming of Christ is at hand, when the signs, as here given, shall appear.

Then ought we not to keep out a watch, that these signs may not pass unobserved,—and Christ coming suddenly find us asleep? (Mark xiii. 36.) Let us open our eyes and see if these signs of the coming of our Lord have yet appeared. For our not knowing the time is never given as an excuse for indulging in idle repose, but is always urged as a reason why we should watch. (Matt. xxiv. 42.) We will first inquire whether the sun has yet been darkened; and as the exact date at which it was to be darkened is also given, it will be necessary first to find the date before we can learn whether this sign has appeared. According to our

Saviour, it was to happen immediately after the tribulation of those days (Matt. xxiv. 29); and by reference to ver. 21, we learn that the tribulation here spoken of commenced with the war at Jerusalem; and by its commencing with the Jews, we learn that it is a tribulation which was to befall them: so that it only remains now to find the particular time at which this tribulation ended, to ascertain the date of the darkening of the sun; and to do this, we must trace the history of the Jews from that time until we find the end of the tribulation.

We now approach a crisis in their history which is truly painful to contemplate,—that over which our Saviour wept: "O Jerusalem, Jerusalem, thou that killest the prophets, and stonest them which are sent unto thee, how often would I have gathered thy children together, even as a hen gathereth her chickens under her wings, and ye would not!" Behold, your house is left unto you desolate. For I say unto you, ye shall not see me henceforth, till ye shall say, Blessed is he that cometh in the name of the Lord. (Matt. xxiii. 37–39.)

In view of the dark cloud of horror which hung over that city, he admonished his little flock to flee to the mountains (Luke xxi. 21): "for," says he, "there shall be great distress in the land, and wrath upon this people. And they shall fall by the edge of the sword, and shall be led away captive into all nations: and Jerusalem shall be trodden down of the Gentiles, until the times of the Gentiles be fulfilled." (Luke xxi. 23, 24.) "For these be the days of vengeance, that all things which are written may be fulfilled." (Luke xx. 22.)

Fleetwood, in his "History of the Jews," thus speaks of their "tribulation":—"When Titus accomplished the destruction of Jerusalem, the political existence of the Jewish nation was annihilated. We now see the Temple smouldering in ruins, and the high-priesthood buried under its rubbish. Those who did not perish during that war, were made captives, and were dispersed to the four winds of Heaven. And now, to give a narrative of the Jews, we must follow them, despised, persecuted, and forsaken as they were, into almost every part of the world; and collect from the histories of the nations, the broken and scattered details of their eventful history. During the five years which Adrian spent in avenging the Romans, we are informed that five hundred and eighty thousand Jews were butchered. Now indeed they were nearly exterminated. They seemed to have reached the very extremes of degradation, suffering, and wretchedness."

"This," says Edward Robinson, "was the final war and catastrophe of the Jewish nation. It was a catastrophe far more terrible than that of the destruction of Jerusalem, though the latter, in consequence of the vivid description of it by Josephus, has come to be usually considered as the last act in this great tragedy. Such, however, it was not."

This proves that the time of trouble, such as never should be again, is not to be restricted to the narrow limits of the war at Jerusalem. (Matt. xxiv. 21.)

Tertullian, during the reign of Severus, thus describes them. "Dispersed and vagabond, exiled from their native soil and air, they wander over the face of the earth, without a king, either human or divine: and even as strangers they are not permitted with their footsteps to salute their native land."

Fleetwood says:—"For many centuries the Jews beheld in the Church of Rome their worst and most cruel tormentors. The Greek general, Belisarius, put to death every Jew, male and female, that he could find. During the reign of Justinian many Jews were murdered, and their property confiscated.

"It is truly sickening to think of the misery the Jews suffered from the Crusaders. Men were seen murdering their own children, to keep them from falling into the hands of their enemies. Women would bind their children fast to their own bodies and plunge into a watery grave, to escape a more cruel end. This dreadful carnage spread to all the cities on the Maine and Danube. The blood of the Jews marked the footsteps of the Crusaders wherever they went.

"On the 14th of February, A.D. 1198, the Jews were in their synagogues at Paris. Suddenly they were surrounded by the troops. Their property was confiscated. They, their wives, and children, destitute of clothes, provisions, or means to travel, were all compelled to depart the kingdom." In the twelfth century, persecution raged in England. "When Richard went off to the Crusade the people rose and murdered multitudes of Jews. The intention was to murder every one in the kingdom. About fifteen hundred of them retired to York, and tried to defend themselves; but were overpowered. They first offered to ransom their lives with money: but there was no mercy in the relentless mob. They then deliberately killed their wives and children; and retiring to the palace, they fired it, and thus became their own executioners, as their brethren at Bither had done, under the persecution of Adrian, more than one thousand years before.

"During the year in which Spain was enriched with the discovery and possession of a new world, A.D. 1492, the Inquisition was committing the most dreadful outrages upon the Jews. 'Incidents, which make the blood run cold, are related of the miseries which they suffered.' The number of Jewish inhabitants in Spain at this time is estimated at from three hundred thousand to eight hundred thousand. An edict appeared in this year, commanding all unbaptized Jews to quit the realm in four months. They now scattered in various directions. Many perished on the ocean. Multitudes perished with famine. They at first encamped on the sandy plains; for they could not obtain admission into Fez. Here they lived for a while on the few roots they could find. 'Happy,' says a Jewish writer, 'would they have been, if grass had been plentiful.' In this dreadful state of suffering, some killed their children to put them out of their misery; and others sold them into captivity for bread. One party of the Jews who were thus driven out of Spain, were barbarously set on shore on the coast of Africa, naked and destitute. The first who went up to view the country, were devoured by wild beasts, which came howling furiously upon them. Multitudes also were eaten by the wild beasts in Africa. (Compare all this with what had been threatened in the days of Moses. Deut. xxxii. 2–4.) This century saw them barbarously used in Naples, Venice, and Portugal. In very many instances, mothers were seen throwing their children into wells and rivers, to keep them out of the hands of their merciless oppressors. Many were sent off to the unwholesome climate of St. Thomas as slaves. The Dominicans were extremely severe upon them. On one occasion, in Lisbon, these men came into the streets with crucifixes in their hands, exclaiming, 'Revenge! revenge! Down with the heretics! Root them out! Exterminate them!' It is said that they even offered as a reward to every one that would kill a Jew, that his soul should remain but one hundred days in purgatory. The kings of Europe having driven them out of their kingdoms by force or cruelty, they generally bent their course towards the east and north.

"From 1663 to 1666, the murder of the Jews in Persia became general. Some made their escape to Turkey.

"Up to the commencement of the EIGHTEENTH CENTURY THE WORLD SCARCELY AFFORDED THEM A REFUGE. For seventeen centuries every man's hand seemed against them. Like the bush which Moses saw, surrounded with flames, but not consumed,—afflicted, persecuted, despised, and villified in every land, they fled from place to place. A general gloom overspread their affairs, with only here and there a gleam of light that served not to guide their footsteps, but to bewilder them in the way.

"Though we have but little to say about the Jews during the eighteenth century, yet that little, we hope, will be more agreeable to our readers than the foregoing details of murder and robbery. The condition of the Jews began EVERYWHERE TO IMPROVE. During the reign of Queen Anne, the Jews began to be viewed as HUMAN BEINGS in England; and an act was passed to facilitate conversions from Judaism. In A.D. 1753, a bill was passed in the time of George II. for the naturalization of the Jews."

We have now traced the sons of Abraham through the appointed time of their tribulation. And as a dark and doleful night giving place to the morning light, we see this once-despised and suffering people now considered as HUMAN BEINGS AND ELEVATED AT LEAST TO AN EQUALITY WITH MANKIND. "The bill as passed in A.D. 1753 for the naturalization of the Jews seems to have been the FIRST STEP TOWARDS THE AMELIORATION OF THEIR WRETCHED CONDITION. The people, however, were not yet enlightened enough to support such a measure. The mayor and citizens of London were very clamorous against it. The bill had to be rescinded. A respectable minister of the gospel, named Tucker, was abused by the populace for having written a defence of the measure."

"In the year 1780, the imperial avant-courier of the Revolution, Joseph II., ascended the throne. Among the first measures of this restless and universal reformer was a measure for the amelioration of the condition of the Jews. He published his edict of toleration, by which he opened to the Jews the schools and the universities of the empire, and gave them the privilege of taking degrees as doctors in philosophy, medicine, and civil law. It enforced upon them the wise preliminary measures of establishing primary schools for their youth. It threw open the circle of trade to their speculations. In 1790 the Jews were recognized as free citizens of the great republic."—*Rev. H. H. Millman's History of the Jews.*

"The Emperor Napoleon convened an assembly of them in Paris, May 30, 1806, that he might learn their principles; and the next year the grand Sanhedrim (composed, according to the ancient custom, of seventy members) convened for the establishment of a civil and religious polity. A synagogue and a consistory were established in every department."

Thus, it appears that as early as 1807 this people were again granted the privilege of worshiping God according to the dictates of their conscience. The time of the tribulation had not reached its end as early as 1753, and it had ceased before the year 1808. It would therefore appear that the time of the darkening of the sun cannot be earlier than 1753, nor later than 1808.

Let us now inquire whether the sun was darkened at any time between the years 1753 and 1808. "It has. . . . I refer to the dark day of A.D. 1780, May 19. That was a day of supernatural darkness. It was not an eclipse of the sun, for the moon was nearly at the full; it was not owing to a thickness of the atmosphere, for the stars were seen. The darkness began about 9 A.M. and continued through the day. Such was the darkness that work was suspended in the field and shop; beasts and fowls retired to their rest, and houses were illuminated at dinner-time. . . . The sun was supernaturally darkened from morning till night,—in some places it being cloudy and the sun entirely invisible, and in others being visible, but having the same appearance as when totally eclipsed: and the stars being visible. I have both these accounts from many living witnesses in different parts of the country. It being cloudy in the north and clear in the southern part of New England."—*Litch's Prophetic Expositor.*

"We have no evidence," says the objector, "that this was a universal darkness, shrouding the whole globe in the blackness of night; and, even if it had been, we have seen other dark days."

In answer to this we ask, Who said this was to be a universal darkness, or that it was to be the only dark day that the world should ever witness? Shall we first imagine what ought to be, and then resolve that if the prophecy does not accord with our supposition we will not credit it? Who has given us authority to prescribe for God what he ought to do? Surely, it is enough for us to behold, with wonder and reverence, his word literally fulfilled.

It is the precise date at which the sun was to be darkened that proves this to be the one our Saviour meant. Had the sun been darkened twenty-five years earlier, it could not have answered; for the tribulation had not then reached its end. Neither would it verify his prediction were it to become to-day as black as the darkest night; for the tribulation has long since ended, and he declares that it was to be immediately after the tribulation.

It appears to be morally impossible to reconcile the three evan gelists, except by placing the darkening of the sun at about the year 1780. According to Luke, the Jews were to "fall by the edge of the sword, and should be led away captive into all nations;

and Jerusalem shall be trodden down of the Gentiles, until the times of the Gentiles be fulfilled." (Luke xxi. 24.) Now, there is nothing in Luke which forbids placing the darkening of the sun at the end of the time of the Gentiles. The parallel passage in Mark, however, shows that it cannot be as low as the time of the Gentiles, but must be looked for within "those days after the tribulation." (Mark xiii. 24.) The only limit to which we are restricted by Mark is, that it must be found between these two points,—that is, between the end of the tribulation and the end of the times of the Gentiles; but according to Matthew, we can look for it nowhere else but "immediately after the tribulation of those days." (Matt. xxiv. 29.) Were it not for Mark, and the expression in Matthew, the tribulation of "those days SHALL BE SHORTENED" (that is, shorter than the times of the Gentiles), we could evade the precise time to which Matthew confines us by making the expression, "tribulation," cover the whole of Luke's "times of the Gentiles." But Mark draws us back to some period *within those days;* and, as soon as we are within those limits, Matthew restricts us to the period *immediately "after the tribulation of those days.* Therefore, the only possible way to avoid placing the darkening of the sun at about the year 1780, is to show that the tribulation of the Jews has not yet ended.

How that can be done, we cannot see; for, so far from the Jews being despised at the present day, no people can claim a larger share in the sympathies of the world, than these wandering sons of Abraham. If their time of trouble has not yet terminated, why is it that so much sympathy is now manifested for them, when a few years ago they were despised and trodden upon by all nations, as if they were inferior to brutes.

When the present condition of the Jews is compared with their past, we are compelled to place the darkening of the sun at about the year A. D. 1780.

Some writers affirm that the darkening of the sun is to occur at the time of the second coming of Christ; but Joel, with Matthew and Mark, places it "Before the great and the terrible day of the Lord's coming" (Joel ii. 31); and so far from our Lord's placing it after the time of his coming, he mentions it as one of those signs by which we may know his coming "is near even at the doors."

The next sign is that the moon should not give her light. As the precise date at which this was to happen is not given, we cannot be so certain that we have the right time, or the exact darkness to which our Saviour alluded; but we find a darkness of the moon in the same year, which clearly answers to his prediction.

"At the time of the dark day, May 19, 1780, there was a full moon, or nearly so (the moon fulled the 18th), yet the night was as dark as Egyptian darkness: 'the moon did not give her light.' The darkness of the following evening was probably as gross as has ever been observed since the Almighty gave birth to light. I could not help conceiving at the time that if every luminous body in the universe had been shrouded in impenetrable darkness, or struck out of existence, the darkness could not have been more complete. A sheet of white paper held within a few inches of the eyes was equally invisible with the blackest velvet." — *Litch's Extracts from Rev. Tenny.*

The third sign was that "the stars shall fall from heaven." Having seen this literally fulfilled, the author is not dependent on another for testimony. Never shall I forget the morning of November 13, 1833, when, but a boy, I went and told my grandmother that all the stars were falling. The scene was both awful and sublime. The heavens were literally filled with brilliant falling bodies which so much resembled those planets which we are wont to call stars, that many persons believed the stars were really falling.

Professor Olmstead, in his work on Falling Stars, speaks of this phenomenon as follows:—"Those who were so fortunate as to witness the exhibition of shooting stars on the morning of November 13, 1833, probably saw the greatest display of celestial fireworks that has ever been seen since the creation of the world, or at least within the annals covered by the pages of history."

We now ask the reader to consider whether this be not a fulfillment of our Saviour's prediction. If it is not, in what way can it ever be fulfilled? Are we to expect the great planets to fall? The stars were to fall to the earth "as a fig-tree casteth her untimely figs, when she is shaken of a mighty wind" (Rev. vi. 13), which those planets, being larger than our world, could not do,—for more than one could not strike the earth. Surely, that could be no sign to us of the immediate coming of Christ; for no one would be left alive to know by this sign that his coming was "near, even at the very doors." We are therefore compelled either to admit that this did answer to our Saviour's prediction, or that it never can be fulfilled.

That these falling meteors were called stars, at that day, Dr. Clark shows in his essay on Matthew xxiv. 29: the bodies we designate as stars, are called worlds by Paul in Hebrew xi. 3.

Truth has nothing to fear from investigation. The more we reflect upon this subject, the more are we convinced that these are the signs which our Saviour has given that we may know his coming is near. Hence we are commanded, saying, "Now learn a parable of the fig-tree; when his branch is yet tender, and putteth forth leaves, ye know that summer is nigh: so likewise ye, when ye shall see all these things, *know that it is near, even at the doors. Verily, I say unto you, This generation shall not pass, till all these things be fulfilled.*" Now, notice what follows: "Heaven and earth shall pass away, but my *words shall not pass away.*"

As the "generation" here mentioned is connected with the preceding verse, and evidently intended to limit the expression, "even at the doors," it cannot mean the generation living at that time,—as some try to construe it,—for this would break the connection, and no longer show how near his coming is at the door when these signs appear: but merely show how near it was from the time at which he delivered these words,—thus making the signs of no worth. Others, observing the absurdity of supposing that he meant the generation then living, conclude that he meant the Jewish nation. This, however, is a very lame conclusion, and is yet more absurd than the former; for, our Saviour was directing the attention of his disciples to the signs which were to precede his coming, and not to any thing concerning the Jewish nation. Hence he could not, consistently with the laws of language, have used the word "this," if he had meant the Jewish nation: and, while it is evident that he used these words, in order to show how near to the doors his coming is when these signs appear, this would give no limit at all: it were as well had he said nothing. The only construction, therefore, that can be made in connection with the preceding verse, and in harmony with the general scope of the whole chapter, is to suppose that he meant the generation in which these signs are seen.

The first sign was the darkening of the sun, in 1780; consequently, the generation spoken of by our Saviour must be commenced there. As a generation is equivalent to one hundred years (compare Gen. 15, 16, with ver. 13), this generation will end in 1880: therefore we may expect the coming of Christ in the clouds of heaven somewhere within this limit,—that is between the years 1780 and 1880.

Having thus discovered that we are indeed living in the time of the end, we may now proceed to examine the book of Daniel. "For at the time of the end, *shall be the vision.*" (Dan. viii. 18.) This is the time the seal shall be loosed. At the end of 1290 days from the setting up of the abomination that maketh desolate, the wise are to UNDERSTAND. (Dan. xii. 10, 11.) This abomination which has made the Church so desolate was set up in A.D. 533; and since the year 1823, we have been living in the time of the end. In that very year (A.D. 1823) the watchmen on the walls of Zion commenced proclaiming the coming of Christ, the midnight cry was made, and the wise virgins commenced trimming their lamps. (Matt. xxv. 6.)

It was not until after the seventh trump began to sound, that the little book was eaten: which beginning to sound, we understand to be the same thing with the "midnight cry,"—not "sounded," but "begin to sound." The difference between "sounded" and "begin to sound" (Rev. xi. 15 and x. 7) is an important one. When the seventh angel "shall begin to sound, the mystery of God shall be finished." What mystery? That which "he hath declared to his servants the prophets." (See Dan. xii. 4–10; Hab. ii. 2, and 2 Pet. i. 19.) Observe, that at the time the midnight cry was made, the "little book had not been read,—it was merely open; for those who ate the little book or read it, must prophesy again before "many people and nations and tongues" after the beginning to sound of the seventh trumpet; but when it had sounded, then it was said the "kingdoms of this world, are become the kingdoms of our Lord and his Christ."

We may pause here to ask the considerate and reflecting reader if the movement of 1843 was not the beginning to sound of the seventh trumpet, or at least the midnight cry? Can any one imagine how the words of our Saviour can have a more perfect fulfillment than they had at that time.

We should remember that, after the midnight cry is made, there must yet be time enough for the virgins to trim their lamps before the bridegroom arrives (Matt. xxv. 7); which trimming of lamps must signify the searching of the Scriptures (Psalms cxix. 105); and eating of the little book must mean to understand the same. (Jer. xv. 16; Ezek. iii. 1.)

CHRONOLOGY EXAMINED.

THE chronology of our world, as far back as the time of the Peloponnesian War, is a settled period of time. Those who have examined the matter with the light of astronomy are willing to admit that this portion of chronology is settled to absolute certainty; but after passing this point,—that is, the year B.C. 431,—there is much darkness and uncertainty. Ptolemy of Alexandria, the Egyptian astronomer, born A.D. 138, collected and left on record a catalogue of kings, mentioning the number of years during which each reigned, from the year B.C. 747 down to the year A.D. 137. This canon is valuable in establishing chronology, and is sufficiently correct for ordinary purposes; but it is nine years too short from the first of Nebuchadnezzar, King of Babylon, to the first of Cyrus, King of Persia; and forty-eight years too long from the first of Cyrus to the time of the Peloponnesian War, B.C. 431. We are abundantly prepared to prove this both by God's holy volume of truth, and the unerring records of astronomy. As the time at which Ptolemy lived was from five to eight hundred years after the death of these kings, who reigned during the disputed part of his chronology, we observe that he was as dependent on history as we are; and there is too much clashing among historians as to the length of different reigns for any reasonable man to believe that an exact chronology could thus be obtained without the aid of astronomy, or some other means of getting the correct time. For example: Herodotus says that Cambyses reigned seven years and five months, while Clemens Alexandrinus makes it ten, and the Jews give him sixteen. Berosus says that Evilmerodack reigned two years only; but Josephus gives him eighteen. The Jews say Darius, the last King of Persia, reigned thirty-two years; but Ptolemy gives him only four. According to Ptolemy, Cyrus reigned nine years. Herodotus says he reigned twenty-nine, and Xenophon gives him seven. This, we know, is owing to the fact that they commenced the reigns from different epochs; yet it proves that we cannot get a correct chronology from the mere mention of the number of years a king reigned, unless we have some means of knowing from what epoch that reign is commenced. For example: Ptolemy says Augustus Cæsar reigned forty-three years, while Josephus gives him fifty-seven and a-half. According to Ptolemy, Tiberius reigned twenty-two; but others give him twenty-five. So, during the reign of these two kings, we would have a difference of seventeen years, had we no other means of settling the chronology. But after we enter the disputed ground,—that is, when we go beyond the year B.C. 431,—we have not the same light by which to establish the particular epoch from which each king's reign is to be commenced.

To show the uncertainty of that portion of chronology which extends through the kingdom of Persia, we will here give the views of several persons, as to the length of time from the destruction of the first temple by Nebuchadnezzar, to the destruction of the second by the Romans, in the year A.D. 70. According to the generally received chronology, it was 657 years: Josephus makes it 702; the modern Jews say it was only 490 years; and Nicodemus, 475. Some make it 479; others, 586; and the learned Matthew Henry was himself of the latter opinion. In his comment on Daniel (ix, 25), he says:—"I should most incline to understand this of the edict of Cyrus mentioned Ezra i. 1; for by it the people were restored. And there is nothing to be objected against this but that, by this reckoning, the Persian monarchy, from the conquest of Babylon by Cyrus to Alexander's conquest of Darius, lasted about 130 years; whereas, by the particular account given of the reign of the Persian emperors, it is computed that it continued 230 years. So Thucydides, Xenophon, and others reckon. Those who fix it to the first edict, set aside these computations of the heathen historians as uncertain and not to be relied upon."

Now, when we observe men thus differing from 44 to 227 years as to the duration of the kingdom of Persia, it will not be considered presumption on our part to say that Ptolemy's canon of the kings of Persia makes the duration of that kingdom 48 years too long, which, by the authority of Ptolemy himself, we intend to prove.

But says one, "Our chronology is established by astronomical demonstrations." If this be true, we confess we must yield the point; for an eclipse of the sun or moon can be calculated with great precision; but we shall examine for ourselves and see whether your chronology can stand the great error-detecting and truth-establishing power of astronomy.

We will commence with the Roman era, which dates from the laying of the foundation of Rome which, according to Varro, was laid on the 12th of the calends of May, or April 20, B.C. 753.

Varro is known as the most learned of the Romans, and wrote about A.D. 52.

Cicero, born about B.C. 107, relates that on the day of the founding of Rome there was a total eclipse of the sun. Plutarch, who died about A.D. 140, also affirms that on the day of the foundation of Rome there was a total eclipse of the sun, which he places in the third year of the sixth Olympiad, which, according to Scaliger, dates from the 23d of July, B.C. 754 to 753. (This is in exact harmony with Varro.) In S. Bliss's Sacred Chronology he copies a catalogue of eclipses from Dr. Hales's work. The first eclipse in this catalogue is dated April 21 B.C. 753, "the day of the foundation of Rome." Now, if this catalogue is what it professes to be,—that is, "Eclipses which, happening in connection with historical events, are found by astronomical calculation to have occurred in the years assigned,"—it follows that there was a total eclipse of the sun at Rome on the above-mentioned day: and, if so, then the day of the laying of the foundation of Rome is definitely settled: and to question the correctness of the Roman era would but betray ignorance on our part. But since our Saviour commands us to call no man master, we will take nothing on the mere assertion of others: we will at least venture to examine the subject for ourselves. By calculation we learn that the moon was at that time 25 days old, and the sun's distance from the node was 41 degrees. Hence, an eclipse at any place on earth at that time was impossible. If, therefore, the above-mentioned historians can be credited,—both as to the foundation of Rome being laid on the 20th of April, and that, on the day it was laid, there happened a total eclipse of the sun,—then we have positive proof that the year 753 was not the year on which it was laid. Bliss, quoting from Hales, says, "By astronomical calculation there was an eclipse of the sun visible at Rome, B.C. 753, July 5, aft. 4½, dig. 4, agreeing in every respect except the quantity."

But we learn by calculation that the moon was at that time 11 days old, and her distance from the node was 21 degrees 31 minutes. This was evidently a mistake. Dr. Hales, we suppose, meant the 5th of July, 754; for there was an eclipse of 2 digits on July 5th, B.C. 754. But we cannot see how Dr. Hales could say that this "agrees in every respect except the quantity:" for the historian says it was in the third year of the sixth Olympiad, while this was in the second year. Two historians mention that it was on the day of the foundation of Rome, which is said to be on the 20th of April and not the 5th of July.

If this be what is called "the astronomically established chronology," we have no confidence either in the chronology, nor in the assertions of those who say it is thus established. Hence, we shall now examine the subject for ourselves. When the foundation of Rome was laid does not concern us. We shall give attention to that portion of Ptolemy's chronology which clashes with the book of God; and that is the portion which makes it 131 years from the end of the reign of Nebuchadnezzar to the time of the Peloponnesian War; for the Bible makes it only 92,—a difference of 39 years.

Ptolemy lived in the second century of the Christian era. Astronomy was then but imperfectly understood, and hence he was unable to detect errors and thus establish a correct astronomical era. Yet he has given a sufficient number of eclipses—which happened in connection with his catalogue of the reign of kings—to enable us to discover where his record is incorrect.

The Nabonassarean era, from which Ptolemy's canon commences, dates from February 26, B.C. 747. "According to Ptolemy, Hipparchus selected three ancient eclipses of the moon, out of those observed at Babylon, . . . of which the first happened in the first year, and the two others in the second year of Mardok Empadus, the fifth king in succession from Nabonasser." According to Ptolemy's canon, the first year of Mardok was B.C. 721; and his second year answers to B.C. 720. We will now endeavor to ascertain whether those three eclipses really occurred. In Struyk's catalogue of eclipses, as copied by James Ferguson, they are put down thus:

B.C. 721, March 19, 10h. 34m.; total.

B.C. 720, March 8, 11h. 56m.; 1 digit and 5m.

B.C. 720, September 1, 10h. 18m.; 5 digits and 4m.

We learn by calculation that a total eclipse of the moon occurred on March 19, B.C. 721; and in the year B.C. 720 there was a small one of 2½ digits on September 1st; but no eclipse occurred on March 8, B.C. 720,—the moon's latitude at that time being 55m. 38s.; while the semi-diameter of the earth's shade was only 38m. 38s.; hence, the moon could not have touched the earth's shade at all, but passed about 100 miles above the shade that falls on her disc at the time of an eclipse. As Ptolemy's tables made three full eclipses here, it follows that he arranged his chronology according to his imperfect knowledge of astronomy. But since this science is now so much better understood, we know there were but two eclipses there, and one of them was too small to be noticed by those who knew nothing of an eclipse until they saw it. Ptolemy, therefore, was mistaken in supposing that these were the "three eclipses of the moon," which Hipparchus found among the public records of Babylon. Hence, the year B.C. 721 was not the first year of Mardok Empadus, the fifth King of Babylon. And this we shall clearly prove after having examined all the eclipses in Ptolemy's catalogue.

The next, as found on record at Babylon, was in the fifth year of Nabopolasser, which, according to Ptolemy's canon, answers to B.C. 621. In Struyk's catalogue it stands thus:

B.C. 621, April 21, 18h. 22m. eclipsed 2 digits, 36m.

In S. Bliss's catalogue of eclipses, copied from Dr. Hales, it is put down to the same hour and the same quantity eclipsed. If their calculation be correct, then there was no eclipse at all at Babylon: for the moon was down and the sun up before this eclipse commenced; as they have only about 2½ digits eclipsed at 22m. after 6.

According to Ferguson's tables this eclipse was about 45 minutes earlier than they have it: hence, about one digit may have been visible at Babylon at sunrise; but this, being too small to be noticed by the heathen, amounts to nothing.

The next eclipse, according to Ptolemy, happened in the seventh year of Cambyses. This in Struyk's catalogue is as follows:

B.C. 523, July 16, 12h. 47m.; digits eclipsed 7 and 24m.

By calculation there were about 9 digits eclipsed at that time. This is the first eclipse of the moon which has the appearance of being one of those recorded at Babylon. Now, if we can find the one in the 20th, and the other in the 31st of Darius Hystaspes, Ptolemy's canon will here appear to be correct.

The 20th of Darius, according to Ptolemy, answers to B.C. 502. This in Struyk's catalogue is set down thus:

B.C. 502, Nov. 19, 12h. 21m.; digits 1 and 52m.

But this, if seen at all, is also too small to be considered worthy of record among the wonders as discovered at Babylon, or among those eclipses which had so much frightened that people as to cause them to keep a public register of them.

The 31st of Darius Hystaspes, at which time the next eclipse must be found according to Ptolemy's canon, answers to the year B.C. 491. This in Struyk's catalogue is put down thus:

B.C. 491, April 25, 12h. 12m; digits 1 and 44m.

Which amounts to nothing. But there was no eclipse at all; for the moon, according to Ferguson's tables, passed about two hundred miles above the earth's shade. If it be asked, "Might not these eclipses have all been there; for, in going back twenty-five hundred years, our tables may be so far incorrect as not to make them as full as they should be?" We reply, those who wish to see Bible truth triumph over error, are here exceedingly fortunate; for God, who has given the moon "to serve in her season for a *declaration of time and a sign of the world*," has so arranged her motion as to enable us to settle this decisively. We will now show that no astronomical tables properly arranged can be made to make all of those eclipses of the moon. Astronomers will at once understand what we mean by this; but we wish to make it plain to all.

At the time of the eclipse of March 8, B.C. 720, the moon's latitude was north, ascending, and 9 degrees 39m. from the node: while at the time of the eclipse of April 25th, B.C. 491, the moon's latitude was north, descending, and her distance from the node was 18 degrees and 19m. If to her distance from the node we here add one degree, we will have 19 degrees and 19m. This gives us for the moon's latitude in eclipses 55m. and 57s.; and as the earth's shade here was 41m. 55s., we will have for the size of this eclipse a little over one-half of a digit. But this addition to the node throws the moon far above the earth's shade, in the year B.C. 720: for all you reduce her distance from the node to make one eclipse fuller, you add to her distance from the opposite node at the time of the other eclipse, just as if you had a pole not quite long enough to reach two opposite points: if you move it to reach one point, you would move it the farther from the opposite point.

Ferguson's tables come as near making all the ancient eclipses, as it is possible for any to do; but, according to what is known to be the motion of the sun and moon, no tables can be arranged so as to make them all answer to what is said of them by the historians, until we correct Ptolemy's errors.

Dr. Hales, in attempting to prove the correctness of Ptolemy's canon by astronomy, seems to have acted very unfairly in so arranging his tables as to make those eclipses larger which other tables made too small; and such as he could not then make, he copied from other authors. For example, the eclipse of March 8, 720, in Bliss's Chronology, as copied from him, is put down at 3½ digits. Now, if his tables did, at that time, eclipse 3½ digits, then, on April 21, in the year B. C. 621, they made no eclipse at all: so he here copies from Struyk's catalogue of eclipses made by other tables, and put down 2½ digits. Neither could his tables have made any eclipse November 19, B.C. 502; or April 25, B.C. 491; each of these he copies from Struyk's. If honest, it is unfair to palm this off on the ignorant as an astronomical demonstration of the correctness of Ptolemy's Canon.

Ferguson's tables have been so far strained from the truth, as to be unable to make those eclipses correct, which are on undisputed ground, or where the chronology is clearly settled. In proof of this, he makes the eclipse of August 3, B.C. 431, total at Athens; but Thucydides, who saw this eclipse, informs us that it was not total, but only "assumed a crescent form." The eclipse of August 14, B.C. 394, his tables make annular. But Xenophon, the historian, says, "The sun appeared in the form of the crescent of the moon." The eclipse of July 17, B.C. 188, is said by Livy to have been total; but Ferguson's tables make it only about 10 digits. The eclipse of the moon, as seen at Alexandria, April 5, A.D. 125, his tables make only about $\frac{3}{4}$ of a digit, which is too small to be noticed. These eclipses show that Ferguson's tables have been thrown about one degree out of the truth as to the sun's mean distance from the node, in order to come the nearer making those eclipses of Ptolemy. This making a difference of only about half a second, amounts to nothing at the present day; yet, in running back 2000 years, they are about one degree in error.

Ferguson is again in error as to the moon's mean anomaly. At the time of the eclipse of August 3, B.C. 431, according to his tables, the sun set a little more than 4 digits eclipsed: and according to Struyk's Catalogue of Eclipses, the sun went down 6 digits eclipsed.* But Thucydides, who also saw this eclipse, declares that it "became full again after it had assumed a crescent form." The eclipse of August 20, B.C. 31, is said by the historian to have been a great eclipse: but according to Ferguson there was only about 4 digits eclipsed before the sun went down at Rome. According to his tables, the eclipse of the moon in the year B.C. 201, began only about seven minutes before the moon was up at Alexandria: but the historian informs us that it "rose so much eclipsed, that it must have commenced about half an hour before she rose." If those eclipses of the moon, which are said to be found in connection with Ptolemy's canon, be those recorded at Babylon, then Ferguson's tables must be strictly correct as to the sun's mean distance from the node, as we cannot alter it either way without lessening the quantity of some of those eclipses which are already too small to be received as those

* This proves the incorrectness of Struyk's tables, by which he made these eclipses of the moon, which are said to prove the correctness of Ptolemy's canon.

discovered at Babylon; and we cannot correct the moon's mean anomaly; for this would make the size of the eclipse of the sun B.C. 188, less than 10 digits, which eclipse is admitted to have been total; and would throw the eclipse of May 28, B.C. 585, yet later, which is already too late to be seen in Asia.

Now, in order to throw this eclipse as far east as Asia, and to make the eclipse of B.C. 188 total, at Rome, the moon ought to have come to the change about one hour sooner than Ferguson's tables bring it. But strange to say, instead of astronomers having discovered in this the clear proof of the incorrectness of Ptolemy's canon, they have rather attributed the error to the motion of the heavenly bodies.

Says Mr. Smith: "It is particularly to be noted, that eclipses which have happened many centuries ago, will not be found by our present tables to agree exactly with ancient observations, by reason of the great anomalies in the lunar motions; which appears to be an incontestable demonstration of the non-eternity of the universe. For it seems confirmed by undeniable proofs, that the moon now finishes her period in less time than formerly."

But while the above opinion of astronomers finds foundation alone in the errors into which Ptolemy has fallen, we can, by reference to eclipses found on undisputed ground, prove it to be incorrect. For example: at the time of the eclipse of May 21, A.D. 95, Ferguson's tables brings the moon to the change about one half hour too soon for any eclipse; while, therefore, to make the other eclipses by his tables, we must subtract one hour, we must here add at least thirty minutes.

Such eclipses as this proves that the error in Ferguson's tables is not as to the length of the mean lunation, but as to the moon's anomaly. Hence, if we admit that Ptolemy was but a man,—one as capable of falling into error as we are,—we can easily correct the errors in Ferguson's tables, and they will then make all those ancient eclipses with as much precision as they do the eclipses of the present day.

Though some may rather affirm that God has failed to give the revolving worlds of the universe their proper motions than admit the possibility of an error in Ptolemy's canon, yet we can most clearly prove by the authority of Ptolemy himself that his canon is incorrect; and we feel confident that, were he now living, he would frankly admit it. Those who are more familiar with the history of Rome than with astronomy, know that "in B.C. 188 there was a total eclipse at Rome; and prayers were offered up for three days to avert the evil." If there was a total eclipse of the sun at Rome in B.C. 188, then there was no eclipse of the moon on the 8th of March, B.C. 720, neither at Babylon nor any other place on earth: and if there was no eclipse of the moon at Babylon on the 8th of March, B.C. 720, then Ptolemy's canon is incorrect; for he admits that there were two eclipses of the moon observed at Babylon in the second year of Mardok, the fifth King of Babylon, which, according to his canon, answers to the year B.C. 720.

This is worthy of particular attention. It is a settled question in history that there was *a total eclipse of the sun at Rome in the year* B.C. 188; and if so, then there *could not* have been an eclipse of the moon on the 8th of March, B.C. 720. We can again prove the incorrectness of Ptolemy's canon by an eclipse of the moon as observed at Alexandria, his native place, about thirteen years before his birth,—that is, on the 5th of April, A.D. 125.

We have already observed that, according to Ferguson's tables, there was only 1 digit and 5 minutes eclipsed on the 8th of March, B.C. 720; and on the 5th of April, A.D. 125, there was only about ¾ of a digit. This eclipse was on undisputed ground; and as the moon's latitude was north, ascending, it is impossible to make either of these eclipses any larger without reducing the size of the other. Hence, about one digit is as large as the eclipse of March 8, B.C. 720, can possibly be made; and so far from this causing alarm if all Babylon had been out that night, they would have failed to discover one so small, or at least to have thought of this being an eclipse. On the 27th of February, 1858, the author ascended to the summit of the Southwest Mountains to see the moon rise a little more than two digits eclipsed. Although the moon appears much larger when rising than when overhead, it was difficult to discover any eclipse. The moon appeared a little clouded on one side, and not entirely round. Had we not known the earth's shade was at that time on the moon, we would not have noticed it. How, then, can we believe that the heathen, who knew nothing of an eclipse, could have discovered one only half this size, and that at the time of midnight? We once asked an old practical astronomer what was the smallest eclipse of the moon he thought would be likely to attract the notice of one who knew nothing of the eclipse until he saw it. The answer was: "Three digits: and I do not think one under three digits would be noticed by any except those who—knowing that an eclipse would happen at a given time—were looking out for it." Said another—who has made calculations for almanacs for about forty years—in answer to the following question: "Do you think that any one, by frequently looking at the moon, would be likely to notice an eclipse of less than two digits?" "No," he replied; "I do not think he would notice one less than three digits." He continued: "I once saw an eclipse of three digits, and, while looking at it, the eclipse would sometimes seem to disappear so that I could not see it at all: then it would appear again." We may, therefore, safely set down all eclipses under three digits, at that age, as invisible.

We will now show that even if all of the eclipses given us by Ptolemy could have been found at their respective places, we would yet have abundant proof that his canon is incorrect as to the reign of Evil-merodach. This portion of his canon seems to have been gathered from Berosus's History of Chaldea, who says Evil-merodach "reigned but two years." This difficulty is easily solved when we compare Berosus with Daniel and Josephus. The truth appears to be that Evil-merodach in the second year of his reign acted in a manner as, the Chaldeans told him, "no king, lord, nor ruler should act;" and because they could not show him his dreams, he "was angry and very furious, and commanded to destroy all the wise men of Babylon." (Dan. ii. 10, 12.) This Berosus calls "governing public affairs after an illegal and impure manner." (See Josephus against Apian.) About the 11th year of his "reign he had a plot laid against him by Nerriglisar, his sister's husband," "and he was driven from men, and did eat grass as oxen." (Dan. iv. 33). After this Nerriglisar had reigned four years, his son took the kingdom; and when he had reigned only nine months, the kingdom was taken from him and given to Beltshazzar, the son of Evil-merodach; and, in the second year of his reign, Evil-merodach (his seven-years exile being completed) returned again to his kingdom. (Dan. iv. 36.) But finding the way the kingdom had been made sure unto him (Dan. iv. 26) was by his son's being placed on the throne, he did not think proper to displace him: therefore, while Josephus is correct in placing his death at the end of eighteen years from the time he first took the kingdom, the Chaldeans might well say that he had, properly speaking, reigned only two years. Berosus, who wrote about two hundred years after the day of Evil-merodach, was under no obligation to mention the interval filled up by the Hebrews in governing Babylon (Dan. ii. 49); for he was not giving a chronology of the time, but simply writing a history; and could therefore properly say that Evil-merodach was slain "when he had reigned only two years," after the manner of the other kings of Babylon, though the time that had elapsed from the commencement of his reign was eighteen years. This view of it reconciles Daniel, Berosus, and Josephus, who are undoubtedly the best authorities. This view is proven to be correct by the seventy-years captivity commencing on the tenth day of the fifth month in the eighth year of the reign of Nebuchadnezzar (2 Kings xxiv. 12); and it is singular that Christian writers have thus far suffered Ptolemy's canon to outweigh the Bible.

As Berosus passed over the period of time the Hebrews governed Babylon, it was natural for Ptolemy to suppose that the two years Berosus gives Evil-merodach was intended to fill up the interval between Nebuchadnezzar and Nerriglisar. It appears, however, that Ptolemy discovered a difficulty here, and was unable to reconcile this portion of his canon with the Hebrew chronology. Hence, Syncellus, a Christian author who lived about A.D. 780, "has given two copies of the canon: the one, he calls a Mathematical and Astronomical copy; the other, was an Ecclesiastical copy, partly taken from Josephus, and partly from Africanus, and other Christian historians."

Let it now be borne in mind that however correct Ptolemy's canon may be in every other part, it is not so here; for we have clearly proved that the Evil-merodach of Berosus is the Nebuchadnezzar of Daniel. (See at the year B.C. 521.) Hence, his reign could not have been less than nine or ten years: and that Evil-merodach's reign continued at least fifteen years, we can prove by the duration of the captivity. Then, placing the seventy-years captivity against the first of Cyrus, B.C. 536, we shall have B.C. 606, for the commencement of the captivity, in the eighth year of Nebuchadnezzar. (See 2 Kings xxiv. 12.)

According, then, to Ptolemy's canon revised, Merodach's first year will be B.C. 730; his second, B.C. 729; and the fifth year of Nabopolassar, B.C. 630; no eclipse of the moon was visible at Babylon in either of those years.

Again: according to Ptolemy's canon, the second year of Darius —at which time the Jews commenced building their temple (Haggai i. 15)—falls in their sabbatical year. As it is absurd to suppose that they commenced building in that year, we must therefore make the first year of the reign of Darius one higher. With this revision, the 7th of Cambyses synchronizes with the year B.C. 524; the 20th of Darius with B.C. 503; and the 31st of Darius with B.C. 492. But by calculation there was no eclipse of the moon seen at Babylon during either of the above-mentioned years. Thus, out of the seven eclipses observed at Babylon, we have not found one in harmony with Ptolemy's revised canon.

We will now examine those eclipses of the sun which are referred to in proof of the correctness of Ptolemy's canon. The first is called the eclipse of Thales, because foretold by him. Herodotus speaks of it as follows: "A war commenced between the Lydians and the Medes, which continued five years: and it is remarkable that one of their engagements took place in the night. In the sixth year, when they were carrying on the war with nearly equal success, on the occasion of an engagement, it happened that in the heat of the battle, day was suddenly turned into night." (*Herod.* b.i. s. 74.)

The same historian informs us that while Cyaxares, the King of Media,—during whose reign this eclipse happened,—"was engaged in the siege of Nineveh, he was surprised by an army of the Scythians; and from this time they possessed the dominion of Asia for the space of twenty-eight years. Cyaxares reigned forty years, and then died; but in this period is to be included the time in which the Scythians possessed the empire." (*Herod.* b. i. s. 106.)

According to Ptolemy, the reign of Cyaxares commenced B.C. 634. It would thus appear that the twenty-eight years during which the Scythians possessed the dominion cannot date higher than B.C. 633; from which, if we subtract twenty-eight, we will have B.C. 605 for the end of the dominion of the Scythians: from this it would appear that the war between the Medes and Lydians could not have commenced before B.C. 604 or 605: and by subtracting the six years during which the war continued, we will have B.C. 599 for the earliest period at which this eclipse, according to Ptolemy's chronology, is to be found; and as it occurred during the forty-years reign of Cyaxares, it could not have been later than B.C. 594.

Being thus restricted to five years for the time of this total eclipse of the sun, which so seldom happens at a given place, this becomes a very important eclipse,—one that, if found within the limits of the above-mentioned time, must greatly strengthen Ptolemy's canon; but, if not, must expose its incorrectness.

We are not informed as to the location of the battle-ground over which the centre of this eclipse passed. The war commenced at Sardis; but where it ended we cannot tell, as it continued between five and six years: all that we can certainly know is that it was either in Media or Lydia. So a total eclipse at any place between these two kingdoms within the limits of the above-noticed time will answer.

In the "Bible Companion" this eclipse is put down thus: "B.C. 585. A battle upon the river Halys between Cyaxares and Halyattes, interrupted by a total eclipse of the sun, on the 28th of May." But by calculation this eclipse did not commence there until about sundown,—that is, according to Ferguson's tables: hence, so far from being total, it could not have been seen there at all. The total form went but little farther east than Spain,—on the latitude of Sardis. My tables carry it on the latitude of Sardis as far east as Italy, but not to Asia. This eclipse, therefore, amounts to nothing; and even if it had passed centrally through Asia, it could in no way strengthen Ptolemy's canon, as it falls nine years below the lowest limit to which his canon could place "the eclipse of Thales."

Dr. Hales, and others, discovering that this could not be "the eclipse of Thales," sought another. The one they selected happened on the 18th of May, B.C. 603. According to Ferguson's tables, this eclipse passed centrally through Asia Minor; but as the other one fell nine years below the lowest, so this one is four years above the highest, limit of Ptolemy's canon; therefore, if this be "the eclipse of Thales," instead of strengthening, it is an additional proof of the incorrectness of Ptolemy's canon.

My tables eclipse but 9 digits at Sardis, and still less as we go towards Media. That my tables are more correct than Ferguson's is proven from the fact that they *make all known eclipses on undisputed ground according to the express language of the historian, which his do not.*

But desiring to give Ptolemy's canon a fair trial, we have examined whether a total eclipse of the sun passed through Asia Minor, or Media, between the years B.C. 599 and 594. But by calculation there was no total eclipse of the sun within the limit of those five years,—another proof of the incorrectness of Ptolemy.

The next eclipse of the sun as offered in support of Ptolemy's canon is in S. Bliss's catalogue, dated thus: "B.C. 547, October 22, aft. 0. 35 m. total,—when Cyrus took Larissa in Media." He gives Xenophon as authority, who says:—"At the time the Persians were wresting the empire from the Medes, the King of Persia could not make himself master of the city Larissa until it happened that the sun, obscured by a cloud, disappeared, and the darkness continued till, the inhabitants being seized with consternation, the town was taken. (See his "Expedition of Cyrus," b. iii. s. 4.)

From the language of Xenophon, we may conclude this was not an eclipse of the sun, but what we call a dark day, caused by a thick cloud passing over the sun. This, therefore, proves nothing. We will, however, give it a passing notice. According to Ferguson's tables there were about 10½ digits eclipsed; but my tables make about 8 digits.

The next eclipse of the sun found in history is recorded by Herodotus. He says: — Xerxes's army having spent the winter at Sardis, on the opening of spring commenced their march towards Greece. "But as they were on the point of setting out, the sun, quitting his seat in the heavens, disappeared, though there were no clouds, and the air was perfectly serene, and night ensued in the place of day." (*Herod.* b. vii. s. 37.) So this could have been nothing short of a total eclipse of the sun; the expression, "the sun, quitting his seat in the heavens, disappeared, though there were no clouds," shows that it was central there, and one of the darkest eclipses. Dr. Stukely, in describing the eclipse of A.D. 1724, which passed central over him, says: "The trace of the sun we could now no more discover than if it had never existed." So those who were in the army of Xerxes, being unable to discover the least appearance of the sun, not knowing what caused it to be thus obscured, might well say it appeared to quit its place in the heavens. William Beloe translates it thus: "The sun, which before gave his full light, in a bright, unclouded atmosphere, withdrew his beams, and the darkest night succeeded."

Herodotus further informs us that when Xerxes reached Greece, the people were celebrating "the Olympic games." (*Herod.* b. viii. s. 26.) This proves the eclipse to have happened in the fourth year of those games, which makes it one of the most important in detecting error and establishing a correct chronology: for, as we have already mentioned, a total eclipse but seldom happens at the same place. By this eclipse we will now test Ptolemy's canon; for if it can be found at the time his chronology gives us, then the correctness of his canon may be thus far admitted; but if it cannot, then this is a positive proof of its incorrectness. According to Ptolemy, the reign of Xerxes commenced B.C. 485, which was the fourth year of the Olympic games. But by calculation, there was no eclipse of the sun seen at Sardis during that year. The next fourth year of the Olympic games was B.C. 481,—that is, commencing in July, B.C. 481, and ending in July, 480. There was no eclipse at that time. The succeeding fourth year dates from July, 477, to July, 476; the next, commences July, B.C. 473 and ends July, 472; the following from B.C. 469 to 468; the next from B.C. 465 to 464. But there was no eclipse there. And here, according to Ptolemy's canon, ends the reign of Xerxes.

We have now passed through the reign of Xerxes, from the first to the last year, and have been unable to find the smallest eclipse at Sardis during the fourth year of the Olympic games, within the limits of the time as given Xerxes by Ptolemy. What will its advocates have to say now? Strange as it may appear, Dr. Hales runs back twelve hundred miles to Susa, and places this eclipse in the third, instead of the fourth, Olympiad. While we are willing to admit that Herodotus was liable to be mistaken as to the places at which events occurred, it happens that, connected with this eclipse, is a circumstance that forbids the possibility of such an error on his part, which is as follows:—

"The troops throughout the continent, that were to march with Xerxes himself, having assembled at Critalla in Cappadocia, crossing the river Halys, they entered Phrygia, marching through that country, arrived at Celænæ, a city in Phrygia. In the city lived a man named Pythius, a native of Lydia. This man, being in waiting, entertained Xerxes and all his army with great magnificence. (*Herod.* b. vii. s. 27.) And this man Pythius, the Lydian, was present at the time this eclipse happened."

This eclipse, passing over the army of Xerxes, proves that it could not have occurred before he reached Cappadocia, for there "it was ordered that all the troops throughout the continent that were to march with Xerxes himself, should be assembled." (*Herod.* b. vii., s. 26.) And the fact that Pythius, who was present at the time, was "at Celænæ, waiting for the arrival of Xerxes," shows that it was not before Xerxes reached Celænæ.

The only question worthy of controversy is as to whether the eclipse was seen at Celænæ or Sardis. If Xerxes was at Celænæ, then it happened in the fall of the year; for he spent the winter at Sardis. But if he was at Sardis, then it occurred in the spring. Hence, in running through the reign of Xerxes, we examined the whole of each fourth year of the Olympic games. If we possessed positive evidence that this eclipse happened when Xerxes was at Sardis, then it would have been only necessary to have examined the spring of each year; or, if Herodotus had said positively that Xerxes was at Celænæ at the time, then we would have examined only the fall of each year. But whether it happened in the spring or fall, it was in the fourth year of the Olympic games, and not before Xerxes reached Cappadocia.

Though Herodotus does not say positively that this eclipse occurred while Xerxes was at Sardis, yet it is quite clear that he was either of this opinion, or, having forgotten to mention this circumstance at its proper place, did not bring it in until he had reached that point in his history. But that this eclipse happened when Xerxes "was on the point of setting out" from Celænæ appears almost conclusively from the circumstance of Pythius being present at the time; for it is very unreasonable to suppose that this old man, owning large possessions as he did, would have left all to follow Xerxes more than one hundred miles up to Sardis, and there spend the winter, while his sons and all those active men who had the management of his large estate had been drawn off in the army of Xerxes.

It being so clear and certain that the eclipse did not happen before Xerxes reached Celænæ, the one as found by Dr. Hales is unworthy of notice: yet we will see what it amounts to. This eclipse, as copied from Dr. Hales by S. Bliss in his chronology, stands thus: "B.C. 481, April 19, aft. 2·27, digits 7, when Xerxes left Susa to invade Greece." You will observe that the doctor has but seven digits eclipsed, covering but little more than one-half of the sun, causing little or no darkness at all. But the one recorded by Herodotus so completely obscured the sun that Xerxes and his army believed it had ceased to exist:—"having entirely disappeared, the darkest night succeeded." So, even if this eclipse had happened at Celænæ, it could not have been the one recorded by Herodotus. According to Ferguson's tables, there were only about 3¼ digits eclipsed. My tables make about 3½; which, so far from causing darkness, could not be seen with the naked eye.

Now, when we observe learned men—those whom we look up to as guides—thus endeavoring to palm this off upon us as an astronomically-established chronology, ought we to be stigmatized for being unwilling to take any thing on trust, or for being anxious to examine every subject for ourselves? But, however absurd it may appear to one who has any reason, it has that strong argument which is, of all others, the most weighty with the large majority of the people, which is, that the learned Dr. So-and-so said it.

Since we are forbidden to acknowledge any man as "father upon the earth" (Matt. xxiii. 9), it becomes us to inquire "whether these things were so" (Acts xvii. 11), that we may be enabled to give "a reason of the hope that is in us." (1 Pet. iii. 15.)

We will now see whether the next eclipse of the sun as recorded by Herodotus, can be found in harmony with Ptolemy's chronology. The circumstances connected with the time are as follows:—"As soon as the Peloponnesians heard of the ruin of Leonidas and his party at Thermopylæ, they assembled at the isthmus all the force they could collect from their different cities, under the conduct of Cleombrotus. Having stationed themselves, therefore, at the isthmus, and having blocked up the Scironian Way, they then, as they determined on consultation, built a wall across the isthmus." (*Herod.* b. viii. s. 71.) At the completion of this wall, Cleombrotus "conducted back from the isthmus the detachment which had constructed the wall. He had brought them back because, whilst offering a sacrifice to determine whether he should attack the Persians, an eclipse of the sun had happened." (*Herod.* ix. 10.)

We find, therefore, that the particular place at which this eclipse was seen was at the isthmus in Greece. The time was after the construction of the wall,—hence in the spring of the second year of the Persian War: for, early in the spring, "when Alexander arrived at Athens, this work was not completed, although, from terror of the Persians, they eagerly pursued it." But in a short time after this, "the wall of the isthmus was finished, and therefore they did not want the aid of the Athenians." (*Herod.* b. ix. s. 8.) The spring of the second year of the Persian War was in the first year of the Olympic games. (*Herod.* b. viii. s. 26.)

Since we have not only the place at which this eclipse was seen, and the year of the Olympic games, but also the exact season of the year during which it was seen, this becomes another very important eclipse. We will, therefore, once more give Ptolemy's canon a trial.

According to Ptolemy, the reign of Xerxes began with the year B.C. 485. The spring of the first year of the Olympic games after the beginning of his reign was B.C. 483; the next was 479, and the next 475; the following 471, and the next 467, with which ends the last first year of the Olympic games during the reign of Xerxes. No eclipse was seen in Greece during the limits of this time.

If Ptolemy's advocates now refuse to yield, do they not show an unwillingness to acknowledge the truth, even when the judgment has been fully convinced. Had these two eclipses of the sun been found, we would frankly acknowledge that Ptolemy's canon —at least up to the time Xerxes invaded Greece—was reliable. But since they have not been, we must either disbelieve Herodotus, or acknowledge that Ptolemy's chronology is now crushed beneath the truth-testing power of astronomy. We have already, in many different ways, exposed the error of Ptolemy's canon; and, under the head of "Chronology Established," we intend to prove the truthfulness of our historian by showing that each of the above-mentioned eclipses happened at the time Xerxes invaded Greece. But how have the supporters of Ptolemy's canon smoothed over this? As if resolved that it shall stand, right or wrong, they have made it in the first, instead of the second, year of the Persian War, and that not only without the least authority, but even by contradicting the express words of Herodotus,—on whom they are dependent for all their information on the subject; for he tells us positively that there was no intermission from the commencement to the completion of the wall. His words are these: "without *intermission, either by night or by day.*" (*Herod.* viii. 71.) As it was impossible for Cleombrotus to have conducted from the isthmus all those that worked on the wall, and yet there should have been no intermission, *this eclipse cannot be placed in the first year of the war.* It cannot be urged that Cleombrotus conducted portions of the men away and left others at work; for Herodotus says: "This wall was soon finished, as not one of so many thousands was inactive; for, without interruption, either by night or by day, they severally brought stones, bricks, timber, and bags of sand." (*Herod.* viii. 71.) So those who place the eclipse in the first year of the war first contradict Herodotus, and then place an eclipse where no historian says there was one. If the clause, "without intermission," be clipped out of the book of Herodotus, yet we can establish the time at which this eclipse happened; for Herodotus informs us that Cleombrotus "died very soon after having conducted back from the isthmus the army that had built the wall." (*Herod.* ix. 10.) Now, it is impossible that he could have conducted from the isthmus those who had built the wall before the time the wall was built. And this wall was not finished when Alexander arrived at Athens (*Herod.* ix. 8), which was early in the spring of the second year of the war.

If Cleombrotus conducted this army from the isthmus before the completion of the wall, at what time did he do it? Not before the battle of Salamis; for at that time, his army was yet there (*Herod.* viii. 71): not at the time of the battle; for they were then engaged in another at the isthmus (*Herod.* viii. 74.): not soon after the battle; for Herodotus informs us that they yet remained there. (*Herod.* viii. 123.) Neither could this eclipse have happened after the army of Xerxes had fled; for it happened at the time Cleombrotus was "offering a sacrifice to determine whether he should attack the Persians." (*Herod.* ix. 10.) But after the Persians had left, no Persians were there to attack. What absurdities those who place this eclipse in the first year of the war are driven to! And yet, in S. Bliss's catalogue of eclipses, copied from Dr. Hales, this eclipse is placed in the first year of the war, thus: "B.C. 480, Oct. 2, aft. 2, digits 8, soon after the battle of Salamis."

It is so clear, however, that this eclipse could not have happened as early as the 2d of October, B.C. 480, that most of the advocates of Ptolemy's canon seem to prefer passing it over in silence. For example: in the "Bible Companion" the battle of Salamis is dated on "the 20th of October." If that be the true date, the eclipse on the 2d of October of the same year could not have been after the battle.

William Baloe says: "The festival of the mysteries of Ceres was celebrated on the 20th of the month Boëdromion, which answers to our October." And the 20th day of the moon's age did on that year fall on the 23d of October. If Baloe is correct,—first, that the month "Boëdromion answers to our October," and, second, that the celebration was "on the 20th of the month Boëdromion,"—then the celebration of the "mysteries of Ceres" came off on the 23d of October in that year. According to Herodotus, "the mysteries of Ceres" was celebrated on that year before the battle of Salamis. (*Herod.* viii. 65); therefore, this eclipse could not have been after the battle, if as early as the 2d of October; and as Cleombrotus left the isthmus at the time of the eclipse, it could not have been before the battle.

Is not this positive proof that the eclipse of the 2d of October, B.C. 480, could not have been the one recorded by Herodotus? And is not the error of Ptolemy now clearly exposed?

The next eclipse of the sun recorded in history took place at the beginning of the Peloponnesian War, and is thus introduced by Thucydides:—"The same summer, at the beginning of a new lunar month (the only time at which it appears possible), the sun was eclipsed after midday, and became full again after it had assumed a crescent form, and after some of the stars had shone out."

The first year of the Peloponnesian War, according to Ptolemy, was B.C. 431; and this eclipse is in S. Bliss's catalogue put down thus: "B.C. 431, August 4, aft. 5; 53, total." Excepting the quantity, this answers to the description of Thucydides, who saw the eclipse, and who says it was not total, but only "assumed a crescent form." Ferguson's tables make it total; and, according to them, the sun set 4 digits eclipsed; but Thucydides informs us that it "became full again." My tables eclipse 11 digits, which was a crescent form; and the eclipse ended about 28 minutes before sunset. This precisely corresponds with what is said of it by the historian.

Having now traced Ptolemy's canon down to a point up to which it is by astronomical demonstration proven to be correct, it is unnecessary to go any farther; so we shall now go back and inquire as to whether we can settle the correct Bible chronology.

CHRONOLOGY ESTABLISHED.

By the authority of that unerring Word of God from which "one jot or tittle" cannot "pass," we now intend to show the exact chronology of our Bible. We shall establish our position by astronomy; and thus put to silence those who oppose, or at least meet them on their own ground: for none doubt the truth-testing power of astronomy.

In Daniel ix. 25, we read thus: "Know, therefore, and understand that from the going forth of this commandment to restore and build Jerusalem, unto the Messiah the Prince, shall be seven weeks, and threescore and two weeks." Since both Jew and Gentile understand Daniel to mean 483 years, the only unsettled point is as to where they are to be commenced; and all that has made this a controversial point is that God in his wisdom saw proper to seal up the book of Daniel "until the time of the end:" for a plainer text cannot be found in the Bible. The book of Daniel was to remain sealed "until the time of the end;" and in ver. 25 of Chapter ix. is the key for the opening of the same to the understanding of those who shall live at the time of the end. To make this clear, let the reader first call to mind that Daniel has informed us that this vision was not intended for his own information, and Peter has also reminded us of the same fact: "No prophecy of the Scripture is of any private interpretation" (2 Pet.

i. 20): "for unto the prophets," says he, "it was revealed that not unto themselves, but *unto us they did minister the things which are now reported.*" (1 Pet. i. 12.)

With this light, it is plain that we are to receive that knowledge committed in charge to Daniel as something addressed to us, while Daniel is only the source through which that information is communicated: that is, we are to receive the words of the heavenly messenger, not as something addressed to Daniel individually, but something addressed to us collectively, while Daniel is our representative.

In Daniel viii. we have recorded in a few words a large portion of the history of our world, which has only in part been explained to our understanding; for Daniel says: "And it came to pass, when I, even I Daniel, had seen the vision, and sought for the meaning, then behold, there stood before me as the appearance of a man. And I heard a man's voice between the banks of Ulai, which called, and said, Gabriel, make this man to understand the vision." Remember, that Daniel being only our representative, Gabriel is here by the authority of heaven commanded, not to make Daniel individually, but us collectively, understand this vision. Through Daniel he says to us: "*Understand, O son of man; for at the time of the end shall be the vision.*" (Ver. 7.) After telling us that the beast which he had seen in the vision represented different kingdoms of the earth, he left, having only given us this much information, and told us that this vision was to reach to the "*last end of the indignation.*" (Ver. 19.) Hence, this much is all that any of us have ever been able to understand. "I was astonished at the vision, *but none understood it.*" (Ver. 23.) How is this? Has the God of heaven been disobeyed? This is hard to believe; yet we are compelled to admit it, if Gabriel does not open to our understandings the mystery of this vision; for he and no other has been commanded to do it. Let us, therefore, again consult our representative, and see if we can get any additional information. "*I heard,*" says Daniel, "*but I understood not:* then said I, O my Lord, what shall be the end of these things? And he said, *Go thy way, Daniel; for the words are closed up and sealed till the time of the end.*" (xii. 8, 9.) It is therefore useless to inquire further. We are here told to go our way; that these things are "sealed up and closed till the time of the end:" and it is useless to try to frustrate the purpose of God by endeavoring to understand that which he, in his wisdom, has thought proper to conceal from us. Until the time of the end, we will have to content ourselves with understanding other portions of the Word of God.

But before the angel Gabriel left, he informed us that at the "*time of the end should be the vision*" (viii. 17): and by referring to the "Signs of the Times," it will be seen that we are now living in the time of the end (see p. 28). We are, therefore, the very persons for whom the vision was intended: and if the "*wise shall understand*," may we not exercise faith to believe that Gabriel may yet obey the mandate of heaven, and open to us these things? (Dan. viii. 16.)

Then where is our representative: for it is now time to awake out of sleep. He is searching books (ix. 2); he is engaged in prayer (ver. 4); he knows that the angel Gabriel has been commanded to explain these things to us; and he will not be put off. "I set my face unto the Lord God, to seek by prayer and supplication, and sackcloth and ashes." Let us follow his example in searching books. Let us join him *in prayer*. Shall we be less concerned for our welfare than he for us? Remember, the knowledge of the vision is for our benefit, not for his. Listen to his fervent appeals: "O Lord, hear; O Lord, forgive; O Lord, hearken, and do; defer not, for thine own sake, O my God: for thy city and thy people are called by thy name." (ix. 19.)

His effectual, fervent petition has reached heaven. God has heard. Behold! the winged messenger returns swiftly now: "Yea," says Daniel, "while I was speaking in prayer, even the man Gabriel, whom I had seen in the vision at the beginning, being caused to fly swiftly, touched me about the time of the evening oblation. And he informed me, and talked with me, and said, O Daniel, I am now come forth to give thee skill and understanding. At the beginning of thy supplications the commandment came forth, and I am come to show thee; for thou art greatly beloved: therefore, understand the matter, and consider the vision." (ix. 21–23.)

Remember that Daniel is only our representative,—that we are they who are to "understand the matter, and consider the vision." "KNOW, THEREFORE, AND UNDERSTAND," says this heavenly messenger to us, "*that from the going forth* of the commandment to restore and build Jerusalem, unto the Messiah the Prince shall be seven weeks, and threescore and two weeks." All now is plain. We have the necessary information; for the heavenly messenger has obeyed the precept of heaven,—he has made us "UNDERSTAND THE VISION." (viii. 16.) That which was before a sealed book, is now opened; and we here discover the wisdom and power of God. "O the depth of the riches both of the wisdom and knowledge of God! how unsearchable are his judgments, and his ways past finding out." (Rom. xi. 33.)

This heavenly messenger does not say from the time some commandment shall be given: but "from the going forth of the commandment;" and, as if to direct our attention to the words used, he emphatically says, "KNOW, THEREFORE, AND UNDERSTAND," or, as the Douay Bible has it, "take NOTICE." If, as directed, we "take notice," it will be observed "THE" supposes some commandment already framed which had not gone forth; or at least it restricts us to the commandment with which Daniel was familiar. As this divine instructor does not first inform Daniel that a commandment would go forth, it would have been an abuse of language for him to have used the word "the," if he alluded to any other. If it be true, then, that from the word of God "one jot or tittle shall not pass," we are necessarily bound to look for that commandment which Daniel knew was to go forth; and, in order to do this, we will first inquire who was to give it; and, second, to whom it was to be given. By reference to 1 Esdras vii. 4, we learn that it was not to be given by the kings of the earth, but by the God of heaven. We refer to Esdras instead of Ezra, because the word "commandment" of Cyrus, Darius, and Artaxerxes, as mentioned in Ezra vi. 14, is not properly translated. In the original, the words used are different: the one translated "the commandment of the God of Israel," means a "royal decree or edict;" while "the commandment of Cyrus, and Darius, and Artaxerxes," means "respect, permission, or consent," as properly translated in Esdras.

In the next place, to whom was this commandment to be given? Not to the Jews,—for they had no power to restore and build Jerusalem; and it is required of a man to do acccording to that which he hath, and not that which he hath not. Had they possessed this power, there would have been no use for a commandment, as all they wanted was the privilege. As none possessed this power except the Kings of Babylon, and after them the Kings of Persia, it is clear that this commandment must have been given to one of them. We must now ascertain to which one. "Thus saith the Lord, the King of Israel, who, as I shall call, and shall declare it and set it in order for me. CYRUS, he is my shepherd, and shall perform ALL MY PLEASURE: *even saying to Jerusalem,* Thou shalt be built; and to the temple, Thy foundation shalt be laid (Isa. xliv. 6, 7, 28): and "I will direct all his ways: *he shall build my city, and he shall let go my captive.*" (Isa. xlv. 13.)

We will now inquire whether Cyrus ever received this commandment? "Thus saith Cyrus, King of Persia, The Lord God of heaven .... hath charged me to build him a house at Jerusalem." (Ezra i. 2.) Isaiah has not only informed us that this commandment was to be given by the Lord to Cyrus, but we have the acknowledgment from Cyrus that he received it; and it is impossible to evade the fact by saying that he has only acknowledged that he was commanded to build the temple; for that was not only a part of Jerusalem, but constituted the most essential portion of the city; and in the same verse through which he received the authority to build the temple, he is commanded to BUILD JERUSALEM. (Isa. xliv. 28.)

It now remains to ascertain the exact time at which the commandment went forth; for we are not authorized to commence the sixty-nine weeks with the framing of it, but from the time it went into execution, which could not have been as early as the time at which it was framed, for that was many years before Cyrus was born. It was not before he conquered Babylon; for until then the Jews were subject to that kingdom: nor until after the death of Darius, the Median; for up to that time Cyrus did not possess the full power of obeying this commandment. But it went forth into full force soon after the death of Darius,—that is, "in the first year of Cyrus"(Ezra i. 1); and this could not have been later than the end of Jeremiah's seventy-years captivity; for the object of the commandment was "that the word of the Lord by the mouth of Jeremiah might be fulfilled." (Ezra i. 1.)

Ezra omits the proclamation of Cyrus for the building of Jerusalem. But this apparent difficulty at once vanishes when we observe who was to give the commandment and to whom it was to be given; for we here have the exact words: "even saying to Jerusalem, Thou shalt be built;" for saith the Lord of Cyrus, "HE SHALL BUILD MY CITY, AND HE SHALL LET GO MY CAPTIVES." (Isa. xlv. 13.) By comparing Ezra i. 1–4 with vi. 34, we learn that he has not given us the full edict as issued by Cyrus; but, the full copy having coming down to us through Josephus, we find that as much was said about building Jerusalem as the temple. Josephus not only declares that Cyrus "gave them leave to go back to their own country, and to rebuild their city Jerusalem;" but, by virtue of that privilege, we find them employed on that very work. (See Ezra iv. 12.) This commandment, therefore, properly went forth, accomplishing the object of its original design, when Cyrus, who was required "to restore and to build Jerusalem," having overthrown those nations to whom the Jews were in bondage, granted them the full privilege of restoring and building their city; for Josephus says, Cyrus "permitted them to have the same honor which they were used to have from their fathers;" and they restored their former worship according to the law of Moses. (Ezra iii. 1–6.) So far from the least hint being in the Bible of "the Lord God of Israel" (1 Esd. vii. 4) ever commanding any one except Cyrus "to restore and to build Jerusalem," he "saith of Cyrus, He is my shepherd and shall perform all my pleasure" in this, "even saying to Jerusalem, Thou shalt be built" (Isa. xliv. 28); for while Cyrus did in nothing else "perform all" the pleasure of the Lord, he did in this: for, saith the Lord, "he shall build my city and he shall let go my captives." (Isa. xlv. 13.)

Is it not strange that those who set themselves up as masters in Israel should, rather than admit the incorrectness of Ptolemy's canon, yet contend that there were three other commandments for the building of Jerusalem, and that Darius or Artaxerxes performed the most essential part of that pleasure of the Lord which he declared should be performed by Cyrus?

The one called a commandment, as given by Darius, was only a prohibition written to the adversaries of the Jews, who were trying to hinder them from accomplishing that which Cyrus had granted them the privilege of performing. It was thus: "Let the work of this house of God alone." (Ezra vi. 7.) Now, what is there about this which has any appearance of a command "to restore and build Jerusalem"?

The next edict is said to have been delivered by Artaxerxes Longimanus in the seventh year of his reign. So far from this having the least appearance of a command either to build Jerusalem or any thing else, Ezra expressly says, "the king granted him all of his request." (Ezra vii. 6.) There is not a word here about Jerusalem, which had been built long before. Hence, those who date the sixty-nine weeks here have ingeniously evaded the expression, "to restore and to build Jerusalem," by telling us it must be taken in a figurative sense. But it is morally impossible to restrict the meaning of Gabriel to only a figurative sense without laying aside that universal and only rule by which we can ever make any sense of the Bible. We allude to the rule of gathering the meaning by the context and general scope of the subject. If suffered to depart from this rule, we can prove that there is no God: "Yea, there is no God; I know not any." (Isa. xliv. 8.) It is impossible by this rule to twist and strain the expression, "restore and to build Jerusalem," to mean only a second reformation which took place among the Jews seventy-nine years after they had been fully restored to their land. The angel enjoined upon Daniel to "Know therefore and understand that from the going forth of the commandment to restore and to build Jerusalem;" and the only one that Daniel knew any thing of was the one as delivered in charge to Cyrus. As he died in "the first year of King Cyrus" (Dan. i. 2), it is certain that he never knew any thing of any other. But to put an end to this controversy, if it is "impossible for God to lie" (Heb. vi. 18), we are compelled to admit that Cyrus was not only commanded, "even saying to Jerusalem, Thou shalt be built" (Isa. xliv. 28), but that he did build Jerusalem; for saith the Lord, "He shall build my city, and he shall let go my captives." (Isa. xlv. 13.) And Daniel was informed that the sixty-nine weeks are to be commenced not at a commandment, but "from the going forth of THE commandment to restore and to build Jerusalem." (Dan. ix. 25.)

To him who can evade this, the word of God is of no worth. The sixty-nine weeks commence with "The going forth of the commandment to restore and to build Jerusalem," which went forth (Ezra iv. 12) "in the first year of Cyrus, King of Persia." (Ezra i. 1.)

While the book of Daniel remained sealed, it was supposed that God had left it to men to conjecture as to what command was meant, or which selection to make from those which are scattered over a period of from seventy-eight to one hundred and fourteen years, using their own choice as to the particular king in whose reign they would have it issued. And it is remarkable that, after taking this unbounded liberty as to the beginning of Daniel's prophetic dates, learned divines have been unable to get a single period in the vision to reach its proper end. For example: while the seventy weeks were too long for those who commenced them in the reign of Darius, those who preferred Artaxerxes found them thirty-two years too short to span the time as "determined upon" the "holy city." (Dan. ix. 24.) The sixty-nine weeks are thirty years too long for those who use the reign of the latter king; and those who prefer the former are the more perplexed, as they overshoot the time at which the Messiah came by sixty-nine years, while the sixty-two weeks are deficient by seventeen years; and those who begin the sixty-two weeks with the seventh of Artaxerxes want fifty-six years more to reach the time at which they say the

Messiah was cut off. To supply this deficiency, they borrow forty-nine years from that period which was to reach "the Messiah the Prince," and seven years more from Antichrist, "the prince" who was to "confirm the covenant with many for one week." (Dan. ix. 27.) In addition to these gross absurdities in sustaining Ptolemy's canon, in their writings they have been continually clashing with various authors both sacred and profane; for their maxim was that "the canon of Ptolemy is not to be receded from for the authority of any other writing whatsoever." (*Prideaux.*) But He who commanded the author, the least of all his servants, to "write the vision," would allow him no such liberty. Without the privilege of his own selection, "the going forth of the" one definite "commandment" was pointed out. (Dan. ix. 25.) Being allowed the choice of none, he was restricted to the reign of a particular king (Isa. xliv. 28); forbidden to contradict any of God's sacred writers (Rev. xxii. 18, 19), he was confined to the very letter or form of words used (2 Tim. i. 13), even to the jot and tittle. (Matt v. 18.) But, notwithstanding these narrow limits, we find that every part comes together like the portions of a wonderful piece of machinery, previously constructed, but now for the first time properly connected. Behold! every prophetic date occupies its correct place, thus declaring the solemn truth that the sealed book of Daniel is now indeed opened. When the light first broke over the soul of the author, he, like Daniel, "fainted and was sick certain days." (Dan. viii. 27.) For knowing that the learned had for eighteen hundred years been vainly employing every effort of the intellect to pry into the mystery of this volume, he saw this could be no fancy dream, as it was clearly demonstrated that this book, which had been sealed, was now opened, turning "wise men backward," and making "their knowledge foolish." (Isa. xliv. 25.) We are no longer compelled to contradict both sacred and profane authors as our fathers have done, as if they were resolved to make the Bible and all ancient history give place to the authority of Ptolemy.

That empty shadow called "a command to restore and to build Jerusalem," over which so much ado has been made, is simply this:—Xerxes having "stirred up all against the realm of Grecia" (Dan. xi. 2), his son, in the seventh year of his reign, making "a release to the provinces" (Esth. ii. 18), granted the Jews the privilege of returning home. (Ezra vii. 7.)

The next one called a commandment was only a privilege granted Nehemiah to build the wall that enclosed Jerusalem. Nehemiah expressly says, "the houses were not builded" (vii. 4),—that is, not built by him, but by Cyrus about ninety years before; for in the same verse he says, "the city was large and great,"—and without houses there could be no city.

But, as the vision of Daniel was sealed up, our fathers are to be excused for holding views which are now so clearly incorrect. If we had no other reason for commencing the sixty-nine weeks at the first of Cyrus, the fact that the vision was to be sealed up until the time of the end is a sufficient reason; for our fathers, for hundreds of years, have commenced them at the last three so-called commandments. To show that no one has commenced them at the first of Cyrus, we will refer to Prideaux, who says:—"None who understand this prophecy to relate either to the cutting off, or the coming of the Messiah, do begin from the first of Cyrus; for, according to this computation, no chronology can reconcile them."

We have now said enough on this subject to convince all who are willing to receive the truth. As for those who are resolved to "wander and perish," they would "in no wise believe though a man declare it unto them." (Acts xiii. 41.) We cannot see how any one can be so actuated by prejudice as to examine the argument we have advanced, and yet believe that the sixty-nine weeks can be commenced anywhere but with the first of Cyrus.

We shall now consider the following question: Where did the sixty-nine weeks end? The angel did not inform Daniel that they were to end at the baptism of Christ, nor when he should enter on his ministry, or the Holy Spirit should be seen descending on him like a dove; but, when "the Messiah the Prince" should appear. The day of his birth was the time at which he was introduced to Daniel's people as "Christ the Lord." (Luke ii. 11.) It was at this glorious introduction that the "multitude of the heavenly host" were heard praising God, saying, "Glory to God in the highest, and on earth peace, good will toward men." (Luke ii. 14.) "For behold, I bring you good tidings of great joy, which shall be to all people." (ii. 10.) As it was revealed unto Daniel that the sixty-nine weeks were to reach to "the Messiah the Prince," so it was revealed to Simeon "that he should not see death, before he had seen the Lord's Christ." (Luke ii. 26). When he had embraced the babe of Bethlehem, he did not crave to see his baptism, as if he thought that would be the time of the appearing of the promised Consolation of Israel; but, as if his every anxiety was now satisfied, he says, "Lord, now lettest thou thy servant depart in peace, according to thy word: for mine eyes have seen thy salvation, which thou hast prepared before the face of all people; a light to lighten the Gentiles, and the glory of thy people Israel." When Herod "had gathered all the chief priests and scribes of the people together," and "demanded of them where Christ should be born," they answered, "In Bethlehem of Judea: for thus it is written by the prophet." (Matt. ii. 5.) No prophecy in the Bible speaks of the baptism of Christ as the time of the appearing of the Messiah. With one consent they all thus point to the babe of Bethlehem: "For unto us a child is born, unto us a son is given: and the government shall be upon his shoulder; and his name shall be called Wonderful, Counsellor, The mighty God, The everlasting Father, The Prince of Peace." (Isa. ix. 6.)

The Messiah was to be of the house of David; it was necessary that he should be "made under the law to redeem them that were under the law;" and necessary also that he should have a body. It was his birth, not his baptism, that made him of the house of David, placed him under the law, and gave him his body. Daniel was informed that the sixty-nine weeks were to reach to "the Messiah the Prince," who was "born King of the Jews" (Matt. ii. 2), in Bethlehem, and not in the river Jordan. If they reach to his baptism, they extend thirty years beyond the time he came into the world, and was introduced to Daniel's people as the Messiah:—"For unto you is born this day" (not thirty years hence) "in the city of David" (not in the river Jordan) "a Saviour, which is Christ the Lord." (Luke ii. 11.) Thus "when the fullness of time was come," or at the end of Daniel's sixty-nine weeks, "God sent forth his Son, made of a woman, made under the law, to redeem them that were under the law." (Gal. iv. 4.) Hence, the sixty-nine weeks can extend nowhere else but to the time when he was thus made of a woman. The only apparent authority for extending them to the baptism of Christ is that our fathers did so, which, indeed, is no authority at all; for, as the vision of Daniel was to be sealed up until the time of the end, the fact of their thus extending them is a proof that they ought not to reach that period; for, if they have been able to explain the vision of Daniel, then the book itself is false, as it professes to be sealed up till the time of the end. Hence, if as much authority existed for extending the sixty-nine weeks to his baptism, as to his birth, this would be sufficient to throw us back to the time of his birth. That we can, consistently with the truthfulness of the book of Daniel having been sealed, extend them to the birth of Christ, we refer to

Prideaux, who says:—"For his coming here predicted must be interpreted, either of his coming at his birth, or of his coming on his ministry. No one saith it of the former, neither will the term of years predicted of it ever meet it there."

It now remains to find the exact year of his birth. This having been already settled, we merely refer the reader to Luke ii. 42. By noticing the date as placed in the margin of a reference Bible, it will be seen that Jesus was twelve years old, A.D. 8. Eight and four are twelve; but, in crossing the Christian era, we must always diminish one: this, then, gives us the year B.C. 5, for the time of the birth of Christ. The seventy-years captivity, ending there, gives us the year B.C. 558 for the time of its beginning, in the eighth year of Nebuchadnezzar (2 Kings xxiv. 12): and from the time of the captivity the Bible gives its own chronology back to the Creation. So with the Creation we will now commence; and by the chronological dates, as given in our Bible, establish the true chronology,—the correctness of which we will prove by the records of those unerring astronomical demonstrations which, crushing Ptolemy's canon, opened the sealed book of Daniel to the understanding of our heavenly Father's children.

THE

CHRONOLOGICAL ORDER OF OUR BIBLE ESTABLISHED.

PROPHETIC DATES, TYPES, AND SHADOWS, DISCLOSED.

B.C. 4126. THE BEGINNING OF CREATION.—At the time our Bible was written, the word month meant moon; for "the month is called after her name" (Ecclesiasticus xliii. 8); and since He who made the moon calls the month Abib *"the first month"* (Lev. xxiii. 5), it follows that this was the first month of creation. Hence, he who made the sun and moon "for days and years" (Gen. i. 14) "to serve in their season for a declaration of times and a sign to the world," positively enjoins upon his people to use "the month Abib" (Ex. xiii. 4) as *"the first month of the year."* (Ex. xii. 2.) And why? Because "this month is unto you *the beginning of months,"* as it was the first month or moon of Creation. According to the chronological dates as found in our Bible, Creation commenced in the year B.C. 4126; and from Genesis i. 5, we learn that Creation began on the first day of the week; and by calculation we find that the first day of the month Abib, in the year B.C. 4126, fell on the first day of the week,—that is, Sunday, April 30, O.S.. or March 29, N.S. Thus we prove by astronomical demonstration that Creation began on Sunday, March 29, B.C. 4126.

All nations, from the time of the fall of man to that of the exodus, continued to reckon time from the fall of the year. With them the fifteenth day of the seventh month was the end of the year (Ex. xxiii. 16); from which we conclude that this was the day on which Adam fell, and the end of his first year in the garden of Eden. If so, the day he fell the moon began to wane, the leaves to fall, the chilling winds to howl; the earth, laying aside the loveliness of spring, put on her wintry robe,—the emblem of death.

The unhappy race of Adam continued to reckon time from this epoch until "the time of the promise drew nigh," when the Lord enjoined it upon Israel, his "first-born" to reckon time as at the beginning of creation; that with them the first month should be the first month of the year. (Ex. xii. 2.)

Under that dispensation, which was "a shadow of good things to come" (Heb. x. 1), he, who from the time of the fall was to toil and live by "the sweat of his face," was required to "labor and do all" his "work" in "six days" and rest "the seventh day" (Ex. xx. 9); from which we conclude that after six thousand years of toil and sorrow in this world, the true Israel shall rest during the millennial sabbath. Thus our God, "declaring the end from the beginning" (Isa. xlvi. 10), teaches his children that at the end of six thousand years the great sabbath of rest will begin. (Rev. xx. 4.) If to the year B.C. 4126 we add 1875 diminished by 1, we will have 6000. Therefore, on the 15th day of the seventh month in the year A.D. 1875, the world will be 6000 years old, reckoning from the fall of man; or 6000 years, 6 months, and 14 days, from the beginning of Creation.

The 15th of the seventh month in the year B.C. 4126 fell on Friday, October 5th, which was the sixth day of the week,—the same day on which man was formed of the dust of the earth, six months and nine days before. Within the limits of about two months before the fall of man, both the sun and moon were eclipsed.

A.M. 1656. THE FLOOD.—As Methuselah lived 969 years, the flood could not have commenced earlier than the 17th of the second month (Gen. vii. 11), in the year of the world 1656. According to Josephus (*Ant.* b. i, c. iii. s. 3), this is the second month of the civil year, which is the eighth month of the sacred year; and that they then began the year with the month Tisri will appear from Isaac having reaped the same year in which he sowed (Gen. xxvi. 12), which he could not have done had they commenced the year with the month Abib, as the Israelites did when they left Egypt.

A.M. 2085. ABRAHAM GOES TO CANAAN.—"In the second month, on the seventh and twentieth day of the month," in the year of the world 1657, "was the earth dried" (Gen. viii. 14); and if to this we add 427 years, we will have the 27th of the same month, in the year of the world 2084, for the time of the death of Terah. If we allow thirty days for Abraham to mourn for his father (Num. xx. 29), eighteen more to make arrangements to leave for the land of Canaan, we will have the 15th of Tebeth, the tenth month, for the time Abraham left Haran. "Abraham was seventy and five years old when he departed out of Haran" (Gen. xii. 4); "And after Abraham had dwelt ten years in the land of Canaan," he took Hagar "to be his wife" (Gen. xvi. 3); "and Abraham was fourscore and six years old when Hagar bare Ishmael to Abraham." (Gen. xvi. 16.) From this it would appear that Abraham reached the land of Canaan in about three months from the time he left Haran. These three months bring us to the 15th of Abib, which was the day on which Abraham reached Canaan. (Ex. xii. 41.) Josephus says, the Israelites "left Egypt on the month Xancticus, in the 15th day of the lunar month, 430 years after our father Abraham had come into Canaan; but 215 years only after that Jacob removed into Egypt." (*Josephus* b. ii. c. xv. s. 3.) A short time after Abraham reached the land of Canaan, the Lord appeared to him and said, "Unto thy seed will I give this land;" and from this promise, Paul has 430 years to the giving of the law (Gal. iii. 17), which law was given "in the third month, when the children of Israel were gone forth out of the land of Egypt." (Ex. xix. 1.) The Samaritan Pentateuch reads thus: "Now the sojourning of the children of Israel and of their fathers, which they sojourned in the land of Canaan and in the land of Egypt, was 430 years." (See Dr. Clark on Ex. xii. 41.) These four months and odd days will be considered unworthy of notice by some; but as the correctness of our tables are to be tested by astronomy, we must reduce them to the most exact precision by adhering strictly to the express language of inspiration.

According to the chronology as given by Moses, the death of Terah was 427 years after the flood. (Gen. xi. 10.) If full years, they bring us to the 27th of Marchesvan, A.M. 2084; and as Abraham reached Canaan on the 15th of Abib, those who place his going there in the year A.M. 2084 have the chronology seven months and odd days short of the Mosaic account.

A.M. 2515. THE PASSOVER.—The passover was first observed on Wednesday, April 4, N.S., or April, 8, O.S., B.C. 1611; and on the "morrow after the passover," which was Thursday the 15th of the first month, the Hebrews left the land of Egypt. (Num. xxxiii. 3.)

B.C. 1611. THE SABBATH GIVEN TO MAN.—In the year B.C. 1611, the new moon of the second month fell on April 19, at 26 m. after three in the morning, on the meridian of Mount Sinai in Arabia. So the moon could be seen on the evening of the 20th of April; hence, the first day of the second month was on April 21, and the 15th fell on May 5, N.S., or 19, O.S. "And all the congregation of the children of Israel came unto the wilderness of Sin on the 15th day of the second month." (Ex. xvi. 1.) This was on Saturday, May 5. "At evening the quails came up and covered the camp, and in the morning," May 6, which was Sunday, "the dew lay round about the host." (Ex. xvi. 13.) And now the people were "to gather a certain rate every day" for six days (Ex. xvi. 26),—that is, until Friday. "And it came to pass on the sixth day, they gathered twice as much bread." And Moses "said unto them, This is that which the Lord hath said, To-morrow is the rest of the holy sabbath unto the Lord." So the people rested on the seventh day,—that is, on Saturday, May 12. (Ex. xvi. 22, 23, 30.) Thus, the year B.C. 1611 is astronomically proven to be the year the children of Israel left the land of Egypt. To make this clear, it will be necessary to show that no other year within the limits of the dispute among chronologists will answer. As the ninth year of Joshua, the third of David, the twelfth of Solomon, and the eighteenth of Josiah, were years of the jubilee, if we add or diminish here, it must be by entire cycles of forty-nine years. The following table shows the day of the week and month on which the 15th day of the Jewish second month falls for the first year, through ten cycles of forty-nine years:—

B.C.	N.S.	O.S.	
1856	May 11	May 26	Tuesday.
1807	" 10	" 25	Friday.
1758	" 9	" 23	Monday.
1709	" 7	" 21	Friday.
1660	" 6	" 20	Tuesday.
1611	" 5	" 19	Saturday.
1562	" 4	" 17	Tuesday.
1513	" 1	" 14	Friday.
1464	" 1	" 13	Tuesday.
1415	April 30	" 12	Saturday.

Within the limits of the above table, which runs through a period of 441 years, 1611 and 1415 are the only two years on which the 15th of the second month falls on Saturday,—the only two years on which the Jewish sabbath falls on the 22d of the second month; and as the year 1415 is too short, and the year 1856 too long, it will be observed that this table runs through the limits of the dispute among chronologists, thus proving that B.C. 1611 was the year the Hebrews left the land of Egypt.

B.C. 1611. MANNA THE TYPE.—As the manna was a type of Christ (John vi. 48; Rev. ii. 17), the children of Israel gathering manna for six days and resting on the seventh, seems "to be a sign" (Ezek. xx. 12) that the sons and daughters of Adam may gather the bread of life (John vi. 57) for 6000 years and rest on the seventh millennium or great sabbath, which remaineth for "the people of God" (Heb. iv. 9; Rev. xx. 4); and, as on the seventh day, there was no manna found, so it would appear that when 6000 years shall have rolled around, the bread of eternal life will cease to be offered to man,—"the fullness of the Gentiles" will have come in. (Rom. xi. 25.)

B.C. 1605. SABBATICAL YEAR.—Under the Mosaic dispensation every seventh day was a sabbath, and every seventh year was a sabbatical year. (Lev. xxv. 4.) As this law was given the first year of their leaving the land of Egypt, it follows that the seventh year from that time was a sabbatical year. Since there was a positive law, enjoining it upon the Jews to begin their year with "the month Abib" (Ex. xiii. 4), saying, "This month shall be unto you the beginning of months: it shall be the first month of the year to you" (Ex. xii. 2), there need be no doubt as to what was the first month of this year. (See at the year B.C. 548.)

B.C. 1571. END OF THE FIRST CHASTISEMENT.—As a chastisement for disobedience, the Lord "drove out the man from the garden of Eden" (Gen. iii. 23, 24), the place of his inheritance. (Gen. ii. 8.) Man continued to wander in exile for 2555 years: at the end of which the sons of Abraham returned to the land of their inheritance,—"a land that floweth with milk and honey." (Josh. v. 6.)

When Israel was about to enter this land, the Lord promised to be with them on the condition of obedience: "And I will walk among you, and I will be your God, and ye shall be my people. But if ye will not hearken unto me, and will not do all these commandments, then I will punish you seven times more for your sins." (Lev. xxvi. 12, 14, 18.) The expression "more" as used here, saying, "I will punish you seven times more," declares that they had once been thus punished for their sins. According to our table of chronology, in which we have followed the Hebrew, Moses's "seven times" must mean a period of 2555 years; but according to the Septuagint, the interval between the fall of man and the time the Hebrews entered the land of Canaan was 3983 years. This makes it necessary to look for some other rule by which to ascertain the number of years in Moses's "seven times," which, if we can find, we shall be enabled to decide which is the correct chronology,—that of the Hebrew, or the Septuagint.

That the expression "seven times" was the Chaldean term for seven years, we thus learn: "A holy one came down from heaven" and addressed a Chaldean king in the Chaldean language, thus: "Let seven times pass over him" (Dan. iv. 16); and while Daniel, in explaining this to the king, must employ such terms as were familiar to him, he uses the same expression, "seven times shall pass over thee." (Dan. iv. 25.) But, instead of "seven times," the Greeks used the expression, seven years. So, Josephus, who professed "to do no more than translate the Hebrew books into the Greek language," instead of "seven times" used the expression "seven years." (*Ant.* x. c. x. s. 6.)

Now, the Chaldean year consisted of just 365 days: so, in seven Chaldean times, or years, there were 2555 days;—and "each day for a year shall ye bear your iniquity" (Num. xiv. 34); and according to the Hebrew chronology, the interval between the time of the fall of man and the time Israel entered the land of of Canaan was just 2555 years. This decides that the Hebrew is the correct chronology. (See more on this at the year B.C. 681.)

B.C. 1571. THE SEVEN-YEARS SERVICE OF JACOB.—As Hagar and Sarah were types of the "two covenants" (Gal. iv. 24), so the two wives of Jacob seem to be types of the same. When Jacob had "served seven years" (Gen. xxix. 20), for the one he loved, he received one whom he did not love (Gen. xxix. 31); so when he who "must work the work of him that sent" him (John ix. 4), had thus been employed for seven prophetic years, he received "a wife" which was not beloved. (Jer. iii. 20; Rom. ix. 13.) But Jacob served "yet seven other years" for the object of his love (Gen. xxix. 27): from this may we not conclude that Christ will serve seven other prophetic years, and receive the object of his love,—"the bride, the Lamb's wife." (Rev. xxi. 9.) The seven years during which Jacob served were spent in the service of Laban, "the Syrian" (Gen. xxviii. 5), whose year consisted of just 365 days; and the expression, "my days are fulfilled" (Gen. xxix. 21), shows that the time was fulfilled to the day. So the period of time which Jacob served was 2555 days, answering to the 2555 years from the fall of man to the time "Israel after the flesh" (1 Cor. x. 18) entered the land of Canaan. Jacob's second service of "seven other years" seems to be dated from the time he openly manifested his displeasure with his first wife: "What is this thou hast done unto me?" (Gen. xxix. 25.) From this we may infer that there must be just 2555 years from the time "the Lord removed Israel out of his sight" (2 Kings xvii. 23)—and thus manifested to all the world his displeasure towards that people—to the end of the service of Christ for the recovery of man.

This happened "in the sixth year of Hezekiah" (2 Kings xviii. 10), B.C. 681. The Julian period for the year B.C. 681 is 4033, to which if we add 2555, we will have 6588, which is the Julian period for the year A.D. 1875. According to this type, the last service for the redemption of man ends in A.D. 1875.

B.C. 1570. SABBATICAL YEAR.—That the year B.C. 1570, or the second year after the children of Israel entered the land of Canaan, was a sabbatical year, we learn from Joshua viii. 35: "Moses commanded them, saying, At the end of every seven years, in the solemnity of the year of release, in the feast of tabernacles, when all Israel is come to appear before the Lord thy God in the place which he shall choose, thou shalt read this law before all Israel in their hearing" (Deut. xxxi. 10, 11); and "there was not a word of all that Moses commanded which Joshua read not before all the congregation of Israel. (Josh. viii. 35.)

B.C. 1565. DIVISION OF THE LAND.—Says Dr. Clark: Joshua "spent about seven years in the conquest of the land, and is supposed to have employed about one year in dividing it." (See on Josh x. 1.) As Caleb's forty-five years ends about August, 1565 (Num. xiii. 21, 23), it would appear that they spent one year and six months in dividing the land. This brings us to the sabbatical year 1563, which was also the year of jubilee, during which they returned unto their possession.

B.C. 1563. FIRST JUBILEE.—"The Lord spake unto Moses," "saying, When ye come into the land which I shall give you, then shall the land keep a sabbath unto the Lord." (Lev. xxv. 1, 2.) The falling of the walls of Jericho, and the ruin of the city Ai, throwing terror over the inhabitants of the land, the Israelites were enabled to observe in peace and quietness a sabbatical year on the second year of their entering the promised land, at which time, in obedience to their law, they "read all the words of the law." (Josh. viii. 34.) "When all the kings which were on this side Jordan" "heard thereof" (Josh. ix. 1),—that is, heard that the Hebrews were reading their law and observing a sabbatical year, in which they did not go forth to battle (*Jose. Ant.* xiii. c. vii. s. 1), "they gathered themselves together to fight with Joshua (Josh. ix. 2); but, on learning that the inhabitants of Gibeon had made peace with Israel, and were among them, they feared greatly, because Gibeon was a great city." (Josh. x. 1, 2.) It accordingly appears that the Hebrews were not molested during this sabbatical year: the land, therefore, kept the first sabbath in the year 1570. Now, from this, their first sabbath, the law required, saying: "Six years thou shalt sow thy field, but in the seventh year shall be a sabbath of rest unto the land, a sabbath for the Lord" (Lev. xxv. 4); and, at the time of this second sabbath, "thou shalt number seven sabbaths of years unto thee, seven times seven years; and the space of the seven sabbaths of years shall be unto thee forty and nine years. Then" (in this forty-ninth year) "shalt thou cause the trumpet of the jubilee to sound, on the tenth day of the seventh month" (Lev. xxv. 8, 9): and "In the year of this jubilee ye shall return every man unto his possessions." (Lev. xxv. 13.) Hence, those who received their inheritance on the east of Jordan, eight years before the jubilee, were forbidden to go to their possession "until the Lord hath given rest unto your brethren, as well as unto you; and until they also possess the land which the Lord your God hath given them beyond Jordan;" and then, "In the year of this jubilee" (Lev. xxv. 13) "shall ye return every man unto his possession which I have given you." (Deut. iii. 20.) Therefore, at the time of this jubilee, Joshua said to them. "Now return ye, and get you unto your tents, and unto the land of your possession, which Moses the servant of the Lord gave you on the other side Jordan." (Josh. xxii. 4.) "And the Lord gave them rest round about," insomuch that, during this sabbatical year of jubilee, "there stood not a man of all their enemies before them." (Josh. xxi. 44.) "The land had rest from war." (Josh. xiv. 15.)

B.C. 1563. END OF THE YEAR OF JUBILEE.—As this year commenced with the 10th day and the forty-ninth sabbatical year, it must end on the 10th day of the seventh month in the fiftieth year; for its duration was one year: "ye shall hallow the fiftieth year." (Lev. xxv. 10.) For this reason, it was unnecessary for the sixth year before the jubilee to yield a larger supply of bread than for the ordinary sabbatical year. Had the sabbatical year commenced with the seventh month, as did the jubilee, then a supply for two years would have been sufficient for the Seventh-year Sabbath; but as it commenced with the month Abib (see at the year 1605), it was necessary for the supply of the sixth year to be sufficient for three years (Lev. xxv. 21); for the autumn of the eighth year was the earliest period at which they could sow their grain, and they could not reap it before the spring of the ninth. (Lev. xxv. 22.) As the year of jubilee commenced in the seventh year, and ended on the 10th of the seventh month of the eighth year, it interfered in no way with their crops; and it ended early enough for them to sow their grain; for the law enjoined it upon them to "sow the eighth year." (Lev. xxv. 22.)

B.C.1563. THE ANTITYPE OF THE JUBILEE.—That law, from which "one jot or one tittle" cannot pass away "till all be fulfilled" (Matt. v. 18), required, saying, "In the year of this jubilee ye shall return every man to his possession" (Lev. xxv. 13); yet it appears that during this jubilee, only two tribes, "and the half tribe of Manassah" returned unto the land of their possession. (Josh. xxii. 4.) "There remaineth yet very much land to be possessed" (Josh. xiii. 1): for though the other tribes had their land divided to them by lot, it was yet in the hands of the Canaanites. Hence, this law, "ye shall return every man unto his possession" (Lev. xxv. 13), remaineth to be fulfilled by him who came to fulfill the law (Matt. v. 17); and since the Jubilee Sabbath, under the Mosaic dispensation, was but "a shadow of things to come" (Col. ii. 17), we are unable to discover how the law can be accomplished but in that of the true Israel's returning unto their everlasting possessions, in the year of the world's great jubilee. "If Joshua had given them rest," if the law concerning the matter had received its accomplishment here, "then would he not afterwards have spoken of another day;" but now he hath spoken of another: "There remaineth therefore a rest" (keeping of the Sabbath) "to the people of God." (Heb. iv. 8, 9.) From Leviticus xxvi. 43, we learn that the land was to "enjoy her sabbaths while she lieth desolate without them;" and seventy years was the interval in which the land enjoyed her sabbaths; "for as long as it lay desolate, it kept sabbath to fulfill three-core and ten years." (2 Chron. xxxvi. 21.) If the law was fulfilled in a rest of seventy years, then there must be just seventy jubilees to answer the end of the law; for the sabbath of the jubilee was a rest of one year. In seventy jubilees there are 3430 years; and the first jubilee was in the year B.C. 1563. The Julian period for the year 1563 is 3151; and if we add 3430 to 3151, we will have 6581, which is the Julian period for A.D. 1868. Thus, apparently, the year 1868 will be the world's last jubilee.

B.C. 1547. JOSHUA'S DEATH.—Joshua "died, being a hundred and ten years old" (Josh. xxiv. 29), which, according to Josephus was twenty-five years after the death of Moses. (*Jose.* b. v. c. i. s. 29., As this twenty-five years adds eighteen to the age of Joshua after the time he is called "old and stricken in years" (Josh. xiii. 1), it appears to be a period long enough; and as it makes Joshua forty five years old at the time he is called "a young man" (Ex. xxxiii. 11), we cannot reasonably make it less, as all we take from the twenty-five years, we add to the age of Joshua when called "a young man," and also diminish that period which Joshua called "a long time." (Josh. xxiii. 1.) Josephus cannot be far from the truth here; but should there be an error, it will be corrected by the forty-nine years cycle, or the year of jubilee.

B.C. 1546. THE ANARCHY.—"After the death of Joshua," says Josephus, "for eighteen years in all, the multitude had no settled form of government, but were in an anarchy; after which they returned to their former government." (*Ant.* vi. c. v. s. 4.) The cycle of forty-nine years to the year of jubilee proves that Josephus is here correct. (See "Table of Chronology.")

B.C. 1528. THE FIRST SERVITUDE.—"The children of Israel did evil in the sight of the Lord;" "therefore the anger of the Lord was hot against Israel, and he sold them into the hand of Chushan-rishathaim" (Judg. iii. 8) during their sabbatical year, at which time they did not fight. (*Jose. Ant.* xiii. c. viii. s. 1.)

B.C. 1528. BEGINNING OF JUDGES.—Some writers on chronology date the commencement of Paul's 450 years from the division of the land by Joshua, because that was the last circumstance mentioned by the apostle. It must be observed that Paul was not giving a connected chronology of the world, but only alluding to historical matters of fact,—one of which was that the Lord "gave them judges, about the space of four hundred and fifty years, until Samuel the prophet." (Acts xiii. 20.) As the 450 years measures the time of the judges to that of "Samuel the prophet," they cannot begin before the time of the judges. As that time did not commence before the division of the land (Acts xiii. 19, 20), we learn that Joshua was not included as one of them. And as Joshua, at the time of his death, "let the people depart every man unto his inheritance" (Josh. xxiv. 28), without appointing over them any particular judge, or ruler, the time of the judges did not commence as early as the time of his death. And for some length of time after the death of Joshua, they were yet without a judge to "lead the armies of the people;" hence, "the children of Israel asked of the Lord, saying, Who shall go up for us against the Canaanites;" and having at this time no judge to lead their armies, "the Lord said, Judah shall go up." (Judg. i. 2.) Since there was no change of government from the death of Joshua to the time the Lord "sold them into the hand of Chushan-rishathaim" (Judg. iii. 8), the time of the judges could not have commenced earlier than that epoch; for Othniel (Judg. iii. 9) being the first judge whose name is recorded either in sacred or profane history as a ruler of Israel, where is the authority for commencing the time of the judges before his day? The time of the judges, from this epoch to the judgeship of Samuel the prophet, was 450 years; and Paul says, the Lord "gave unto them judges, about the space of four hundred and fifty years, until Samuel the prophet." (Acts xiii. 20.) Josephus also dates the commencement of the judges here. He says: "In the days of Moses and his disciple Joshua, who was their general, they continued under an aristocracy; but after the death of Joshua, for eighteen years in all, the multitude had no settled form of government, but were in an anarchy; after which they returned to their former government, they then permitting themselves to be judged by him who appeared to be the best warrior, and most courageous; whence it was that they called this interval of their government, The Judges." (*Ant.* vi. c. v. s. 4.)

B.C. 1462. THE ERA OF EHUD.—With this epoch—that is, with the eighty-years rest, during the judgeship of Ehud—the Israelites commenced a new era. (See Dr. Clark on this subject.) This epoch is proven to be the one with which this new era commenced by the apostle Paul having assigned 450 years for the duration of the time of the judges to that of Samuel the prophet.

B.C. 1078. "Samuel judged the children of Israel in Mizpeh;" and to this the commencement of Samuel's judgeship there are just 450 years from the time of Othniel their first judge. Hence, Paul and the book of Judges are in exact harmony. (Acts xiii. 20.)

B.C. 1024. THE ELEVENTH JUBILEE.—As Ish-bosheth, Saul's son, lived seven years and six months after the death of his father, we are unable to account for the author of the second book of Samuel allowing him but two years (2 Sam. ii. 10); but upon the supposition of David's having been duly anointed king (1 Sam. xvi. 1, 13) by the God of Israel, the kingdom was properly his as soon as Saul was removed; for, though Saul's son fell heir to the kingdom at the death of his father, it must "go out" "in the jubilee" (Lev. xxv. 28); for "in the year of this jubilee ye shall return every man unto his possession." (Lev. xxv. 13.) The author of the second book of Samuel only allows for the reign of Saul's son that number of years which brings him to the year of jubilee: at which time, according to their law, his heirship ended. This proves that the third year of David was a year of the jubilee.

B.C. 983. THE 480TH YEAR OF THE ERA OF EHUD.—According to the punctuation of our English Bible, we would at first conclude, from 1 Kings vi. 1, that Solomon commenced building the temple on the 480th year from the time Moses led the children of Israel out of the land of Egypt. But this verse will admit of two constructions:—*first*, that this was the 480th year from the time Moses led the Israelites from Egypt; *second*, that it was in the 480th year of the era of Ehud. If the Hebrews were at that time using the era of Ehud, it is natural to suppose they would date by this era; and by examining our table of chronology, it will be seen that the fourth year of Solomon synchronizes with the 480th year of the era of Ehud; but the fourth year of Solomon, according to the same table, was 628 years from the time Moses led Israel from Egypt. Josephus must have understood this to be the "four hundred and eightieth year" of the era of Ehud; for, according to his calculation, it was 592 years from the time Moses led Israel from Egypt. That Paul understood this to be the "four hundred and eightieth year" of the era of Ehud, he affirms that the time of the judges to that of Samuel the prophet was 450 years, which could not be had it been only 480 years from the leaving of Egypt to the fourth year of Solomon's reign. David "could not build a house unto the name of the Lord his God, for the wars which were about him on every side." (1 Kings v. 3.) Hence, Solomon, in order to secure "rest on every side" (1 Kings v. 4), until he had accomplished the great work, "made affinity with Pharaoh, King of Egypt, and took Pharaoh's daughter, and brought her into the city of David, until he had made an end of building." (1 Kings iii. 1.) As he, at this time, brought out of Egypt "horses for all the kings of the Hittites and for the kings of Syria," also merchandize of "linen yarns" for "the king's merchants" (2 Chron. i. 16, 17), a large number of the Israelites must have gone with him to celebrate his marriage in Egypt. The time was "at the end of three years" (1 Kings ii. 39), hence, during "the fourth year of Solomon's reign," which synchronizes with the 480th year of the era of Ehud. And they did not commence building the temple until "after the children of Israel were come out of the land of Egypt." (1 Kings vi. 1.) "And it came to pass in the four hundred and eightieth year,"—that is, the 480th year of the era of Ehud,—"after the children of Israel were come out of the land of Egypt,"—that is, those of Israel who had just returned from the celebration of Solomon's marriage in Egypt,—"in the fourth year of Solomon's reign over Israel," "he began to build the house of the Lord." (1 Kings vi. i.) That the reader may have no doubt that the author of the first book of Kings could not have meant the 480th year from the time Moses led the children of Israel from the land of Egypt, we will here add a table giving the interval between the time:—

				YEARS.
Wilderness	....	Josh. v. 6	....	40
Division of land	....	" xiv. 10	....	6
First Servitude	....	Judg. iii. 8	....	8
Rest	....	" iii. 11	....	40
Second Servitude	....	" iii. 14	....	18
Rest	....	" iii. 30	....	80
Third Servitude	....	" iv. 3	....	20
Rest	....	" v. 31	....	40
Fourth Servitude	....	" vi. 1	....	7
Rest	....	" viii. 28	....	40
Abimelech	....	" ix. 22	....	3
Tola	....	" x. 2	....	23
Jair	....	" x. 3	....	22
Fifth Servitude	....	" x. 8	....	18
Jephthah	....	" xii. 7	....	6
Ibzan	....	" xii. 9	....	7
Elon	....	" xii. 11	....	10
Abdon	....	" xii. 14	....	8
Sixth Servitude	....	" xiii. 1	....	40
Eli	....	1 Sam. iv. 18	....	40
Seventh Servitude	....	" vii. 2	....	20
Saul	....	Acts xiii. 21	....	40
David	....	2 Sam. v. 4	....	40
Solomon	....	1 King vi. 1	....	4
Total	....		....	580

From the exodus to the building of the temple, the dates as given in the Bible make 580 years, without allowing any time either for Joshua after the division of the land, for the anarchy after the death of Joshua to the First Servitude, or for Samuel the prophet. Josephus allows for the government of Joshua twenty-five years, the anarchy eighteen years, and the judgeship of Samuel the prophet twelve years. Though Josephus has given us a correct copy of what he found in books then extant, he has here made a slight mistake,—not in copying, but in his omissions; for, as we have before observed, the Bible dates make 580 years. Josephus makes it 592 by adding twelve years for the judgeship of Samuel; but he seems here to have forgotten the twenty-five years which Joshua governed Israel, and the eighteen years of the anarchy. If we allow Josephus to correct himself, we must to this 592 add 25 years for the government of Joshua, and 18 for the anarchy, which makes 635; and from this we must subtract 6,—for the 6 years to the division of the land is included in the 25,—and 6 from 635 leaves 629; but these are years current: to make them years complete, we must reduce 1, which leaves 628 for Josephus's period of time from the leaving of Egypt to the building of the temple, as corrected by his dates.

B.C. 975. THE THIRTEENTH JUBILEE.—The temple was completed in "the eleventh year" of Solomon's reign. "The dedication did not take place till the following year, the twelfth of Solomon," because, according to Usher, that was the Jubilee. We know not what authority Bishop Usher and others had for believing the twelfth of Solomon was a year of the jubilee; but we can draw many good reasons from the Bible for believing they were correct in this. As "the house was finished" in "the eighth month," "in the eleventh year" of Solomon's reign, it is impossible to account for its not being dedicated until the seventh month of the following year—that is, not until eleven months after it was completed—but upon the supposition that they were awaiting the coming jubilee.

B.C. 925. THE REIGN OF NADAB commenced in "the second year of Asa," and reached its end "in the third of Asa, King of Judah." (1 Kings xv. 25, 28.) He must have reigned one year, conjointly with his father.

B.C. 901. THE REIGN OF ELAH.—Elah's first year began "in the twenty-sixth of Asa," and reached its end "in the twenty-seventh of Asa." (1 Kings xvi. 8, 10.) His reign was mostly in conjunction with his father.

B.C. 900. THE REIGN OF TIBNI AND OMRI.—"In the twenty and seventh year of Asa, King of Judah," Zimri slew Elah, the King of Israel; and when he had reigned "seven days," the armies of Israel, which were at that time absent, "heard say, Zimri hath conspired, and hath also slain the king: whereupon all Israel made Omri, the captain of the host, king over Israel that day in the camp." (1 Kings xvi. 10, 15, 16.) After the death of Zimri, "Then were the people of Israel divided into two parts: half of the people followed Tibni, to make him king, and half followed Omri." (1 Kings xvi. 21.) But at the end of three years, "Tibni died, and Omri reigned." This was in the thirty-first of Asa (1 Kings xvi. 22, 23); and when he had reigned about five years, it appears that he associated a man by the name of Baasha with him in the kingdom: this was "in the six and thirtieth year of the reign of Asa." (2 Chron. xvi. 1.)

B.C. 891. THE REIGN OF BAASHA.—As "there was war between Asa and Baasha, King of Israel, all their days" (1 Kings xv. 16), Baasha did not live more than about one year; for it is clear that this war was soon brought to a close. (1 Kings xv. 16–21.) In thus transferring the kingdom to Baasha for one year, Omri's object apparently was to use this means of continuing the war through the Jewish sabbatical year, which he had commenced in the thirty-fifth of Asa (2 Chron. xv. 19), which was the Jewish sixth year; hence, the thirty-sixth was the seventh year. As the Jews did not fight during this year, Asa procured the services of the King of Syria. (1 Kings xv. 18.) After the death of Baasha, Omri reigned one year more alone, making six in which he had thus reigned out of the seven he had been on the throne.

B.C. 889. THE REIGN OF AHAB.—In the eighth year of Omri's reign,—the thirty-eighth of Asa,—he associated his son Ahab with him in the kingdom. Hence, out of the twelve years he was in possession of the kingdom, he reigned only "six years" alone, "in Tirzah." (1 Kings xvi. 23.)

B.C. 884. SABBATICAL YEAR.—From 2 Chronicles xvii. 7–10, it would appear that the third year of Jehoshaphat was a sabbatical year; but, according to our table of chronology, the second year of his reign, synchronizes with the sabbatical year. This difficulty may be easily removed by supposing that his reign commenced as early as the seventh month of "the fourth year of Ahab, king of Israel." (1 Kings xxii. 41.)

B.C. 869. THE REIGN OF AHAZIAH.—When Ahab, King of Israel, and Jehoshaphat, King of Judah, were about to engage in the war against the Syrians (1 Kings xxii. 4), Ahab placed Ahaziah, his son, on the throne, to "reign over Israel," and Jehoshaphat, King of Judah, also placed Jehoram, his son, on the throne of Judah, until their return from the war. (2 Kings i. 17.) In about two years from this time Ahab was slain, when "Ahaziah, his son" took full possession of the kingdom,—a short time after which he died. (2 Kings i. 2, 17.)

B.C. 868.—JEHORAM, THE SON OF AHAB, began to reign in the eighteenth year of Jehoshaphat (2 Kings iii. 1), which was "the second year of Jehoram, the son of Jehoshaphat." (2 Kings i. 17.)

B.C. 863. THE REIGN OF JEHORAM.—In the twenty-third year of Jehoshaphat, which was "the fifth of Joram," he associated his son Jehoram with him in the kingdom. Though we have had so many similar associations, this is the first one thus mentioned. (See 2 Kings viii. 16.)

B.C. 782. THE REIGN OF AMAZIAH.—"Amaziah, the son of Joash, King of Judah, lived after the death of Joash, King of Israel, fifteen years," at which time "they made a conspiracy against him in Jerusalem; and he fled to Lachish," where he seems to have remained concealed twelve years; after which "they sent to Lachish, and slew him there." (2 Chron. xxv. 25, 27.) So Azariah's reign commenced in "the twenty and seventh year of Jeroboam, King of Israel" (2 Kings xv. 1), or B.C. 770.

B.C. 758. THE PROPHECY OF AMOS.—As the Seventh-year Sabbath was the only one that ended with the appearing of the new moon, or with the end of the Jewish month, the prophecy of Amos must have been made during the sabbatical year (Amos viii. 5); and the expression, "When will the new moon be gone?" or, according to the Douay Bible, "When will the month be over" (Amos viii. 5), shows that it was during the last month of the sabbatical year. It was also two years before the end of the reign of Jeroboam; for two years after the prophecy was delivered, the earthquake happened (Amos i. 1), when Jeroboam fled from the kingdom. (Zach. xiv. 5.)

B.C. 755. AN ECLIPSE OF THE SUN.—Two years after the prophecy of Amos, there was a great earthquake (Amos i. 1), called the trembling of the land. "Shall not the land tremble for this? And it shall come to pass in that day, saith the Lord God," —that is, on the same day of the trembling of the land, or the day of the earthquake,—"that I will cause the sun go down at noon, and I will darken the earth in the clear day." (Amos viii. 8, 9.) A. Clark says, "This may either refer to that darkness which accompanies earthquakes, or to an eclipse;" but Bishop Usher, Dr. Hales, and others, understand it to be an eclipse of the sun. We are unable to see how it can answer to any thing short of a total eclipse of the sun. It is never said that the sun is down when behind a cloud; but when it is hidden from us by the revolution of the earth, we then say it is down, although it still occupies the same place in the heavens, and gladdens with its brightness another portion of our globe. Then, why may we not as properly say the sun is down when it is totally eclipsed, or hid from our view by the moon? That there was an actual trembling of the land,—a real earthquake,—all admit. If the expression regarding the earthquake be taken literally, why should we apply another rule when the sun is spoken of. The sun was to go down at the middle of the day on which the earthquake occurred, while the light of that people did not go down or pass away until more than eight hundred years after. It is added, "and I will darken the earth in the clear day." (Amos viii. 9.) This settles two points: first, that the going down of the sun cannot be taken in a figurative sense, but must refer to the darkening of the earth on that particular day; secondly, that this darkness could not have been caused by a cloud. Hence, there must have been a total eclipse of the sun at Samaria on that day. The eclipse was to happen on the day of the earthquake, which was at the end of the forty-first year of Jeroboam (Amos viii. 8; Zach. xiv. 5; 2 Kings xiv. 23); it was two years after the sabbatical year (Amos viii. 5; i. 1); the specified hour and minute was at the middle of the day (Amos viii. 9),—not the middle of the artificial day, or "at noon," as our translators have it, but at the middle of the natural day, or twelve hours from sunset; for while the sun, according to the Douay translation, was to "go down at midday," this midday darkness was to be in the morning. (Amos iv. 13.) As we have here not only the exact year during the reign of the Kings of Israel, but also the particular date, reckoning from the last sabbatical year, and even the exact hour and minute of the day, we may well say it is impossible to counterfeit this eclipse. Hence, it must prove either that our chronology is strictly correct or erroneous. Bishop Usher, Dr. Hales, and others, suppose that the eclipse foretold by Amos occurred B.C. 791. We may here remark that by their chronology this was six years before the end of the forty-first year of the reign of Jeroboam, while the Bible places it at the end of his forty-first year. Besides, it was at the end of the day; while the eclipse, as predicted by Amos, was to be at "midday" (Amos viii. 9),—that is, the middle of the natural day, which was in the morning. (Amos iv. 13.) In addition, our astronomical tables show that it began ten minutes after sundown: hence, could not have been seen in Samaria.

According to our chronology, the forty-first year of Jeroboam's reign in Samaria ended B.C. 755. This was the Jewish third year; hence, two full years from their last sabbatical year. By calculation, on July 9th, N.S., or the 16th, O.S., B.C. 755, there was a total eclipse of the sun in Samaria. On July 8th, the sun set at five minutes after seven, at which time the day, according to Jewish reckoning, commenced (Lev. xxiii. 32; Mark i. 32); and as twelve hours from the beginning of the day bring us to the middle, this gives us five minutes after seven in the morning for the middle of that day at which time the sun did "go down" behind the moon; and, according to our astronomical tables, the middle of this eclipse—at which time the sun was darkened by the moon—was exactly at five minutes after seven in the morning,—the exact middle-point of the day, according to Jewish reckoning. And does not this, being found in such exact harmony with every other portion of Bible Chronology, as proven by astronomy, definitely settle the correctness of our chronology,—found in harmony, we say, with other portions of Bible Chronology; for we had written our table of chronology before we thought of this eclipse; and as it is found in the right year, we have not altered our chronology a single day to reconcile it with this eclipse. Concerning the eclipse of 791, Dr. Hales remarks:—"Such a curious coincidence of astronomical computation with prophecy affords a strong presumption, bordering on certainty, that the chronology of the reigns of the Kings of Israel is here rightly assigned." If an eclipse, with all of the above-mentioned objections—one which cannot be made at all by those tables with which we make all other eclipses—be considered as evidence of the correctness of chronology, how clear must be the proof of the one we have found, answering not only to the year, but to the hour and minute at which it was foretold it should occur. Since it is impossible to find another eclipse of the sun answering to the exact year, hour, and minute, as pointed out by Amos, this does appear to prove to absolute certainty that our chronology here is strictly correct. By the errors into which Ptolemy fell, the book of Daniel has been sealed; but, by the unerring authority of heaven, it is now opened.

A total eclipse of the sun resembles its "going down." In speaking of the eclipse of 1729, Dr. Stukely says:—"On each side the horizon exhibited a blue tint, like that at the close of day. Scarcely had we time to count ten, when Salisbury spire, six miles to the south, was enveloped in darkness. The hill disappeared entirely, and the deepest night spread around us. We lost sight of the sun, whose . . . trace we could now no more discover than if it had never existed. . . . The whole picture presented an awful aspect that seemed to announce the death of nature. We were now involved in a total and palpable darkness. . . . It was the most awful sight I had ever beheld in my life." Alluding to the eclipse of 1560, Clavins remarks:—"The darkness . . . was greater, or at least more striking, than that of night, and the birds fell to the earth through terror." After these descriptions of a total eclipse of the sun, we ask how Amos and Jeremiah

(xv. 9) could, in as few words as they have used, have described one more fully. Writers use the language of the people among whom they live. As late as the day of Herodotus, the expression, "a total eclipse of the sun" was unknown. He thus describes one:—"Day was suddenly turned into night. This change of the day Thales had foretold." This proves that the expression, "a total eclipse of the sun," to convey an idea of its being thus obscured, was unknown at that day. Herodotus describes another, thus:—"The sun, quitting his seat in the heavens, disappeared, though there were no clouds, and the air was perfectly serene, and night ensued instead of the place of day." Suppose Amos had said, "The sun shall be eclipsed." How could the people of that age have known what he meant? or how could we tell whether he meant a total eclipse, or a partial one? Or suppose he had used the expression, "There shall be a total eclipse of the sun." Then you might explain his language away by saying, "The light of that people was totally eclipsed when Jeroboam with all the people of Samaria were on the day of the earthquake frightened from the kingdom." (Zech. xiv. 5.) But since he said, "I will cause the sun to go down at midday, and I will darken the earth in a clear day" (Amos. viii. 9), there is no room left to explain his words away by saying this must be understood in a figurative sense. For if by the expression, "sun," we are here to understand the clear light beaming through the law of the Lord, then by "clear day" we must understand a full submission or perfect obedience to that law; therefore, to take this in a figurative sense, would be to charge the Lord with taking the light of his favor from that people at "midday," or the time of their most perfect obedience,—that he would "darken the earth" or the mind of his people "in the clear day," or at the time they were of all others the most devoted to his service. This is about the construction those must put upon this text who will admit that Amos meant something, and yet that the something was not an eclipse of the sun. But the words, "that day," which limit the time of the going down of "the sun" to the particular day of the earthquake, forbids any such construction; for it is well known that the light of that dispensation did not pass away on that particular day. It appears to be a gross perversion of the word of God to say Amos here alluded to any thing more or less than a total eclipse of the sun.

B.C. 755. Jeroboam's Absence from Samaria.—At the end of the forty-first year of Jeroboam's reign in Samaria (2 Kings xiv. 23), the Lord did "darken the earth in a clear day;" for he caused "the sun to go down" behind the moon "at midday," or the middle of the natural day. This was followed by a great earthquake,—so dreadful as to cause the people to flee from the land of Samaria (Zech. xiv. 5.), thus "cast out and drowned as by the flood of Egypt" (Amos viii. 8), inasmuch, as "the high places of Israel" were made desolate, "and the sanctuaries of Israel . . . laid waste." When Israel had thus suffered for about twenty-three years, Jeroboam "restored the coast of Israel from the entering of Hamath unto the sea of the plain." "For the Lord saw the affliction of Israel, that it was very bitter. And the Lord said not that he would blot out the name of Israel from under heaven; but he saved them by the hand of Jeroboam." (2 Kings xiv. 26, 27.) As Jeroboam died in the thirty-eighth year of Azariah, King of Judah (2 Kings xv. 8), he lived sixty-four years from the beginning of his reign.

B.C. 690. THE NINTH YEAR OF HOSEA.—Hosea's reign began in the twentieth year of Jotham (2 Kings xv. 30), which synchronizes with the fourth of Ahaz; and having reigned eight years, his ninth year commenced in the twelfth of Ahaz (2 Kings xvii. 1); and from that time his reign continued about nine years more. (2 Kings xvii. 6.)

B.C. 681. THE SAMARITAN WAR.—"In the fourth year of Hezekiah" the "King of Assyria came up against Samaria, and besieged it. And at the end of three years they took it, even in the sixth year of Hezekiah." (2 Kings xviii. 9, 10.) Hence, this war occurred at a time during which three Assyrian years fell within the limits of three Jewish years. The Assyrian year consisted of 365 days; but the Jewish varied from 354 to 383 days. In B.C. 684, the first month commenced on March 17, and in B.C. 681 on April 13. These three Jewish years were twenty-seven days longer than three Assyrian years; hence, the King of Assyria could well continue the war three full years and take Samaria before the end of these three Jewish years. But the three previous Jewish years were two days, and the three following, three days, shorter than three Assyrian years. Thus, by astronomical demonstration, we prove that the end of this war—in the sixth of Hezekiah, at which time the ten tribes of Israel were led captive—was B.C. 681.

B.C. 682, 681. THREE ECLIPSES OF THE MOON.—The year B.C. 565 was the first of Nebuchadnezzar; and, according to Ptolemy's catalogue of the Kings of Babylon, the first year of Mardok Empadus was just 117 years before Nebuchadnezzar's first year. If to the first year of his reign—that is, B.C. 565—we add 117 years, we will have B.C. 682 for the first year of Mardok. "Hipparchus selected three ancient eclipses of the moon out of those observed at Babylon. One happened in the first year, and the two others in the second year of Mardok Empadus." These are very important eclipses for testing the correctness of our chronology; for three full eclipses but seldom happen within the limits of two years. By calculation, there was one in the first year and two in the second of Mardok, thus:—

B.C. 682, August 3, aft., 7h. 35m.; digits 11½.
B.C. 681, January 28, morn., 3h. 49m.; total.
B.C. 681, July 22, aft., 7h. 42m.; total.

Having in search for these three eclipses of the moon examined every year from B.C. 721 to B.C., 681, we discover that the year 682 is astronomically proven to be the first year of Mardok,* or Merodach-baladan. (Isa. xxxix. 1.)

B.C. 681. MOSES'S "SEVEN TIMES."—We have observed that the ten tribes of Israel were torn from their home and kingdom in the year 681, since which time they have never been restored to the land of their fathers, concerning which the Lord saith: "I will chastise them as their congregation hath heard." (Hos. vii. 12.)

---

* Ptolemy places the beginning of the reign of Mardok in the twenty-seventh year of the era of Nabonassar, which synchronizes with B.C. 721. But we may here ask, What historian has recorded any such era as in existence before the day of Ptolemy? Do not Jeremiah and Daniel's dating by the years of the reign of the different Kings of Babylon, seem to prove that it did not exist in their day? Have we not the same proof that there was no such era in the day of Haggai, Zachariah, Ezra, and Nehemiah? Berosus, Herodotus, Thucydides, and Xenophon are also silent as to its existence. If there had been such an era in the day of Hipparchus, surely that "great astronomer" could not have failed to notice it, when he was so careful to inform us that one of the eclipses he brought from Babylon, happened "in the first year, and the two others in the second year of Mardok Empadus, the fifth king in succession from Nabonassar. There was no such era in the day of Josephus; or, at least if there was, he had no confidence in its correctness; for, so far from using this era in his history, according to his chronology, he would place the beginning of the reign of Merodach about fifty-five years higher than the time as given in the Nabonassarean era. That the Babylonians knew nothing of such an era, would appear from Dr. Hales's own acknowledgment. He says, the "Chaldean era only marked the succession of kings, and the number of years each reigned. The collective years might have been added afterwards by the Egyptian astronomer." Says Sir Isaac Newton: "It was sixty years after the death of Alexander before chronology was reckoned by the number of years in which kings reigned."

That which "their congregation" had heard read "in the solemnity of the year of release" (Deut. xxxi. 10) was this: "And I, even I, will chastise you seven times for your sins." (Lev. xxvi. 28.) At the year B.C. 1571, we notice that the expression, "seven times," was the Chaldean* term for seven years; hence, a period of 2555 days, for their year consisted of 365 days. If these "seven times" span the period the people of God are to remain in their "enemies' land" (Lev. xxvi. 34), they must begin with the scattering of that people,—"I will scatter you among the heathen" (Lev. xxvi. 33),—and they must end with the accomplishing "to scatter the power of the holy people." (Dan. xii. 7.) They were scattered among the heathen in the sixth year of Hezekiah. (2 Kings xviii. 10.) "And ye shall be plucked from off the land whither thou goest to possess it. And the Lord shall scatter thee among all people from the one end of the earth unto the other." (Deut. xxviii. 63, 64.) The sixth year of Hezekiah synchronizes with A.M. 3445, to which, if we add 2555, we will have 6000. From which we conclude that when the world is 6000 years old "the times of the Gentiles" will "be fulfilled" (Luke xxi. 24), and Israel return home, "That in the dispensation of the fulness of times"—Moses's "seven times"—"he might gather together in one all things in Christ, both which are in heaven, and which are on earth." (Eph. i. 10.)

B.C. 681. THE LAND WENT OUT IN THE YEAR OF JUBILEE.—The ten tribes were taken captive at the end of the sixth of Hezekiah,—that is, about the 15th of the seventh month, B.C. 681. By reference to the table of chronology, it will be seen that the land of Israel went out of their possession in the year of jubilee; and in Leviticus xxvii. 21, we read that "the field, when it goeth out in the jubilee, shall be holy unto the Lord, as a field devoted; the

* If it be urged that the Hebrews, having left the idolatrous worship of the Chaldeans, these "seven times" must be according to their new method of reckoning time, we answer: Then they must be according to their average year; for, at the time this prophecy was delivered, the epoch from which they were to be commenced was unknown, and the length of the first year is not given; hence, it was impossible either for Moses, or those to whom he spoke, to have known the length of time, but upon the supposition that he meant average years. With him the average year consisted of 365 days, which, multiplied by seven, gives us 2555. This amounts to the same thing with the Chaldean "seven times." And that Moses's "seven times" means a period of 2555 years, neither more nor less, we have this clear proof that they have been once thus fulfilled. (See at B.C. 1571.) Having at A.D. 26 exposed the error of supposing that "a time, times and a half" means a period of only 1260 days, the opinion that Moses's "seven times" means only 2520 days, or years, is proven to be erroneous.

possession thereof shall be the priests." On the word, "devoted," Dr. Clark makes the following observations: "So devoted to God as never more to be capable of being redeemed." From this we infer that the Hebrews can never again come in possession of their land. And yet this land, having gone out of their possession in the year of jubilee, must be the possession of the priests,—not the Levitical priesthood; for this would violate that law, "Thou shalt have no inheritance in their land." (Num. xviii. 20.) They are slain, and the servants of God called by a new name. (Isa. lxv. 15.) The priesthood now being changed (Heb. vii. 12), the royal priesthood passes over to the Christians (1 Pet. ii. 9), or spiritual Israel (Rom. ii. 29); for they are the priests that are to "inherit" (Matt. v. 5) "and reign on the earth." (Rev. v. 10.) But though the promised inheritance has passed over to the Christians (Gal. iii. 29), they are not yet in possession of the land. (Gen. xiii. 15.) The particular time at which the people of God will come into this promised inheritance may be inferred in the following way.

B.C. 681. THE SEVENTH-YEAR RELEASE.—In Deuteronomy xv. 1, the Hebrews were required at the end of seven years to make a release; which law, Jeremiah informs us, they did not observe. "Thus saith the Lord, the God of Israel; I made a covenant with your fathers, in the day that I brought them forth out of the land of Egypt, out of the house of bondmen, saying, At the end of seven years, let ye go every man his brother a Hebrew, which hath been sold unto thee; . . . but your fathers hearkened not unto me, neither inclined their ear." (Jer. xxxiv. 13, 14.) From this we learn that this portion of the Mosaic law, as late as the time of the Babylonish captivity, had not been observed; and the Jews have never had it in their power to make such a release since that time; hence, it is yet unfulfilled. And since "one jot or tittle" cannot pass from the law "till all be fulfilled," this must be accomplished by Him who came not to destroy the law, but to fulfill (Matt. v. 17); therefore, he has been anointed "to preach deliverance to the captives" (Luke iv. 18, 19), "to preach the acceptable year of the Lord," which, according to the law, must be at the end of seven years.

The time Israel was led into captivity was about the 15th of the seventh month, B.C. 681. Seven years such as those—at the end of which Jacob, the father of Israel, was released from his services (Gen. xxix. 20)—consisted of 2555 days (see at B.C. 1571), which, omitting fractions, is the same with seven average Jewish years. B.C. 681 is A.M. 3445, to which, if we add 2555, we have 6000. Thus it appears that "THE LORD'S RELEASE"

(Deut. xv. 2) will be in the beginning of the great Sabbath of rest "which remaineth to the people of God." (Heb. iv. 9.) Now, this is no vain speculation; for if the law was a "shadow of good things to come" (Heb. x. 1), surely this is that foreshadowed by the year of release. That this year was typical of our release from the thraldom of sin, is universally admitted. But let it be borne in mind that the Jewish year of release had respect to time, and that the type must resemble the antitype; or, the shadow that which is shadowed forth. As it was at the end of seven common years, that which is thus foreshadowed must be at the end of seven prophetic years. This deliverance from the last enemy, even death, is that glorious promise to which the "twelve tribes, instantly serving God day and night, hope to come." (Acts xxvi. 7.) And they date the commencement of their sore trials and afflictions from "the time of the Kings of Assyria." (Neh. ix. 32.)

B.C. 681. THE TWO DAYS OF HOSEA.—To these captives Hosea says, "Come, and let us return unto the Lord; for he hath torn, and he will heal us: he hath smitten, and he will bind us up. After two days will he revive us; in the third day he will raise us up, and we shall live in his sight." (Hos. vi. 1, 2.) As those who returned unto the Lord are not yet raised up (Acts ii. 34), as they are not yet living in his sight (1 Pet. i. 8; 1 John iii. 2), we must understand these days to be such as those alluded to by Peter, in writing on this same subject. "Beloved, be not ignorant of this one thing, that one day is with the Lord as a thousand years, and a thousand years as one day." (2 Pet. iii. 8.) If we place these two days against the year B.C. 681,—at which time Israel was carried into captivity,—they reach to A.D. 1320. After these two days, and at sometime "in the third day, he will raise us up, and we shall live in his sight." And if "his going forth is prepared as the morning" (Hos. vi. 3), then about one-half of this third day must also pass before we are raised up. They commenced the day in the evening (Lev. xxiii. 32), at the going down of the sun (Mark i. 32); hence, about one-half passed before the beginning of the morning. One-half of the above-mentioned day is 500 years, which if we add to A.D. 1320, we will have A.D. 1820. From this it would appear that we are now living in the morning of the third day,—in that "morning" in which the saints of God shall be "redeemed . . . from the power of the grave." (Ps. xlix. 14, 15.) And that particular point of time during this morning is "at the" time of the sounding of the "trump: for the trumpet shall sound," "the great trumpet shall be blown" (Isa. xxvii. 13), "and the dead shall be raised." (1 Cor. xv. 52.) And the time "the trumpet shall sound" is on the 10th of the seventh month of the forty-ninth sabbatical year,—the year of Jubilee. "Then shalt thou cause the trumpet of the jubilee to sound, on the tenth day of the seventh month, in the day of atonement shall ye make the trumpet sound throughout all your land." (Lev. xxv. 9.) These things being "a figure for the time then present," and "the law having a shadow of good things to come" (Heb. ix. 9; x. 1), our God must come in the "jubilee, and the Lord with the sound of a trumpet." (Ps. xlvi. 6, Douay Bible.) The first year of jubilee following A.D. 1820 is in A.D. 1868. Though the trumpet must sound throughout all the land "on the tenth day of the seventh month," Israel must first keep the feast of tabernacles (Lev. xxiii. 34) before they can return unto their possession; for if the "law" was "a shadow of good things to come" (Heb. x. 1), each portion of this law must have its proper bearing in that which is shadowed forth. Hence, it is nowhere said that they are to return unto their possession on the 10th day of the seventh month; but "in the year of this jubilee ye shall return every man unto his possession." (Lev. xxv. 13.) The jubilee beginning in A.D. 1868 is the antitype found at the end of a jubilee of jubilees; hence, it must be forty-nine years long; and Israel can at the end of the seven-years feast of tabernacles return unto their possession in the year of this jubilee. "When once the Master of the house is risen up, and shut to the door" (Luke xiii. 25) of salvation at the time of "the resurrection of the just" (Luke xiv. 14),—that is, on the 10th of the seventh month A.D. 1868,—those who are not by that time prepared to go up "to keep the feast of tabernacles" (Zech. xiv. 19), "even upon them shall be no rain" of grace. (Zech. xiv. 17.) Hence, the seven-years feast, as kept by the people of God, after the ingathering of souls (Lev. xxiii. 39) in the end of the world, will be to them "a time of trouble, such as never was since there was a nation" (Dan. xii. 1); for while the people of God, as shadowed forth by "the feast of tabernacles," shall be "in the clouds" of heaven, (1 Thess. iv. 17) they will be crying "to the mountains and rocks, Fall on us, and hide us from the face of him that sitteth on the throne, and from the wrath of the Lamb." (Rev. vi. 16.)

B.C. 674. SABBATICAL YEAR.—It will be remembered that during the siege of Samaria three eclipses of the moon occurred which being considered a favorable omen, the King of Assyria immediately after the total eclipse of September 3, B.C. 674 marched to attack Jerusalem. This being the sabbatical year

Hezekiah tried to satisfy him with a present, instead of meeting him in battle. (2 Kings xviii. 14–16.) The king having taken from Hezekiah the three-years supply then in store (Lev. xxv. 21), he must "eat this year such things as grow of themselves;" and as the law forbade their sowing "their fields during the sabbatical year (Lev. xxv. 4), they must "in the second year"—that is, during B.C. 673—eat "that which springeth of the same; and in the third year," B.C. 672, "sow ye and reap." (2 Kings xix. 29.) As this was to be "a sign" to Hezekiah, these years must, of course, precede the slaying of the Assyrian army. Therefore the time they were slain could not have been earlier than B.C. 671. From this event may be dated the ruin of the Assyrian empire and the building up of the Babylonish kingdom; for "at this time it was that the dominion of the Assyrians was overthrown by the Medes." (*Jose. Ant.* b. x. c. 2, s. 2.) Hence, in B.C. 671, if our chronology be correct, we must find that "total eclipse of the moon" which James Ferguson informs us dates "the Assyrian empire at an end, and the Babylonish established." By calculation, there was a total eclipse of the moon on January 7th, at fifty minutes after five in the afternoon, on the meridian of Babylon, in B.C. 671. These eclipses and the sabbatical year prove that we have properly placed the reign of Hezekiah.

B.C. 666. KINGDOM OF THE MEDES.—After the Medes revolted against the Assyrians they set up a republican form of government, under which they continued six years, when they elected their first king. For the Medes "ruled over all Asia beyond the river Halys for the space of one hundred and twenty-eight years, excepting the interval of the Scythian dominion." (*Herod.* b. i. s. 130.) Which chronology stands thus:—According to Herodotus, Deioces reigned 53 years; Phraortes, 22; Cyaxares, 40; Astyages, 35; total duration, 150; from which subtract 28 years that the Scythians reigned, and we have 122; to which add the 6 years of their democracy, and the result is 128,—the space of time during which they were in possession of their dominion. According to Herodotus, the kingdom of the Medes was in existence 150 years when Cyrus, King of Persia, began to reign, who reigned 29 years, and died B.C. 482. If to B.C. 482 we add 179, we will have B.C. 661 for the beginning of the kingdom of Media. The six years of their republic gives us B.C. 667 as the time when they achieved their independence. Allowing about three years for the duration of that war in which they "exchanged servitude for freedom," we have B.C. 670. This was the seventeenth of Hezekiah, which, according to Josephus, was about the time that the Medes revolted from the Assyrians. They had not revolted as early as the fourteenth of Hezekiah (2 Kings xviii. 33), which synchronizes with B.C. 673, and did not before the King of Assyria returned to Nineveh. The Assyrian army did not leave the land of Judea until after the Jewish second year from their last sabbatical year (2 Kings xix. 29), or the sixteenth of Hezekiah, which answers to B.C. 671; for the King of Assyria remained in Egypt about three years. (Isa. xx. 3.) About the sixteenth, or the beginning of the seventeenth, of Hezekiah, when the King of Assyria returned out of Egypt, "then the angel of the Lord went forth and smote in the camp of the Assyrians a hundred and fourscore and five thousand. So Sennacherib, King of Assyria departed, and went and returned and dwelt at Nineveh" (Isa. xxxvii. 36, 37); "and there passed not five and fifty days before two of his sons killed him." (Tob. i. 21.) This happened at about the seventeenth of Hezekiah,—that is, B.C. 670. As we may well suppose that the Medes would avail themselves of this favorable opportunity to free themselves, Josephus says correctly: "At this time it was that the dominion of the Assyrians was overthrown by the Medes." (*Ant.* b. x. c. ii. s. 2.) While this is an additional proof of the correctness of our chronology, it also proves the incorrectness of commencing the Babylonish captivity in the third or fourth year of the reign of Jehoiakim; and shows that Evil-merodach reigned at least eight or ten years, while Ptolemy's canon gives him but two. Those who follow Ptolemy's canon, commence the Babylonish captivity in the end of the third, or beginning of the fourth, year of Jehoiakim, which makes the first year of the reign of Deioces, the first King of Media, synchronize with the eighteenth of Hezekiah, at which time it is generally believed Sennacherib's army was destroyed. As this allows the Medes no time for their war of independence, nor for the six years of their republic, Prideaux gives Amon three years, while the Bible gives him but two (2 Kings xxi. 19; 2 Chron. xxxiii. 21), and thus obtains one year.

B.C. 665. AN INTERREGNUM of two years follows the reign of Achian, according to Ptolemy's canon; but as it allows none at the end of the reign of Nabopolasser, where it is evident there was one, we have taken a year from this place and assigned it to that.

B.C. 601. THE REIGN OF JOSIAH commenced about the 15th of the seventh month, B.C. 601, and continued thirty-one years. (2 Kings xxii. 1.)

B.C. 595. NABOPOLASSER, the sixteenth King of Babylon, reigned, according to Berosus, twenty-nine years. (See *Jose. against Apion*, b. i. s. 19.) Ptolemy gives him only twenty-one; hence, he throws in an interregnum of eight years to complete the duration of the kingdom of Babylon. It would appear from Josephus (*Ant.* b. x. c. xi. s. 1) that there were different copies of the works of Berosus, one of which gave Nabopolasser only twenty-one years. This copy having fallen into Ptolemy's hands, may account for his giving Nabopolasser but twenty-one. Having omitted Ptolemy's eight-years interregnum, this addition of eight does not affect the duration of the kingdom of Babylon.

B.C. 591. ECLIPSE OF THE MOON.—According to our chronology, B.C. 591 was the fifth year of Nabopolasser. Ptolemy informs us that during the fifth year of his reign there was an eclipse of the moon at Babylon. Take the light of astronomy, run back through 2450 years, and it will be discovered that on the 22d of March, at forty-seven minutes after eight o'clock in the afternoon, there was a total eclipse of the moon at Babylon.

B.C. 587. JEREMIAH'S TWENTY-THREE YEARS began in the thirteenth year of Josiah (Jer. xxv. 3) between the seventh month, B.C. 589 and 588.

B.C. 583. JOSIAH'S EIGHTEENTH YEAR commenced at about the 15th of the seventh month, B.C. 584; hence, he spent about six months in repairing the house of the Lord (2 Kings xxii. 3–5), and in cleansing the land from the filthiness of the idolatrous Israelites (2 Chron. xxxiv. 33), thus preparing for that great jubilee passover which fell on the 14th of the first sacred month in B.C. 583.

B.C. 583. THE GREAT JUBILEE PASSOVER.—"In the eighteenth year of the reign of Josiah was this passover kept." (2 Chron. xxxv. 19.) "The king commanded all the people, saying, Keep the passover unto the Lord your God." (2 Kings xxiii. 21). "And there was no passover like to that kept in Israel from the days of Samuel the prophet; neither did all the kings of Israel keep such a passover as Josiah kept." (2 Chron. xxxv. 18.) This passover—the greatest ever celebrated at Jerusalem—occurred in the last year of jubilee observed by the people of God; hence, must be the one from which "seven sabbaths," or a sabbath of sabbaths, "shall be complete" to the harvest of this world. Then, raising the vail (2 Cor. iii. 14), let us examine this "shadow of heavenly things" (Heb. viii. 5), as thrown back into the Mosaic dispensation, and see if in that which was a "figure for the time then present" (Heb. ix. 9.), we can discover the antitype. When, before the law, this "shadow of good things to come" (Heb. x. 1) first appeared in the land of Egypt, there was connected with it no "weeks of harvest:" and in every particular the type must resemble the antitype; hence, when, in Christ, it reached its end, it was followed by no week of sabbaths But in those additions made under the law, "seven sabbaths shall be complete" (Lev. xxiii. 15) to "the feast of harvest" (Ex. xxiii. 16),—not from the passover as instituted in Egypt before the law, but from the one which at that time was in the future to be observed: "When ye be come into the land . . . and shall reap the harvest thereof." (Lev. xxiii. 10.) Joshua "kept the passover . . . in the plains of Jericho" (Josh. v. 10); but at that time they had not "reaped the harvest." The next one recorded in the Bible as observed "on the 14th of the first month," was in the eighteenth year of Josiah. (2 Chron. xxxv. 1, 19.) It is remarkable that while this is the first time the word "passover" is to be found in the Bible, from the day of Joshua, as alluding to the legal ordinance of the first month, that it should here be used fifteen times, and in the book of Esdras twelve times more. Not that the Jews had ceased to observe this ordinance; but this is the first time it is recorded in that book through which the Lord has revealed all that is necessary for us to know concerning it,—which points to this as the one from which there must be a great Sabbath of sabbaths, or Jubilee of jubilees to "the harvest of the world." The expression, "When ye be come into the land," forbids our commencing the antitype at a later date; and this being the first one which in every way answers to the law, there is no earlier date; for only that which is written, is "profitable for doctrine." (2 Tim. iii. 16.) The passover was instituted on "the fourteenth of the first month," and on that day it reached its antitype in that "even Christ our passover is sacrificed for us" (1 Cor. v. 7); for a given day of the month marks an epoch, hence, cannot be according to the day-year system. A period of a thousand years as properly begins on a given day of the month as that of a single day; but when a day is mentioned, and the particular day of the month omitted, then it can mark no epoch, hence, must be according to the day-year system; for the "shadow cannot be the same with that which cast the shade." In the type, the law required, saying, "The first day ye shall put away leaven out of your houses." (Ex. xii. 15.) This marks no epoch. Therefore, the antitype cannot be that of a literal day, but answers to the eighteenth year of Josiah, at which time he "put away from" him that wickedness with which his ancestors had polluted the land, even taking up the bones of the idolatrous priests from their graves, and burning them that he might thoroughly "cleanse Judea and Jerusalem," and thus prepare for that last jubilee-passover ever observed. As Josiah commenced preparing "the house of the Lord his God" (2 Chron. xxxiv. 8) for the great jubilee passover, at about the time of the feast of tabernacles (2 Kings xxii. 4), this the first year-day must have reached its end about the same time in the following year, —that is, B.C. 583.

Type. "Seven days ye must eat unleavened bread."

Antitype. These seven days being "a shadow of good things to come," the antitype can no more be restricted to seven literal days than that which cast the shade can be the "shadow;" and yet in the antitype there must be seven definite periods of time; for the shadow must mark the several periods of that which cast the shade: so the antitype must be a period of seven years; and Josiah, having cleansed the land from all pollutions, devoted seven years of strict obedience to the Mosaic law. "The king stood in his place, and made a covenant before the Lord, to walk after the Lord, and to keep his commandments, and his testimonies, and his statutes, with all his heart, and with all his soul, to perform the words of the covenant which are written in this book. And he caused all that were present in Jerusalem and Benjamin to stand to it. And the inhabitants of Jerusalem did according to the covenant of God, the God of their fathers;" and he "made all that were present in Israel to serve, even to serve the Lord their God. And all his days they departed not from following the Lord, the God of their fathers." (2 Chron. xxxiv. 31–33.)

Type. "In the first day ye shall have an holy convocation, ye shall do no servile work therein." (Lev. xxiii. 7.)

Antitype. The year-day, during which Josiah kept the great passover, ended with the beginning of the year of jubilee, which commenced on the 10th day of the seventh month, B.C. 583. This was the year of a holy convocation: "It shall be holy unto you." (Lev. xxv. 12.) And they did no "servile work" in this year: "Ye shall not sow, neither reap that which groweth of itself." (Lev. xxv. 11.)

Type. "In the seventh day is a holy convocation; ye shall do no servile work therein." (Lev. xxiii. 8.)

Antitype. The seventh year-day answers to the twenty-fifth of Josiah, which being the sabbatical year, they did "no work therein;" they were forbidden either to sow their fields. or reap that which grew of itself: "The seventh year shall be a sabbath of rest unto the land, a sabbath for the Lord." (Lev. xxv. 4, 5.) And they also had a holy convocation; for this was the time at which all Israel were to appear before the Lord, "in the solemnity of the year." (Deut. xxxi. 10.) But this being the same thing we saw in the type, cannot be the antitype. The full antitype as to the holy convocation was not reached until during the seventh year after the crucifixion, when the Gentile world commenced assembling into the Church of God (Acts x. 45), as the holy convocation of the first day of unleavened bread reached its antitype by the Jews coming in on the day of Pentecost.

Type. "When ye be come into the land which I give unto you, and shall reap the harvest thereof." (Lev. xxiii. 10.)

Antitype. In the antitype, the harvest is the people (Joel iii. 13); which harvest had now been reaped. The barley-harvest, or ten tribes of Israel had been cut down and lost. "The harvest is past, the summer is ended, and we are not saved." (Jer. viii. 20.) But the whole harvest was not to be cut down: "When ye reap the harvest of the land, thou shalt not make clean riddance of the corners of thy field" (Lev. xxiii. 22),—a sheaf was to remain in the field. (Deut. xxiv. 19.) The tribe of Judah was left (2 Kings xvii. 18) for the benefit of the poor (Lev. xxiii. 22), to whom the gospel is preached (Matt. xi. 5); or to stand as a living monument in proof of the divine origin of our religion. (Deut. xxviii. 46.) It was necessary that they should continue until "the seed should come to whom the promise was made" (Gal. iii. 19); for, "Except the Lord of hosts had left unto us a very small remnant, we should have been as Sodom, and we should have been like unto Gomorrah." (Isa. i. 9.)

Type. "Then ye shall bring a sheaf of the first-fruits of your harvest unto the priest." (Lev. xxiii. 10.)

Antitype. The first-fruits of their harvest was that of the barley (*Jose. Ant.* b. iii. c. x. s. 5), which, in the antitype, answers to Israel in the flesh. Josiah being the first king that had ever carried out fully the Mosaic law, he was properly the first-fruits of that dispensation. "Israel was holiness unto the Lord, and the first fruits of his increase." (Jer. ii. 3.) "And like unto him was there no king before him, that turned to the Lord with all his heart, and with all his soul, and with all his might, according to all the law of Moses; neither after him arose there any like him." (2 Kings xxiii. 25.) "He did that which was right in the sight of the Lord, and walked in the ways of David his father, and declined neither to the right hand nor to the left." (2 Chron. xxxiv. 2.)

Type. "And he shall wave the sheaf before the Lord."

Antitype. To wave, is "to cast away;" and in this sense, the sheaf was waved. "The Lord said, I will remove Judah also out of my sight, as I have removed Israel, and will cast off this city Jerusalem which I have chosen, and the house of which I said, My name should be there." (2 Kings xxiii. 27.)

Type. "To be accepted for you." (Lev. xxiii. 11.)

Antitype. The wave-offerings belonged to Moses. "Wave it for a wave-offering before the Lord, and it shall be thy part." (Ex. xxix. 26.) He was a type of Christ: "For Moses truly said unto the fathers, A prophet shall the Lord your God raise up unto you, of your brethren, like unto me; him shall ye hear in all things whatsoever he shall say unto you." (Acts iii. 22.) Therefore, to wave an offering to be accepted for Moses, must typify the waving or casting off the Jewish Church, or covenant of works to make room for the covenant of grace, that the offering of souls may be accepted for Christ. The Jews having broken the Mosaic law,—they were now under the curse (Gal. iii. 10); and the most perfect obedience being nothing more than their reasonable duty,—or as a debt they owed (Matt. xviii. 25),—this could not atone for the former breach;—and "he will not pardon your transgressions" (Ex. xxiii. 21);—therefore, the only way they could now be accepted, or received unto eternal life, was that this dispensation give place to a new. "Behold the days come, saith the Lord, when I will make a new covenant with the house of Israel and with the house of Judah" (Heb. viii. 8), and "the son of the bondwoman shall not be heir with the son of the free." (Gal. iv. 30.) The whole Jewish world now presents one vast harvest-field, as destroyed by a storm. "We are in desolate places, as dead men." (Isa. lix. 10.) All the grain that can now be gathered into the garner is that which, germinating and springing up again, grows the second time. "Marvel not that I said unto thee, Ye must be born again." (John iii. 7.) "They shall revive as the corn, and grow as the vine." (Hos. xvi. 7.) "If the fall of them be the riches of the world . . . if the casting away of them be the reconciling of the world, what shall the receiving of them be, but life from the dead." (Rom. xi. 12, 15.) The whole Church of God is now waved or passed over to a new dispensation, and Christ is the Foundation on which we pass. The first-born are now slain: and Christ becomes our Passover. (1 Cor. v. 7.) He "has become the first-fruits of them that slept" (1 Cor. xv. 20); and "if we be dead with Christ, we believe we shall also live with him" (Rom. vi. 8); "for if the first-fruit be holy, the lump is also holy: and if the root be holy, so are the branches." (Rom. xi. 16.)

Type. "On the morrow after the sabbath, the priest shall wave it." (Lev. xxiii. 11.)

Antitype. The whole of the seven days, during which they were to offer an offering made by fire,—or the seven days of unleavened bread,—are here called the sabbath; for, to use the words of Alexander Cruden, "Sabbath is likewise taken for all the Jewish feasts, indifferently. 'Keep my sabbaths,'—that is, my feasts. (Lev. xix. 3, 30.)" And this was a feast of seven days, or a week, which is in Luke xviii. 12 called the sabbath: "I fast twice in the week:" the Greek is, "I fast twice in the sabbath." As there is no other sabbath mentioned here, by the expression, "after the sabbath," we must understand, after the seven-days feast of unleavened bread. We are aware that our commentators, following Josephus, place the wave-offering on the second day of unleavened bread; but for this no authority can be found in the Bible. If by sabbath, Moses did not mean the feast of unleavened bread, he must have meant the last day of that feast. As the last day of unleavened bread was the last sabbath mentioned, the definite adjective "the" restricts us to the morrow after this last sabbath; and the last day seems to have been the most sacred of the two. It is mentioned five times (Ex. xii. 16; xiii. 6: Lev. xxiii. 8: Num. xxviii. 25: Deut. xvi. 8), while the former is only mentioned three times. It would appear from Deuteronomy xvi. 8, that the first six days were not as sacred as the seventh: "Six days shalt thou eat unleavened bread" (as if this feast was more for the people); but "the seventh day shall be a solemn assembly to the Lord thy God: thou shalt do no work therein." Also in Exodus xiii. 6, the first day is omitted: "Seven days shalt thou eat unleavened bread, and in the seventh day shall be a feast to the Lord." We learn from Numbers xxviii. 19–24, that the burnt-offerings for each day throughout the seven were the same,—that is, "two young bullocks, and one ram, and seven lambs of the first year," and "one goat for a sin-offering;" and after this manner ye shall offer daily throughout the seven days;" but on the day the sheaf is waved, the law prescribes the offering of but "one lamb without blemish of the first year, for a burnt-offering" (Lev. xxiii. 12); hence, the wave-offering was not within the limits of the seven days. As the law positively enjoined the eating of unleavened bread throughout the feast,—"seven days shalt thou eat unleavened bread" (Ex. xiii. 6),—the prohibition to eat "bread" (Lev. xxiii. 14) cannot be that of the unleavened; and if not, then it is that they should not eat leavened bread,—and if Moses here meant leavened, then the wave-offering could not have been on the second day of unleavened, bread. This settles the question as to the day of the wave-offering.

Type. "And ye shall count unto you from the morrow after the sabbath, from the day that ye brought the sheaf of the wave-offering; seven sabbaths shall be complete: even unto the morrow after the seventh sabbath shall ye number fifty days." (Lev. xxiii. 15.)

Antitype. These seven sabbaths were called the weeks of harvest (Jer. v. 24); and, as we have observed, that the harvest under the Mosaic law was a type shadowing forth the harvest of the people (Isa. xvii. 5), it follows that these weeks of harvest must also be a type, reaching to the time of the harvest of the people, in the same manner in which they under the law reached the harvest of the corn. Under the law, they commenced at the time of barley-harvest, and reached to the time of wheat-harvest. (Esdras xxxiv. 22.) As barley-harvest was the first-fruits of the year, the barley-harvest answers to the harvest of the Jewish dispensation; for they are called "the first-fruits of his increase" (Jer. ii. 3); and the wheat-harvest answers to the harvest of the Christian dispensation,—the first-fruits of which is Christ, the second Adam. (1 Cor. xv. 23, 45.) The harvest of the Jewish dispensation commenced when the King of Assyria subjugated the ten tribes of Israel, and carried them into captivity. "And in that day it shall come to pass, that the glory of Jacob shall be made thin, and the fatness of his flesh shall wax lean. And it shall be as when the harvestman gathereth the corn, and reapeth the ears with his arm." (Isa. xvii. 4, 5.) The Christian "harvest is the end of the world." (Matt. xiii. 39.) Therefore, as these weeks of harvest, under the law, commenced at the time of the passover during barley-harvest, and reached to the wheat-harvest, the antitype must be commenced at the time of the great jubilee-passover, during the harvest of the Jewish, and reach to that of the Christian, dispensation.

B.C. 575. We have observed that in the antitype the seventh year-day of unleavened bread answers to the twenty-fifth of Josiah, B.C. 576, which was the last sabbatical year of release the people of God ever had the privilege of duly observing. This seventh year was expressly called a sabbath,—"A sabbath for the Lord." (Lev. xxv. 4.) "The morrow after the sabbath" synchronizes with the twenty-sixth year of Josiah, B.C. 575. "And ye shall count unto you from the morrow after the sabbath . . . seven sabbaths," or a sabbath of sabbaths, "shall be complete" to "the feast of harvest" (Ex. xxiii. 16),—"the first-fruits of wheat-harvest." (Ex. xxxiv. 22.) "The sabbath days . . . are a shadow of things to come" (Col. ii. 16, 17.); and in the antitype "the harvest is the end of the world." (Matt. xiii. 39.) Hence, "from the morrow after the sabbath" of B.C. 576 there must be a great sabbath of sabbaths, or jubilee of jubilees to the harvest of the Christian dispensation, as the Sabbath of sabbaths under the law reached the harvest of the field. A jubilee of jubilees is 49 times 49, or 2401 years. "Even unto the morrow after the seventh sabbath" (sabbath of sabbaths) "shall ye number fifty days" (Lev. xxiii. 16); which, added to the Sabbath of sabbaths, or 2401 years, gives 2450. The Julian period for B.C. 575 is 4139, to which if we add 2450 we have 6589, which is the Julian period for A.D. 1876; so the fiftieth day of forty-nine years ends with the beginning of the first month, A.D. 1876: "And ye shall proclaim on the self-same day, that it may be a holy convocation unto you." (Lev. xxiii. 21.) A. D. 1868, being the jubilee which occurs within the limits of this fiftieth day of forty-nine years, is thus proven to be that jubilee in which the "trump of God" (1 Thess. iv. 16) will "proclaim" that "holy convocation," or assembling of the people of God, with Christ "in the clouds" of heaven. (1 Thess. iv. 17.) If this be not the antitype of those "sabbath days," which, reaching from the barley-harvest to that of the wheat, "are a shadow of things to come" (Col. ii. 17), then tell us what the true antitype is; for we want the truth, and the truth only. The law being "a shadow of good things to come" (Heb. x. 1), he who came "to fulfill" the law (Matt. v. 17) "can do nothing of himself," (John v. 19) but must "make all things according to the pattern" (Heb. viii. 5), "which was a figure for the time then present" (Heb. ix. 9),—"a shadow of heavenly things." (Heb. viii. 5.) Are we not here clearly taught that the "holy convocation," the solemn assembly of "just men made perfect," the world's great jubilee, will be proclaimed in this fiftieth day of forty-nine years? "And it shall come to pass in that day that the great trumpet shall be blown" (Isa. xxvii. 13); "for the Lord himself shall descend from heaven with a shout, with the voice of the archangel, and with the trump of God" (1 Thess. iv. 16): "in the day of atonement shall ye make the trumpet sound throughout all your land" (Lev. xxv. 9); "and at that time thy people shall be delivered, every one that shall be found written in the book." Daniel "shall stand in his lot" (Dan. xii. 1–13); "in a moment, in the twinkling of an eye, at the last trump . . . the dead shall be raised" (1 Cor. xv. 52); "then we which are alive and remain shall be caught up, together with them in the clouds, to meet the Lord in the air, and so shall we ever be with the Lord. Wherefore comfort one another with these words" (1 Thess. iv. 18); for "He reserveth unto us the appointed weeks of the harvest," which the Jews by transgression lost. "Your iniquities have turned away these weeks, and your sins have withheld good things from you." (Jer. v. 24, 25.) Having lost "the appointed weeks of harvest," the Jews commence their fifty days with the 16th of the first month instead of "from the morrow after the sabbath," as enjoined by the law. This destroying the original institution of Heaven, we, since the days of Josiah, hear no more of "the feast of weeks" (Ex. xxxiv. 22), but Pentecost (Acts ii. 1), which, under the law, was unknown.

In conclusion, we may remark that these things are either true, or they are not. If the latter, then this whole scheme is only that of an ingenious imagination, without any foundation in the book of God: if untrue, then we ask for information; for it is a question which we are unable to solve. How happens it that so many types, shadows, and prophetic dates, over which no man can have any control, are each found reaching its proper period, forming such a wonderful diagram, the one corroborating and confirming the correctness of the other, insomuch as they with one united demonstration all declare the same thing? How does it happen that Moses's "seven times" and the seventh year of release, commencing with the last year of jubilee ever observed in the kingdom of Israel, terminate with the feast of tabernacles, on the day of the beginning of that great sabbath of rest which remaineth to the people of God? Why is it that these "weeks of harvest" do not only date from the greatest passover recorded in the book of God, but also from the last jubilee ever observed by the Jews, while the antitype of the fiftieth day embraces the feast of tabernacles as observed in the end of the world? How is it that the sabbatical year which, following this great passover, answers to the seventh day of unleavened bread, was the last sabbatical year ever observed by the Hebrews, as a free and independent people? If, concerning these matters, there was no original design on the part of our God, is it not one of the greatest mysteries ever known on earth, that all of the types and shadows with all of the prophetic dates in the Bible should be found in such exact harmony? The ceremonial part of the law being prophetic, from which "one jot or one tittle shall in no wise pass . . . till all be fulfilled" (Matt. v. 18), it is clear that these "weeks of harvest" must be the interval between some great passover and the harvest of this world; for it would appear impossible for them in any other way to reach their antitype.

How deeply interesting to contemplate those "patterns of things in the heavens" (Heb. ix. 23), while we behold each, in due order, reaching their antitype in Christ, who came to fulfill the law! When this "shadow of good things to come" (Heb. x. 1) first appeared as thrown back into the Mosaic dispensation, "the feast of harvests," having no sabbaths to point out the time of its observation, was blended with "the feast of ingathering in the end of the year when thou hast gathered in thy laborers out of the field." (Ex. xxiii. 16.) And thus in the antitype, before the beginning of the great Sabbath of sabbaths, Moses's "seven times" and the seventieth jubilee blended these two festivals together in "the end of the world" (Matt. xiii. 39), after the harvest of the gospel dispensation is gathered in (Matt. xiii. 30); for which see the diagram at A.D. 1875. The next time we discover this "shadow of heavenly things" (Heb. viii. 5), it is found yet blended with "the feast of ingathering at the year's end," with this addition, called the "feast of weeks" (Ex. xxxiv. 22); but nothing definite as to the epoch at which they were to be commenced. And so in the antitype we saw that these festivals must, in the end of the world, be blended together, "after your weeks be out" (Num. xxviii. 26), or after a great sabbath of sabbaths; for "He reserveth unto us the appointed weeks of the harvest." (Jer. v. 24.) But the book of Daniel was sealed; and, our chronology being incorrect, we had no epoch from which to begin to reckon. But the third time we saw that "which was a figure for the time then present" (Heb. ix. 9), the definite time was given. They date from the time of the passover, "from the day that ye brought the sheaf of the wave-offering." (Lev. xxiii. 15.) And that there may be no doubt as to the particular passover from which the antitype is to be reckoned, it is added, "beginning to number the seven weeks from such time as thou beginnest to put the sickle to the corn" (Deut. xvi. 9), or when you "shall reap" the barley-harvest. (Lev. xxiii. 10.) This clearly restricts us to the passover as observed by Josiah. That being the only passover of the first month recorded in the book of God as observed at the time of the beginning to reap that barley-harvest, which in the day of Jeremiah was in the "past" (Jer. viii. 20), it is impossible that the antitype can, consistently with those "patterns of things in the heavens," be commenced at a later date than at the time of that great jubilee-passover. After the "weeks of harvest" began to be reckoned from the time of the passover, they in the type were no longer blended with "the feast of ingathering." If the particular day of the month had been given on which this "feast of harvest" was to be celebrated, as that of "the passover" and "the feast of ingathering," these two festivals could not, even in the antitype, have fallen together; for the given day of a month always marks an epoch. But since the only date given for "the feast of harvest" is that it be at the end of "seven sabbaths," it may in the antitype be blended with that of "the feast of ingathering." From Exodus xxxiv. 22, it is evident that in the antitype these "weeks of the first-fruits of wheat harvest," are to point out when these festivals shall be blended together at the end of time. We generally understand Moses to mean that they were to be observed at their proper season; but if we had no further information on this subject than what is to be gathered from this verse, we should conclude from what he says that they must fall together: "Thou shalt observe the feast of weeks, of the first-fruits of wheat-harvest;" and now, with the copulative conjunction "and," he adds, "and the feast of ingathering." When? "At the year's end." According, then, to the language of Moses, in the antitype they must occur at one and the same time:"—"Your threshing shall reach unto the vintage" (Lev. xxvi. 5); "The ploughman shall overtake the reaper." (Amos ix. 13.) And these two festivals do fall together at the time of the end of the world, or from A.D. 1868 to A.D. 1875.

B.C. 570. JOSIAH'S THIRTY-FIRST YEAR.—On Tuesday the 18th of the ninth month,—that is, December 26, B.C. 570, Josiah was slain by Necho, King of Egypt: "And Jeremiah lamented for Josiah; and all the singing-men and singing-women spake of Josiah in their lamentations to this day, and made them an ordinance in Israel." (2 Chron. xxxv. 25.) "So it was a statute in Israel annually to bewail Josiah" (Targum) on the 18th of the ninth month; "and this was given out for an ordinance to be done continually in all the nation of Israel." (1 Esdras i. 32.) For on this day, the 18th of the ninth month, the Hebrews fell into Egyptian bondage; and they have never been an independent people since that time. In commemoration of this their ruin, the Jews, even to the present day, keep an annual fast on the 18th of the ninth month.

B.C. 569. JEHOAHAZ.—We have already remarked that Josiah was slain on the 18th of the ninth month,—Tuesday, December 26, B.C. 570. Consistently with the Jewish custom of mourning for their dead, the time they "anointed . . . Jehoahaz, the son of Josiah, . . . and made him king in his father's stead" (2 Kings xxiii. 30), could not have been within the limits of ten days from the time of the death of Josiah; for, during the first ten days of "weeping and mourning" for the dead, they did neither "wash nor anoint themselves," but "kept their heads covered," and "they did no servile work except in private." Ten full days from the time of the death of Josiah brings us to the 29th of the ninth month,—January 6, B.C. 569; but this was Saturday, the Jewish sabbath. The earliest period, therefore, at which "the people of the land" could, consistently with Jewish customs, have made Jehoahaz king, was on January 7, which was the 1st of the tenth month. He reigned three months. (2 Chron. xxxvi. 2.)

B.C. 569. JEHOIAKIM'S FIRST YEAR.—As the reign of Jehoahaz commenced about the 1st of the tenth month, if we add the three months as given him in 2 Chronicles xxvi. 2, we will have the 1st day of the first month,—April 4, B.C. 569; but the odd days of his reign are not here given. Josephus says he reigned three months and ten days. (*Jose. Ant.* b. x. c. v. s. 2.) These ten days bring us to the 11th of the first month, for the end of the reign of Jehoahaz. Now, if we allow Necho, King of Egypt, some two or three days to make the necessary arrangements to "put the land to a tribute of a hundred talents of silver and a talent of gold," and to make Jehoiakim king (2 Kings xxiii. 33), we will have the 14th of the first month, April 17, B.C. 569, for the beginning of his reign, which was the first day of the passover, at which time "in the beginning of the reign of Jehoiakim," Jeremiah stood "in the court of the Lord's house, and spake unto all the cities of Judah which came to worship in the Lord's house." (Jer. xxvi. 1, 2.) He reigned eleven years and about fifteen days.

B.C. 567. INTERREGNUM.—Nebuchadnezzar was in Egypt when his father died; and he "set the affairs of Egypt and the other countries in order" (*Jose. against Apion,* b. i. s. 19) before he returned home. As Ptolemy allows no interregnum here, we have allowed but one year for the one following Archian,—thus taking one from there, and placing it here, without making any alteration as to the duration of that kingdom.

B.C. 566. NEBUCHADNEZZAR'S FIRST YEAR.—The reign of Nebuchadnezzar commenced in the fourth year of Jehoiakim, which was the twenty-third from the thirteenth of Josiah (Jer. xxv. 1, 3), and not later than the feast of ingathering. (Jer. xxv. 2.) We suppose that his reign commenced about the 1st of the seventh month,—September 25, B.C. 566.

B.C. 566. JEREMIAH IMPRISONED.—"In the fourth year of Jehoiakim, at the feast of ingathering, which commenced about the 8th of October, B.C. 566, "Jeremiah the prophet spake unto all the people of Judah, and all the inhabitants of Jerusalem," the words which we have in Chapter xxv., for which Jehoiakim placed him in prison. So "Jeremiah called Baruch;" and he "wrote from the mouth of Jeremiah all the words of the Lord, which he had spoken unto him. "And Jeremiah commanded Baruch, saying, I am shut up; I cannot go into the house of the Lord; therefore go thou, and read in the roll . . . the words of the Lord in the ears of the people, in the Lord's house upon the fasting-day" (Jer. xxxvi. 4–6), —that is, the day they "lamented for Josiah" (2 Chron. xxxv. 25), which was in the 18th of "the ninth month" (Jer. xxxvi. 9), in the fourth year of Jehoiakim (Jer. xlv. 1), about two months after Jeremiah had been in prison. From this circumstance we learn that the captivity had not commenced as early as the ninth month of the fourth of Jehoiakim.

B.C. 564. JEHOIAKIM'S FIFTH YEAR.—In the fifth year of Jehoiakim, we learn that Baruch again at the same fast of the 18th of the ninth month, read "in the book the words of Jeremiah in the house of the Lord" (Jer. xxxvi. 9, 10), though Jeremiah was not at this time in prison. (Jer. xxxvi. 26.) As this roll contained the prediction of the captivity (Jer. xxxvi. 29), it is certain that it had not commenced as early as that time, which was near the end of the fifth year of Jehoiakim. Is it not strange that rather than admit the possibility of an error in Ptolemy's canon, this authority has been laid aside, and the captivity commenced in the third or fourth of Jehoiakim.

B.C. 561. JEHOIAKIM'S EIGHTH YEAR.—From Jeremiah xxv. 11, 12, we learn that the Jews were to serve the King of Babylon seventy years. This service, according to Josephus, commenced in the eighth year of Jehoiakim, which was the fifth of Nebuchadnezzar (*Jose. Ant.* b. x. c. vi. s. 1); and according to Jeremiah, it must end with the death of Belshazzar, the last King of Babylon (Jer. xxv. 12), who was slain B.C. 491, when Cyrus took the city of Babylon. This seventy-years service apparently commenced on the 10th of the fifth month, B.C. 561. For in 2 Kings xxiv. 1, we learn that Jehoiakim became the servant of the King of Babylon three years, which service, Josephus tells us, consisted in paying tribute. (*Jose. Ant.* b. x. c. vi. s. 1.) Josephus says that he brought this tribute for three years; "but on the third year, when the tribute for the fourth was due, he refused to pay it." Therefore, Nebuchadnezzar came up "in the third year of the reign of Jehoiakim" (Dan. i. 1); for though he had paid the tribute for three full years, the third year of his reign was not out at the time Nebuchadnezzar came up. As the third year for which they paid tribute "expired" with the beginning of the captivity (2 Chron. xxxvi. 10), on the 10th of the fifth month, it follows that this Babylonish service commenced on the 10th of the fifth month three years before,—that is, B.C. 561. Those who commenced the captivity in the fourth year of Jehoiakim make no distinction between this service to the King of Babylon and that called the captivity; but Jeremiah informs us that the Jews were to "serve the King of Babylon seventy years" (Jer. xxv. 11), which cannot reach farther than the death of Belshazzar, the last King of Babylon, nor commence earlier than the fourth year of Jehoiakim, which was the first of Nebuchadnezzar. According to Ptolemy's canon, Nebuchadnezzar reigned 43 years; Evil-merodach, 2; Nericassolassar, 4; Belshazzar, 17: total 66 years. Hence, if they begin the service with the first day Nebuchadnezzar ascended the throne, they will yet require four years to complete it.

B.C. 558. DANIEL TAKEN CAPTIVE.—In the fourth year of Jehoiakim (Jer. xlvi. 2), "the King of Babylon passed over Euphrates, and took all Syria, as far as Pelusium, excepting Judea. But when Nebuchadnezzar had already reigned four years, which was the eighth of Jehoiakim's government over the Hebrews, the King of Babylon made an expedition with mighty forces against the Jews; and required tribute of Jehoiakim, and threatened on his refusal to make war against him. He was affrighted at this threatening, and bought his peace with money, and brought the tribute he was ordered to bring for three years. But on the third year," when the tribute for the fourth year was due, "he did not pay his tribute." (*Jose. Ant.* b. x. c. vi. s. 1.) He thus "rebelled against" the King of Babylon. (2 Kings xxiv. 1.) Then Nebuchadnezzar, King of Babylon, went up "in the third year of the reign of Jehoiakim" (Dan. i. 1), reckoning from the time he became tributary to the King of Babylon, which was eleven years from the time he was first made king by Necho, King of Egypt (2 Chron. xxxvi. 4); "And the Lord gave Jehoiakim, King of Judah into his hands" (Dan. i. 1), and he "bound him in fetters to carry him to Babylon" (2 Chron. xxxvi. 6); and at this time Daniel, with some other children, were carried from Jerusalem. (Dan. i. 3–6.) This being just three months and ten days before the beginning of the captivity, which commenced on the 10th of the fifteenth month, B.C. 558, must have been about the 1st of the second month, May 3, B.C. 558. The supporters of Ptolemy's canon tell us that Daniel meant the third year from the time the King of Egypt, made Jehoiakim king. But this cannot be; for Daniel says:—"In the third year of the reign of Jehoiakim, King of Judah, came Nebuchadnezzar, King of Babylon unto Jerusalem, and besieged it" (Dan. i. 1); but Nebuchadnezzar was not King of Babylon until the fourth year of Jehoiakim, reckoning from the time he was made king by Necho. (Jer. xxv. 1.) Prideaux says that Nebuchadnezzar left Babylon on the third year of Jehoiakim, but did not reach Jerusalem until the fourth. This contradicts Daniel, whose express language is,—not that he started from Babylon, but that he "came unto Jerusalem, and besieged it . . . in the third year of the reign of Jehoiakim." In the second place it contradicts Jeremiah, who informs us that Nebuchadnezzar's first year was in the fourth of Jehoiakim; for if Nebuchadnezzar, King of Babylon, started on this expedition in the third of Jehoiakim, then his reign commenced before his fourth year. As Jehoiakim was not anointed king by the Jews, but was merely a tributary king, made so, first, by the King of Egypt (2 Chron. xxxvi. 4) and, second, by the King of Babylon (2 Kings xxiv. 1), these are two different epochs, from which his reign may properly be dated. The first was important, as it was the beginning of his reign; but the second was more so to the Jews, for with this commenced the seventy-years service to the kingdom of Babylon. And since Daniel was one of the captives, this was the most important one to him; for it marks the epoch from which the seventy-years service to the King of Babylon commenced. It is evident that Daniel did not mean the third year of Jehoiakim, reckoning from the time he was appointed king by Necho: for—1. Nebuchadnezzar was not King of Babylon until the fourth year of Jehoiakim. (Jer. xxv. 1.) 2. The first time Nebuchadnezzar went to Jerusalem was in the eighth year of Jehoiakim. (*Jose. Ant.* b. x. c. vi. s. 1.) 3. Jehoiakim was given into the hand of Nebuchadnezzar, and he carried him "into the land of Shinar to the house of his God" (Dan. i. 2); but, reckoning from the first epoch, we find him at Jerusalem, seated on his throne, as late as the fourth, fifth, and even to the eleventh year. (Jer. xxxvi. 1–9.) 4. Daniel also says a part of the vessels were given into the hand of Nebuchadnezzar, which was not until the end of the eleventh year of Jehoiakim, reckoning from the first epoch. (2 Chron. xxxvi. 7.) 5. While the Jews were to serve the King of Babylon seventy years, only three years of this service was accomplished during the reign of Jehoiakim (2 Kings xxiv. 1); but had Daniel reckoned from the first epoch, then eight years of it must have been accomplished during his reign.

B.C. 558. THE REIGN OF JEHOIACHIN began about the 1st of the second month, May 3, B.C. 558; for he reigned only three months and ten days (2 Chron. xxvi. 5–8), which if we subtract from the 10th of the fifth month, at which time Zedekiah's reign commenced, we will have the 1st of the second month. We have before noticed (p. 98) that Nebuchadnezzar went to Jerusalem in the eighth year of Jehoiakim, and demanded of him tribute, which he paid for three years. So, "Jehoiakim became his servant three years: then he turned and rebelled against him" (2 Kings xxiv. 1) by refusing to bring the fourth year's tribute. So "in the third year of the reign of Jehoiakim" (as tributary to the King of Babylon) "Nebuchadnezzar" went to Jerusalem; "and the Lord gave Jehoiakim, King of Judah into his hand" (Dan. i. 1), and he "bound him with a chain of brass, and carried him into Babylon." (1 Esdras i. 40.) But this being before the end of those three years for which the Jews had "bought their peace with money" (*Jose. Ant.* b. x. c. vi. s. 1), it would have been unjust in Nebuchadnezzar to have made them captives at that time; for it was only Jehoiakim who had rebelled against him in refusing to bring the fourth year's tribute; hence, only a few children were carried off at that time with Jehoiakim. (Dan. i. 2–4.) Jehoiakim, as King of Judah, had "bought his peace with money and brought the tribute he was ordered to bring for three years;" therefore, Nebuchadnezzar suffered his kingdom to continue to the end of the three years for which he had "bought his peace" by being filled with his son Jehoiachin; "and when the year was expired,"—that is, the last of those three years for which Jehoiakim had "bought his peace," and which lacked only three months and ten days of being completed at the time Jehoiakim was carried off,—"Nebuchadnezzar sent and brought him to Babylon" (2 Chron. xxxvi. 10), and made "his father's brother king in his stead." (2 Kings xxiv. 17.) As the three months and ten days during which Jehoiachin reigned were only intended to fill out that time for which his father had "bought his peace," the kingdom yet properly belonged to his father, who was in Babylon. "And when the year was expired," or at the expiration of the time for which Jehioakim had bought his peace, his son was also led captive; hence Jehoiachin was never in possession of the kingdom as his own. "Therefore, thus saith the Lord of Jehoiakim, King of Judah, He shall have none to sit upon the throne of David." (Jer. xxxvi. 30.)

B.C. 558. ZEDEKIAH'S REIGN commenced on Wednesday, the 10th of the fifth month, August 8, B.C. 558, which was the fourth of the Jewish cycle of seven. Jeremiah does not say in the fourth year of the *reign* of Zedekiah, but "in the fourth year" (Jer. xxviii. 1), which points out the fourth year of their cycle,—as the expression, "in the fifth month" (Jer. xxviii. 1), designates the month of the year. When the reign of a given king is alluded to, it is thus expressly mentioned: "In the tenth year of Zedekiah, King of Judah" (Jer. xxxii. 1); but in dating by their cycle only the number was given, thus: "The third year" (Deut. xxvi. 12); "in the sixth year" (Lev. xxv. 21); "in the seventh year." (Jer. lii. 28.) Jeremiah could not have meant the fourth year of the reign of Zedekiah; for he says: "And it came to pass the same year" (Jer. xxviii. 1), which expression evidently points us to the particular year of the last date mentioned; and that was the carrying away "captive Jeconiah, the son of Jehoiakim." (Jer. xxvii. 20.) His language is, "in the beginning of the reign of Zedekiah, King of Judah, in the fourth year" (Jer. xxviii. 1); and it is impossible that the beginning of his reign could have been after he had already reigned three full years. When Hananiah first delivered his prophecy, "even the prophet Jeremiah said, Amen: the Lord do so: the Lord perform thy words which thou hast prophesied, to bring again the vessels of the Lord's house" (Jer. xxviii. 6) "within two full years" (Jer. xxviii. 3); "and the prophet Jeremiah went his way" (Jer. xxviii. 11), as if waiting to see whether this prophecy would be accomplished; but afterwards it was revealed to him that it was untrue,—that the "Lord had not sent" Hananiah. (Jer. xxviii. 15.) This circumstance proves that the prophecy of Hananiah, which was delivered "in the beginning of the reign of Zedekiah" (Jer. xxviii. 1), was in chronological order before that which we have recorded in Jeremiah xxvii.; for at that time Jeremiah had learned that so far from the vessels being brought back within two years, even those "that remain in the house of the Lord . . . shall be carried to Babylon, and there shall they be until the day that I visit them saith the Lord" (Jer. xxvii. 22), which was "after seventy years be accomplished at Babylon." (Jer. xxix. 10.) Had Jeremiah been in possession of this information at the time Hananiah delivered his prophecy, surely he would at once have charged him with falsehood; and to this known untruth he could not have answered, "Amen: the Lord do so; the Lord perform thy words." (Jer. xxviii. 6.) This removing the apparent difficulty, it is now clear that Zedekiah's reign began in the fifth month of the fourth year from their last sabbatical year of release. The words of Jeremiah are: "In the beginning of the reign of Zedekiah, King of Judah, in the fourth year and in the fifth month." (Jer. xxviii. 1.)

Jeremiah further informs us that "the end of the eleventh year of Zedekiah" was at the time of "the carrying away of Jerusalem captive in the fifth month" (Jer. i. 3), which was "in the tenth day of the month." (Jer. lii. 12.) If his eleventh year ended on the 10th of the fifth month, then his first began on the 10th of the fifth month.

B.C. 558. THE CAPTIVITY commenced on the 10th of the fifth month, August 8, B.C. 558, which was the eighth year of Nebuchadnezzar. (2 Kings xxiv. 12.) The reign of Zedekiah began on the same day, in proof of which it is said in 2 Kings xxv. 1: "And it came to pass in the ninth year of his reign, in the tenth month, in the tenth day of the month, that Nebuchadnezzar, King of Babylon, came, he, and all his host, against Jerusalem, and pitched against it." Ezekiel, who dates from the commencement of the captivity, places the time at which Jerusalem was besieged on the same day, thus: "In the ninth year, in the tenth month, in the tenth day of the month, the word of the Lord came unto me, saying, Son of man, write thee the name of the day, even this same day; the King of Babylon set himself against Jerusalem this same day." (Ezek. xxiv. 1, 2.) From Ezekiel xl. 1, we learn that the beginning of the twenty-fifth year of the captivity was on "the tenth day of the month;" and this "tenth day of the month" was that on which "the city was smitten," and "in the fourteenth year." Now, the city was smitten on the 10th of the fifth month (Jer. lii. 12), in "the nineteenth year of Nebuchadnezzar," which was B.C. 547; hence, the thirteenth year after ends on the 9th of the fifth month, B.C. 534; and the fourteenth year commences on the 10th of the fifth month of the same year, which was the "self-same day the . . . city was smitten." (Ezek. xl. 1.) This being "the beginning of the . . . five and twentieth year of" the "captivity," it follows, therefore, that it commenced on the 10th of the fifth month, just twenty-four years before; which, reckoned back from that time, brings us to the 10th of the fifth month, B.C. 558, for the beginning of the captivity. At B.C. 561 we remarked that the Babylonish service commenced in the eighth year of the reign of Jehoiakim, and terminated at the death of Belshazzar, the last King of Babylon, just seventy years from that time; for they were to "serve the King of Babylon seventy years." As Nebuchadnezzar carried no Jews from Jerusalem to Babylon, that was not called the captivity, but the "seventy-years" service to "the King of Babylon" (Jer. xxv. 11); hence, whenever the captivity is mentioned, we understand the writer to mean "Jehoiachin's captivity" (Ezek. i. 2), at which time Nebuchadnezzar carried "all the nobles of Judah and Jerusalem" (Jer. xxvii. 20) "away to Babylon." (Matt. i. 11.) "He carried away all Jerusalem, and all the princes and all the mighty men of valor, even ten thousand captives, and all the craftsmen and smiths: none remained, save the poorest sort of the people of the land." (2 Kings xxiv. 14.) From this carrying "away captive from Jerusalem to Babylon," when "Jechoniah" (or Jehoiachin), "the king, and the queen, . . . the princes of Judah and Jerusalem, and the carpenters, and the smiths, were departed from Jerusalem," Jeremiah dates the commencement of the seventy-years captivity. (Jer. xxix. 1, 2, 10.) From this "removing of" the Jews out of "their own land" to the first year of Cyrus, Josephus says there was seventy years. (*Ant.* b. xi. c. i. s. 1.)

Rather than acknowledge the possibility of an error in Ptolemy's canon, all of this authority as to the time of the seventy-years captivity has been laid aside, and its beginning dated in the third year of the reign of Jehoiakim; and that not only without any authority either sacred or profane, but by closing their eyes, as it were, to the words of Jeremiah, who assures us that the captivity was yet a subject of prophecy in the fifth year of Jehoiakim. (Jer. xxxvi. 9, 29.) The captivity could not have commenced before the end of the reign of Jehoiakim; for when Nebuchadnezzar "came up against him," he "bound him in fetters to carry him to Babylon." (2 Chron. xxxvi. 6.) Prideaux concludes that Jehoiakim "having humbled himself to Nebuchadnezzar" was again restored to his kingdom. But he should have noticed that the adverb "also," as used in ver. 7, shows that he was not only bound in chains to be carried to Babylon, but was also taken there; for it is clear from ver. 7 that, with Jehoiakim, "Nebuchadnezzar also carried off the vessels of the house of the Lord to Babylon." (2 Chron. xxxvi. 7.) At this place the Douay Bible reads thus: "Against him came up Nebuchadnezzar, King of the

Chaldeans, and led him bound with chains into Babylon." In the Apocryphal book of Esdras, we read: "Wherefore against him Nebuchadnezzar, the King of Babylon came up, and bound him with a chain of brass, and carried him into Babylon." (1 Esdras i. 40.)

When we call to mind that the sacred writers—in order to distinguish the time of the beginning of their captivity from that tributary service to the King of Babylon, which commenced in the eighth year of Jehoiakim, and that of the ruin of their city at the end of the reign of Zedekiah—called it "Jehoiachin's captivity" (Ezek. i. 2: 2 Kings xxv. 27; xxiv. 12: Jer. xxiv. 1, 5; xxvii. 20; xxix. 2–4: Est. ii. 6), it is strange that our divines could have been so much influenced by the authority of Ptolemy's canon as to have ever thought of dating the beginning of the captivity anywhere else. Ezekiel makes it a new epoch, from which he dates all his writings, and calls it "our captivity." (Ezek. xxxiii. 21; xl. 1.) The advocates for Ptolemy's canon evade this by saying Ezekiel only calls this "our captivity" because he was at that time carried from Jerusalem; but if Josephus can be credited, Ezekiel was not carried from Jerusalem with "Jehoiachin's captivity." According to Josephus, "Ezekiel, who was then but young" (*Jose. Ant.* b. x. c. vi. s. 3) was carried away with "the children" at the time Daniel was taken captive. (Dan. i. 3, 6.) From the expression "THE CAPTIVITY," as used in the book of Esther (ii. 6), it is evident that this is the epoch from which the Jews dated the beginning of their captivity. Jeremiah also in speaking of those who were carried away at this times, calls them the captives,—"all that are carried away captives." (Jer. xxix. 4.) Jeremiah here informs us that the captivity is to be dated from this epoch. Those who were then carried away—that is, with the captivity of Jehoiachin—were to remain in Babylon seventy years: "For thus saith the Lord, After seventy years be accomplished at Babylon, I will visit you." (Jer. xxix. 10.) But if they had returned at the end of seventy years from the fourth of Jehoiakim, they could have remained but sixty-two years at Babylon. Neither can the seventy years be commenced from a later period; "for thus saith the Lord, That after seventy years be accomplished at Babylon I will visit you, and perform my good word towards you, in causing you to return to this place." (Jer. xxix. 10.) While those who were taken captive at this time were to return at the end of the seventy years, those carried away with Zedekiah were not to return at all, but were to "be removed into all the kingdoms of the earth." (Jer. xxiv. 5, 9.)

The time of the beginning of the seventy-years captivity, being such an important point in chronology, we will in conclusion call the attention of the reader to the undeniable authority we have for commencing it in B.C. 558. The eclipse of the sun as recorded by Jeremiah, and found to have occurred B.C. 549, prevents our beginning the captivity a single year lower, or more than one higher; and the one foretold by Amos forbids our commencing it a single year either lower or higher without adding or diminishing a year more than we have inspired authority for doing. Again, through Ptolemy and Berosus we have settled the chronology of the kingdom of Babylon from the time of Nabonassar, their first king, to the end of the reign of Nebuchadnezzar, which we have proven to be correct by five eclipses of the moon; hence, we cannot begin the reign of Nebuchadnezzar a single year higher nor lower,—and in the eighth year of Nebuchadnezzar the captivity began. (2 Kings xxiv. 12.) At B.C. 666 and B.C. 510 we have adjusted both the beginning and end of the kingdom of Media with Bible chronology. That we have the chronology of that kingdom properly arranged, we prove by the eclipse of the sun which happened during a battle between the Medes and Lydians, as recorded by Herodotus. (See at B.C. 549.) With this combined authority, it may be considered certain that our chronology cannot be far from the truth; and if not, it must be strictly correct; for the captivity commencing in the fourth year of the Jewish cycle of seven, forbids any change as to the arrangement of our table of chronology except by entire cycles of seven full years, which clearly proves that B.C. 558 was the year in which Nebuchadnezzar "carried away all Jerusalem" (2 Kings xxiv. 14) "to Babylon." (Matt. i. 11.) From this epoch, B.C. 558, there must be just seventy years to the end of the captivity, when Cyrus issued the edict for their restoration. (Isa. xliv. 28.) 70 subtracted from 558 leaves 488; hence, it must have been issued B.C. 488. We are required to "KNOW AND UNDERSTAND that from the going forth of this commandment to restore and build Jerusalem unto the Messiah the Prince,"—that is, to the birth of that Prince who was "born King of the Jews" (Matt. ii. 2),—there were just "seven weeks, and threescore and two weeks," of years. (Dan. ix. 25.) 483 years subtracted from B.C. 488, leaves us B.C. 5 for the time of the birth of Christ.

B.C. 554. ZEDEKIAH'S FOURTH YEAR.—"In the third year of the reign of Jehoiakim" (Dan. i. 1), as tributary to the King of Babylon, which was eleven years after the time he had been made king by Necho, King of Egypt (2 Chron. xxxvi. 3), "the King of

Babylon came up and bound him with a chain of brass, and carried him into Babylon" (1 Esdras i. 40), where it would appear he remained quietly until about the fourth year of the reign of Zedekiah, when, escaping, he went "to the Kings of Edom, and of Moab, and of the Ammonites, and of Tyrus, and to the King of Zidon," persuading them to join him in a revolt against the King of Babylon. Expecting their aid he returned to Jerusalem, and again took his kingdom (Jer. xxvii. 1), which the King of Babylon had given to Zedekiah. (2 Kings xxiv. 17.)

But, doubting the propriety of entering rashly into this alliance with Jehoiakim, they sent "messengers unto Zedekiah, King of Judah" (Jer. xxvii. 3) to make inquiry concerning the matter; he, being undecided, consulted Jeremiah, who thus admonished him: "Bring your necks under the yoke of the kingdom of Babylon, and serve him and his people and live. Why will ye die, thou and thy people, by the sword, and by the famine, and by the pestilence, as the Lord hath spoken against the nation that will not serve the King of Babylon." (Jer. xxvii. 12, 13.) Zedekiah then went immediately to Babylon (Jer. li. 59), informing the king of the intention of Jehoiakim, who had already seated himself on the throne as "King of Judah" (Jer. xxvii. 1); and Jeremiah sent a message to those kings who had been almost persuaded to join Jehoiakim in a revolt, saying, "Thus shall ye say unto your masters; ... the nation and kingdom which will not serve ... the King of Babylon, ... that nation will I punish, saith the Lord, with the sword, and with the famine, and with the pestilence until I have consumed them by his hand." (Jer. xxvii. 4, 8.) Those kings being thus deterred from aiding Jehoiakim, he again fell into the hands of the King of Babylon, at which time he was "drawn and cast forth beyond the gates of Jerusalem." Thus he was "buried with the burial of an ass" (Jer. xxii. 19); for "his dead body" was "cast out in the day to the heat, and in the night to the frost." (Jer. xxxvi. 30.)

Jehoiakim's conduct having caused Nebuchadnezzar to cast his son Jehoiachin into prison (2 Kings xxv. 27), and bringing much trouble on the kingdom of Judah, no one mourned his loss. (Jer. xxii. 18.) As the three months and ten days during which Jehoiachin reigned was during the lifetime of Jehoiakim, and before he had this second time been seated on the throne of his kingdom, Jehoiachin never occupied the throne of David as a successor to his father; as Jeremiah spoke of Jehoiakim's "dead body" being "cast out," he evidently meant that he should "have none to sit upon the throne of David" (Jer. xxxvi. 30) after his death, which was strictly true,—for Jehoiakim was yet alive and again in possession of his kingdom after his son Jehoiachin had been carried to Babylon. (Jer. xxvii. 1.) This view of the matter removes the following difficulties:—1. The fulfillment of the words of Jeremiah concerning Jehoiakim: "He shall have none to sit upon the throne of David." (Jer. xxxvi. 30.) 2. How Jehoiakim should have none to "lament for him" (Jer. xxii. 18), while his own son was King of Judah. 3. His dead body being cast forth beyond the gates of Jerusalem" (Jer. xxii. 19), since he was "carried into Babylon." (1 Esdras i. 40.) 4. The reign of Jehoiachin beginning during that of Zedekiah. (Jer. xxvii. 1, 3.) 5. Why Zedekiah should have left the kingdom over which Nebuchadnezzar had given him charge, and gone to Babylon in the fourth year of his reign." (Jer. li. 59.)

B.C. 553. THE THIRTIETH YEAR.—The Jews had two cycles: one of seven, the other of forty-nine, years. By the first, they point out their sabbatical year (Lev. xxv. 4); by the second, the year of jubilee. (Lev. xxv. 8.) From Ezekiel i. 1, 2, we learn that the thirtieth year of their cycle of forty-nine synchronizes with the fifth year of Jehoiachin's captivity, which, commencing the 10th of the fifth month, B.C. 554, ends on the 10th of the fifth month, B.C. 553. Since Ezekiel assures us that the 5th of the fourth month, in the fifth year of the captivity, was in the thirtieth of their cycle, the thirtieth year of their cycle of forty-nine answers to B.C. 553. This, then, proves that in our table of chronology we have the year of jubilee properly arranged, and is also a demonstration of its correctness; for if there is any error, it must be one of forty-nine years.

B.C. 549. ECLIPSE OF THE SUN.—We remarked at B.C. 755 that the expression, "eclipse of the sun," was then unknown. To convey the idea, it would be said, "the sun is gone down while it was yet day" (Jer. xv. 9); "I will cause the sun to go down at noon" (Amos viii. 9); "The sun shall be darkened in his going forth." (Isa. xiii. 10.) During the siege of Jerusalem, Jeremiah thus spoke of a total eclipse: "her sun is gone down while yet day." (Jer. xv. 9.) "It was" is in *italic*, denoting its absence in the original, which reads thus: "Her sun is gone down while yet day." This was apparently written on the day of the eclipse, and clearly after the Lord had "caused" the Chaldeans "to fall suddenly upon" Jerusalem (Jer. xv. 8), and before its destruction; for this was yet the subject of prophecy: "the residue of them will I deliver to the sword before their enemies, saith the Lord." (Jer. xv. 9.) The 10th of the tenth month in the ninth of Zedekiah, when "the King of Babylon set himself against Jerusalem" (Ezek. xxiv. 2), "at noon-day" (Jer. xv. 8), was Tuesday, January 5, B.C. 549, and the city was destroyed on the 10th of the fourth month, B.C. 547. To substantiate our chronology there must have been a total eclipse of the sun at Jerusalem within the limits of the above-mentioned time. By calculation, one occurred there on June 19, B.C. 549, at 30m. past nine in the morning,—five months and fourteen days after Nebuchadnezzar commenced the war. As Zedekiah expected the King of Babylon when "he rebelled against him," we can hardly suppose that his approach caused much surprise in the city; for he came "at noonday." (Jer. xv. 8.) Hence, by the falling of "terrors upon the city" (Jer. xv. 8), we must understand the terror caused by the day being thus suddenly "changed into the darkest night." "I have caused *darkness** to fall upon it suddenly, and terrors upon the city." Dr. Stukely says of a total eclipse of the sun: "It was the most awful sight I had ever beheld." Jeremiah considered this eclipse as a sign of the ruin of that city: "her sun is gone down while it is yet day; she hath been ashamed and confounded: and the residue of them will I deliver to the sword before their enemies, saith the Lord." (Jer. xv. 9.)

B.C. 549. THE ECLIPSE OF THALES.—The war between the Medes and Lydians, during the reign of Cyaxares, continued five years. "In the sixth year, when they were carrying on the war with nearly equal success, on occasion of an engagement it happened that in the heat of the battle day was suddenly turned into night. This change of the day, Thales, the Milesian, had foretold to the Ionians, fixing beforehand this year as the very period in which the change actually took place." (*Herod.* b. i. c. 74.) This undoubtedly was a total eclipse of the sun. Though Cyaxares reigned forty years, this war could not have commenced earlier than his twenty-ninth year,—B.C. 557. (See p. 40.) If we subtract the five years during which it continued, we will have B.C. 552. Hence, the sixth year of the war answers to B.C. 551; and the fortieth of Cyaxares ends B.C. 546. We are thus limited to five years for the time of this eclipse. It must have occurred between B.C. 551 and B.C. 546. Herodotus being silent as to the location of the battle-field, all we can know is that it was either in Media

---

* The word "him" is not in the original. As Jeremiah was here alluding to the eclipse, we supply "darkness" instead of "him."

or Lydia, or at some place between them. By calculation, a total eclipse of the sun passed between these two kingdoms on June 19, B.C. 549. It was central on lat. 35 and long. 40, at 9m. after ten in the morning. The historian informs us that the King of Celicia and the King of Babylon were the mediators, "These were they who hastened the treaty between Cyaxares and the King of Lydia." We may therefore infer that the field of battle was at some place near Babylon or Celicia, or between these places.

B.C. 548. THE SABBATICAL YEAR. — Nebuchadnezzar commenced the siege of Jerusalem in the ninth of Zedekiah, on the 10th of the tenth month (2 Kings xxv. 1),—that is, Tuesday, January 5, B.C. 549; and between the 1st of the seventh month, October, B.C. 549, and the 1st of the first month, April, B.C. 548, "the Chaldeans that besieged Jerusalem," hearing that "Pharoah's army had come forth out of Egypt, departed from the city" (Jer. xxxvii. 5), at which time Nebuchadnezzar, in the eighteenth year of his reign, "carried away captive from Jerusalem eight hundred and thirty-two Jews." (Jer. lii. 29.) When "the King of Babylon . . . fought against Jerusalem" (Jer. xxxiv. 1), Zedekiah, "becoming alarmed, sent to Jerusalem, saying, Pray now unto the Lord our God for us" (Jer. xxxvii. 3); "then Jeremiah the prophet spake" unto Zedekiah, saying, "Thus saith the Lord, Behold, I will give this city into the hand of the King of Babylon, and he shall burn it with fire." (Jer. xxxiv. 2, 6.) At this time the Jews humbling themselves, consented to yield obedience to the law of Moses; and as the year of release was then at hand, Zedekiah "made a covenant with all the people which were at Jerusalem, to proclaim liberty unto them." (Jer. xxxiv. 8.) "But afterwards, . . . when the army of the Chaldeans was broken up from Jerusalem for fear of Pharoah's army" (Jer. xxxvii. 11), "they turned, and caused the servants, and the handmaids, whom they had let go free, to return, and brought them into subjection for servants and for handmaids." (Jer. xxxiv. 11.) "Therefore the word of the Lord came unto Jeremiah from the Lord, saying, Behold, I will command, saith the Lord, and cause" the King of Babylon "to return to this city; and they shall fight against it, and take it, and burn it with fire." (Jer. xxxiv. 12, 22.) We here learn that the sabbatical year had commenced before the army of the Chaldeans returned to Jerusalem, which was in the tenth of Zedekiah and the eighteenth of Nebuchadnezzar. (Jer. xxxii. 1.) As Zedekiah's tenth year ended on the 10th of the fifth month, August 18, B.C, 548, the sabbatical year had commenced before that time. Nebuchadnezzar's eighteenth year ended about the 1st of the seventh month, B.C. 548. And between this and the end of the sabbatical year, he carried off during this the Jewish "seventh year, three thousand Jews and three-and twenty." (Jer. lii. 28.)

B.C. 548. THE SEVENTH YEAR AND YEAR OF JUBILEE ADJUSTED. —The season at which the sabbatical year commenced is thus made clear: "This month shall be to you the beginning of months: it shall be the first month of the year to you." (Ex. xii. 2.) It was called "the month Abib" (Ex. xiii. 4),—that is, the month of "the young ears of corn, or of the new fruit." (*Cruden.*) Six of these years commencing with "the month Abib" were to be spent in sowing and reaping (Lev. xxv. 3); and the seventh was a sabbatical year,—"a sabbath of rest unto the land." (Lev. xxv. 4.) Since it is called the seventh year, it must begin where the sixth ends. We can according to the law commence it nowhere else; for if we commence it with the seventh month of the sixth year, then the Jews would only spend five years and six months in sowing and reaping instead of the six years their law required; or, if they began it with the seventh month of the seventh year, they would thus spend six years and six months, and so continue a state of confusion through every cycle. As the seventh year began with the month Abib, it was necessary for the sixth year to yield a supply sufficient for three years. (Lev. xxv. 21.) But had the sabbatical year commenced with the seventh month, then the sixth year would have had to yield a supply for only two years. Had the year of jubilee commenced with the month Abib as the sabbatical year, then once in forty-nine years it would have been necessary for the sixth year to have yielded a supply sufficient for four years. No such provision having been made in the law, shows that we have the year of jubilee properly arranged. The day on which the jubilee is to be proclaimed is pointed out,—that is, "the tenth day of the seventh month." (Lev. xxv. 9.) To distinguish this from the Jewish forty-ninth sabbatical year, it is called the fiftieth year, which, indeed, it is; for it is another year commencing at a different time, or in another month. And as they were required to hallow this fiftieth year, it must be a whole year, ending on the 10th of the seventh month in the following year. This being called the fiftieth year, some have thought it meant the year following the forty-ninth,—that is, the fiftieth year commencing with the same month with which the forty-ninth began. But since they were required to "cause the trumpet of the jubilee to sound on the tenth day of the seventh month," this will not do; for then the trumpet proclaiming the opening of the jubilee would sound nearly six months before the beginning of the year. Had the year of jubilee commenced with the same month with the other forty-nine years, then once in that period they would have spent only five years in sowing and reaping. The law enjoined: "Six years thou shalt sow thy field." (Lev. xxv. 3.) We have this clear proof that the year of jubilee ended in the year following the forty-ninth, in time for them to sow their grain. The jubilee could not reach farther than the seventh month of the eighth year; for it was positively required: "Ye shall sow the eighth year." (Lev. xxv. 22. See p. 66.)

Having pointed out the month with which the sabbatical year commenced, we are now prepared to adjust it to our chronology. As B.C. 163 and 135 were sabbatical years, there is no room for controversy as to B.C. 548 being a sabbatical year; for if we subtract 163 from 548, we have 385, which, divided by 7, leaves no remainder. (On p. 110 we have observed that the tenth of Zedekiah was a sabbatical year, to which we refer the reader.] The two different times at which the army of the Chaldeans went to Jerusalem may be distinguished by noticing that Jeremiah was not imprisoned the first time; for he was not put in prison until after "the army of the Chaldeans was broken up for fear of Pharoah's army." (Jer. xxxvii. 4, 11, 12, 15.) And he "abode in the court of the prison until the day that Jerusalem was taken." (Jer. xxxviii. 28.) The army returned to Jerusalem "in the tenth of Zedekiah;" for Jeremiah was then "in prison." (Jer. xxxii. 1, 2.) As Zedekiah's tenth year ended on the 10th of the fifth month, August 18, B.C. 548, the army of the Chaldeans had returned before that, and the sabbatical year had commenced (Jer. xxxiv. 15, 16, 22); hence, we cannot place the tenth of Zedekiah, nor the eighteenth of Nebuchadnezzar, a year higher than we have in our chronology, and the sabbatical year of B.C. 674, forbids our placing the fourteenth of Hezekiah a year lower. With this adjustment of the sabbatical year, it becomes a very important means of testing our chronology. For example: the thirty-first year of Josiah ends in the Jewish sixth year; if we move his reign a single year lower, it would terminate in the sabbatical year; but "the Jews observe this rest every seventh year as they do every seventh day." (*Jose. Ant.* b. xiii. c. viii. s. 1.) Therefore, he could not during that year voluntarily have engaged in a war which was declared to be not against him. (2 Chron. xxxv. 21). Having thus adjusted the sabbatical year with the reign of the Kings of Judah, if there be an error in our chronology, it must be one of seven full years. This enables us to settle chronology with great precision. For instance: being limited to five years in which to find the eclipse of Thales (see at B.C. 549), which occurred on June 19, B.C. 549, suppose we strike seven years out of our chronology, we would then lack six of reaching the time of this eclipse. Or, if we add seven years, then the eclipse of B.C. 549 would be four years too late for the one as recorded by Herodotus. Since, then, we can prove that the tenth of Zedekiah was a sabbatical year, we can even by this eclipse of Thales prove that B.C. 548 was the tenth of Zedekiah; for we have adjusted the reign of the Kings of the Medes with our chronology. (See at B.C. 666 and B.C. 510.) Having proven that Zedekiah's reign began in "the fourth year" of the Jewish cycle of seven, and that his tenth was a sabbatical year, the Jewish cycle of seven years enables us to combine our whole catalogue of eclipses both of the sun and moon to prove that Zedekiah's reign began B.C. 558. With this adjustment of the seventh year and the year of jubilee with the reigns of the Kings of Israel, it is clear that our chronology cannot be erroneous.

B.C. 547. ZEDEKIAH'S ELEVENTH YEAR.—"The city was besieged unto the eleventh year of King Zedekiah. And on the sabbath, the ninth day of the fourth month," Saturday, July 7, B.C. 547, "the city was broken up, and all the men of war fled by night." (2 Kings xxv. 2–4.) "And in the fifth month, on the seventh day of the month," Saturday, August 4, B.C. 547, came the "captain of the guard, a servant of the King of Babylon, unto Jerusalem" (2 Kings xxv. 8); and on the third day after,—that is, "in the fifth month, in the tenth day of the month," Tuesday, August 7, B.C. 547, "which was the nineteenth year of Nebuchadnezzar" (Jer. lii. 12)—"they burnt the house of the Lord, and the king's house, and all the houses of Jerusalem." (2 Kings xxv. 9.) As the 9th of the fourth month was in the eleventh of Zedekiah (Jer. xxxix. 2), his eleventh year was not out at that time. His eleventh year ended "in the fifth month," at the time of "the carrying away of Jerusalem captive (Jer. i. 3), which was on the 10th of the fifth month; for the time the "captain of the guard carried away captive . . . the people that remained in the city," was when he "burned the king's house, and the houses of the people" (Jer. xxxix. 9, 8), "in the tenth day of the fifth month." (Jer. lii. 12.) As the eleventh of Zedekiah ends on the 10th of the fifth month, B.C. 547, it must also have commenced on the 10th of the fifth month, B.C. 558.

B.C. 547. EZRA, THE PRIEST, was the son of Seraiah." (Ezra vii. 1.) By comparing Ezra vii. 1–5 with 1 Chron. vi. 3–14, we find that this Seraiah was the high-priest who was slain by Nebuchadnezzar at the time of the destruction of Jerusalem (2 Kings xxv. 18, 21), B.C. 547; hence, Ezra could not have been less than one hundred and fifteen years old when he went to Jerusalem, in the seventh of Artaxerxes, B.C. 431. (Ezra vii. 6.) As Jehoiada was "an hundred and thirty years old when he died" (2 Chron. xxiv. 15), and Tobit "a hundred and fifty-eight" (Tobit. xiv. 11), it is not unreasonable to suppose that Ezra was one hundred and sixteen when he went up from Babylon to Jerusalem; yet it is a further proof of error in Ptolemy's canon; for according to it, Ezra could not have been less than one hundred and eighty at the time he is said to have "reformed the Jewish Church and State. (See p. 11.)

B.C. 546. THE SEVENTY-YEARS INDIGNATION.—(See at B.C. 477.)

B.C. 545. THE SEVENTY-YEARS FAST AND MOURNING.—(See at B.C. 475.)

B.C. 534. THE YEAR OF JUBILEE.—"And the Lord spake unto Moses in Mount Sinai, saying, Speak unto the children of Israel and say unto them, When ye come into the land which I give you, then shall the land keep a sabbath unto the Lord." (Lev. xxv. 1, 2.) Mark the expression: "then shall the land keep a sabbath unto the Lord,"—not the people of the land. When the Jews were in their "enemies' land," the land enjoyed her sabbaths. "For I know," says Moses, "that after my death ye shall utterly corrupt yourselves, and turn aside from the way which I have commanded you; and evil will befall you in the latter days" (Deut. xxxi. 29); "and your land shall be desolate, and your cities waste. Then shall the land enjoy her sabbaths, as long as it lieth desolate, and ye be in your enemies land; even then shall the land rest, and enjoy her sabbaths." (Lev. xxvi. 34.) "For saith the Lord I will remember the land. The land also shall be left of them, and shall enjoy her sabbaths, while she lieth desolate without them." (Lev. xxvi. 43.) This was accomplished during the seventy-years captivity; "for as long as she lay desolate she kept sabbath, to fulfill threescore and ten years." (2 Chron. xxxvi. 21.) Within these seventy-years rest there was but one year of jubilee, which occurred B.C. 534. This was the year of rest to the land for the jubilee-sabbath. From the time the land shall "keep this sabbath unto the Lord" thou shalt "number seven sabbaths of years" (Lev. xxv. 8), "which are a shadow of things to come" (Col. ii. 17); hence, the antitype must be that of a great sabbath of sabbaths, or jubilee of jubilees, which is 49 times 49, or 2401 years. The Julian period for the year B.C. 534 is 4180, to which if we add 2401, we have 6581, which is the Julian period for A.D. 1868. Hence, A.D. 1868 must be the year of jubilee as shadowed forth by the law, at which time "the great trumpet shall be blown" (Isa. xxvii. 13), "in the new moon in the time appointed, on our solemn feast-day" (Ps. lxxxi. 3),—that is, "on the" 10th of the seventh month, "in the day of atonement shall ye make the trumpet sound throughout all your land" (Lev. xxv. 9); for this was a statute for Israel, and a law of the God of Jacob." (Ps. lxxxi. 4.) "The jubilee," says Parkhurst, "is a lively prefiguration of the great consummation of time, which will be introduced in like manner by the trump of God (1 Cor. xv. 52), when the children and heirs of God shall be delivered from all forfeiture, and restored to the eternal inheritance allotted to them by their Father, and thenceforth rest from their labors, and be supported in life and happiness by what the field of God shall supply." (See Clark on Lev. xxv. 11.)

B.C. 522. EVIL-MERODACH'S FIRST YEAR. — Nebuchadnezzar reigned about forty-three years and six months. (2 Kings xxv. 27.) We will then suppose that Evil-merodach's reign began with the 1st of the first month, March 26, B.C. 522, and, according to Josephus, it continued eighteen years. Ptolemy gives him but two. Josephus, however, is the preferable authority; for his people were then in Babylon, while Ptolemy, living six hundred years after, was as dependent upon history as we are. Evil-merodach lived longer than Jehoiachin; and the expression, "all the days of his life" (Jer. lii. 33), certainly conveys an idea that Jehoiachin lived more than two years. If Evil-merodach had reigned but two, then Jehoiachin could not have lived more than about one year after his release from prison; for that was near the end of Evil-merodach's first year. (See further on this subject at the second year of Evil-merodach.)

B.C. 521. THE THIRTY-SEVENTH YEAR OF THE CAPTIVITY.— "In the seven and thirtieth year of the captivity of Jehoiachin, King of Judah, in the twelfth month, in the five and twentieth day of the month,"—March 10, B.C. 521,—"Evil-merodach, King of Babylon, lifted up the head of Jehoiachin, King of Judah, and brought him forth out of prison." (Jer. lii. 31.) If we allow him one day to "change his prison-garments," and to equip himself in a manner suitable to appear before the king, we will have "the seven and twentieth day of the month"—March 12—for his appearance in the presence of the king, who "spake kindly to him, and set his throne above the thrones of the kings that were with him in Babylon." (2 Kings xxv. 27, 28.) While the 25th of the twelfth month dates the time he was delivered from within the walls of the prison, the 27th dates the ratifying of his release by the king.

B.C. 521. EVIL-MERODACH'S SECOND YEAR.—The second year of Nebuchadnezzar, as mentioned by Daniel (ii. 1,) was not that of the king in whose reign he was taken captive, but the one whom we call Evil-merodach. Says Prideaux:—"Nebuchadnezzar was the name among the Babylonians commonly given to their kings as that of Pharaoh was among the Egyptians." Herodotus expressly mentions that the last King of Babylon "bore the name of his father." (*Herod.* b. i. 188.) Though all of the Kings of Egypt were in his day called Pharaoh, he designates none by this name; for his custom was to use their first name; and the king who burned Jerusalem in the nineteenth year of his reign (2 Kings xxv. 8), is by him called Labynetus. (*Herod.* b. i. s. 74.) Evil-merodach's first name was Balthasar (Baruch i. 11); but, on ascending the throne of Babylon, he assumed that of Nebuchadnezzar, which we thus prove:—The Jews were to serve three and only three Kings of Babylon,—that is, "Nebuchadnezzar and his son" [Evil-merodach], "and his son's son" [Belshazzar] (Jer. xxvii. 7); and the father of this last king (Dan. v. 30) is, both by "the queen" and Daniel, called Nebuchadnezzar. (Dan. v. 11, 18.)

Since Daniel expressly says that this, the father of Belshazzar, was the Nebuchadnezzar that "was driven from the sons of men . . . and had his dwelling with the wild beasts" (Dan. v. 21), is it not strange that those who claim to be "masters in Israel" could have had such unbounded confidence in Ptolemy's canon as to follow him in that portion of his chronology which contradicts both Daniel and Jeremiah. It is impossible that the king in whose "second year" Daniel was "made ruler over the whole province of Babylon (Dan. ii. 1–48), can be the one in whose reign he was taken captive; for that Nebuchadnezzar was "King of Babylon" when he went "unto Jerusalem and besieged it" (Dan. i. 1), at which time Daniel was taken away (Dan. i. 6); and it was not until three full years after he reached Babylon that he "stood before the king" (Dan. i. 5); hence, when he first appeared in the presence of that Nebuchadnezzar, it could not have been earlier than the fourth year of his reign. But we here find Daniel standing before this king in his second year's reign (Dan. ii. 1, 27), which makes it impossible that this could have been the same king in whose reign Daniel was taken captive. Berosus says that "Nebuchadnezzar after he had began to build the wall fell sick, and departed this life when he had reigned forty-three years, whereupon his son Evil-merodach obtained the kingdom;" hence, before the reign of Evil-merodach this work was not completed, and the one that built the wall was Nebuchadnezzar, who "was driven from men and did eat grass as oxen." "Is not this great Babylon that I have built?" (Dan. iv. 30.)

Evil-merodach, which signifies "the fool grinds bitterly," was a name given only in derision; for he acted the part of a fool and did grind bitterly when in anger and fury he "commanded to destroy all the wise men of Babylon" (Dan. ii. 12); and seemed to possess an "evil" spirit as "he was driven from men, and did eat grass as oxen, and his body was wet with the dews of heaven, till his hairs were grown like eagles' feathers, and his nails like birds' claws." (Dan. iv. 33.) The Chaldeans charged the king with doing that which "no king nor ruler" did, and with requiring of them that which no "man upon the earth" could do. (Dan. ii. 10.) Berosus seems to allude to this when he says Evil-merodach "governed public affairs after an illegal and impure manner, and had a plot laid against him by Neriglissar, his sister's husband;"—that is, "he was driven from his kingdom." As Daniel wrote at that day and in the Chaldean language, we could not expect him to call this king Evil-merodach,—that is, "the fool grinds bitterly;" but after Babylon was destroyed, and Evil-merodach's kindred were all dead, Ezra, or whoever wrote the last chapter of the book of Jeremiah, calls him Evil-merodach to distinguish him from the one Jeremiah called Nebuchadnezzar. Now, all must admit that the father of Belshazzar, the last King of Babylon, was called Nebuchadnezzar; but this could not have been the one in whose reign the captivity commenced: for the Jews were to serve that Nebuchadnezzar, "and his son, and his son's son." (Jer. xxvii. 7.) If it be asked why Daniel, calling both of these kings by the same name, did not mention that this was another Nebuchadnezzar? We answer: the first chapter has no connection with the second, and was written, as we may suppose, when Daniel was young, while the second chapter, containing the history of what happened about thirty-seven years after, could not have been written so early. From ver. 21 of the first chapter, which was added by some later author, we learn that this was at that time the end of the first book.

B.C. 512. EVIL-MERODACH'S ELEVENTH YEAR.—We have observed at B.C. 521, that Evil-merodach was the Nebuchadnezzar of Dan. ii. To him Daniel said: "They shall drive thee from men, and thy dwelling shall be with the beasts of the field, and they shall make thee to eat grass as oxen, and they shall wet thee with the dew of heaven, and seven times shall pass over thee, till thou know that the Most High ruleth in the kingdom of men, and giveth it to whomsoever he will." (Dan. iv. 25.) Berosus informs us that he was thus driven forth by "Neriglissar, his sister's husband." The reign of Evil-merodach seems to be similar to that of Cyaxares. We may say that Cyaxares died when he had reigned but twelve years, though his death occurred forty years after he first ascended the throne; for in his reign is to be included the twenty-eight years the Scythians possessed the dominion. And thus Berosus could properly say that Evil-merodach "was slain," or "driven from men when he had reigned but two years" (see p. 38); for in the ten years since he ascended the throne is to be included the time "he governed public affairs after an illegal and impure manner," and the time of the Belteshazzar government. If this construction can be received, then we can reconcile Berosus with Josephus and the Bible. It is certain that Josephus either understood this to be the meaning of Berosus, or possessed information showing that he was mistaken; for, with the works of Berosus before him, he says Evil-merodach died "after a reign of eighteen years." (*Jose. Ant.* b. x. c. xi. s. 2.)

B.C. 512. NERIGLISSAR'S FIRST YEAR.—About the eleventh year of the reign of Evil-merodach (Nebuchadnezzar), "he was driven from men" (Dan. iv. 33) by his son Neriglissar, who, ascending the throne of Babylon "reigned four years." With the supposition of Ptolemy that Evil-merodach was slain at the end of two years, and that the kingdom passed from the family of Nebuchadnezzar, we can never reconcile the prophecy of Jeremiah, that the Jews were to serve Nebuchadnezzar, "and his son, and his son's son, until the very time of his land come." (Jer. xxvii. 7.) But that the kingdom did not go out of his family, we have positive proof; for "they were servants to him and his sons until the reign of the Kingdom of Persia." (2 Chron. xxxvi. 20.) This proves Josephus is correct in saying that this Neriglissar, Evil-merodach's sister's husband, was also his own son. He, however, did not assume the position of a king, or deprive his father of the honor of the kingdom, but was one of those counsellors or lords who made the kingdom "sure unto his father." (Dan. iv. 26–36.)

B.C. 510. CYRUS'S FIRST YEAR.—According to Herodotus, the reign of Cyrus followed the thirty-fifth year of the reign of Astyages, King of Media; and from this epoch his reign continued twenty-nine years. His twenty-ninth year synchronizes with B.C. 482. This adjusts the reign of the Kings of Media with our chronology.

B.C. 506. THE SEVENTH YEAR OF EVIL-MERODACH'S INSANITY.—Evil-merodach, having been "driven from men" (Dan. iv. 33) by his son Neriglissar, had his "dwelling with the beasts of the field" until "seven times" (or years) "passed over him" (Dan. iv. 16, 32), which interval was filled up thus: Neriglissar reigned four years and his son nine months, and Belshazzar two years and about three months, at which time, his father's seven-years insanity having expired, he restored to him the kingdom. Says Evil-merodach: "My reason returned unto me . . . and my counsellors and my lords sought unto me and I was established in my kingdom, and excellent majesty was added unto me." (Dan. iv. 36.) Hence, Josephus correctly allows him about eighteen years.

B.C. 503. ECLIPSE OF THE SUN.—As a sign to the kingdom of Babylon that Cyrus was about to overthrow the Eastern "world," Isaiah foretold that the sun should "be darkened in his going forth" (Isa. xiii. 10); but as he said, "the moon and stars of heaven" should also be darkened, he apparently alluded to a darkness such as that caused by a cloud, rather than an eclipse of the sun. Xenophon, alluding to it, says:—"When Larissa was besieged by the King of Persia, at the time the Persians were wresting the empire from the Medes, he could not make himself master of it by any means; when it happened that the sun, obscured by a cloud, disappeared, and the darkness continued till, the inhabitants being seized with consternation, the town was taken." Those who understand Xenophon here to allude to an eclipse of the sun, say it occurred "when Cyrus took Larissa;" and in the eighth year of of Cyrus—that is, B.C. 503—there was a total eclipse of the sun at Rages, in Media, June 21, at 18m. after four in the afternoon. If it happened at the time that the sun was "obscured by a cloud," the darkest night must have ensued, naturally terrifying the Medes.

B.C. 491. THE SEVENTY-YEARS SERVICE to the kingdom of Babylon ended about the 10th of the fifth month, B.C. 491; for Belshazzar, the last King of Babylon was then slain (Dan. v. 30),—as it is written, "When seventy years are accomplished, I will punish the King of Babylon." (Jer. xxv. 12.)

B.C. 490. "DARIUS, THE MEDIAN."—The Medes and Persians, having conquered the Chaldeans, Cyaxares, the uncle of Cyrus, who is by Daniel called "Darius, the Median, took the kingdom." (Dan. v. 31.) We cannot tell whether Daniel had not seen the book of Jeremiah until this time; but before the first year of the reign of this king, Daniel had not discovered the difference between the seventy-years service to the King of Babylon (Jer. xxv. 11), and what Ezekiel calls "our captivity." (Ezek. xl. 1.) The seventy-years service being accomplished at the death of Belshazzar, and the Jews not yet having permission to return and build Jerusalem, may well have excited the deepest emotion in Daniel, causing him to seek by prayer and the searching of books, by which he learned from Jeremiah xxix. 1–10, that they were to remain in Babylon until "seventy years be accomplished" from the time of Jehoiachin's captivity; for they were not only to "serve the King of Babylon seventy years," but the Lord had foretold that "he would accomplish seventy years in the desolation of Jerusalem" (Dan. ix. 2), which commenced with Jehoiachin's captivity when Nebuchadnezzar "carried away all Jerusalem." (2 Kings xxiv. 14.)

B.C. 490. THE FIRST YEAR OF CYRUS begins, according to Ptolemy, with the conquest of Babylon. Daniel commences his reign from the same epoch; for what Ezra (i. 1), and Esdras (1st, ii. 1), and the author of ver. 21 of Dan. i., calls the first of Cyrus, is by Daniel called the third of Cyrus. (Dan. x. i.) Ptolemy makes his reign nine years.

B.C. 488. CYRUS'S FIRST YEAR.—Ezra calls "Cyrus, the King of Babylon" (Ezra v. 13); for he begins his reign after the death of Darius. Says Xenophon:—"At the conclusion of the first year of Darius, Cyrus assembled his army together at Babylon and undertook that expedition in which he is reported to have subdued all those nations which lie from the entrance into Syria as far as the Red Sea." And Ezra could not have commenced the reign of Cyrus before this conquest; for at the time of what he calls the first of Cyrus, we find that he had subdued "all these nations," for Cyrus said: "The Lord God of heaven hath given me all the kingdoms of the earth." (Ezra i. 2.) According to Xenophon, Cyrus reigned seven years from "the acquisition of his empire; and Ptolemy who, omitting the reign of Darius, begins the reign of Cyrus at the conquest of Babylon, gives him nine years. From this we may infer that Darius reigned about two years.

B.C. 488. END OF THE SEVENTY-YEARS CAPTIVITY.—On the 10th of the fifth month, August 15, B.C. 488, the seventy-years captivity ended, and "the commandment to restore and to build Jerusalem" went forth; for the object of the edict of Cyrus was "that the word of the Lord by the mouth of Jeremiah might be fulfilled" (Ezra i. 1),—which word was: "After seventy years be accomplished at Babylon, I will visit you and perform my good word toward you, in causing you to return to this place" (Jer. xxix. 10): "and Cyrus shall perform all my pleasure: even saying to Jerusalem, Thou shalt be built; and to the temple, Thy foundation shall be laid." (Isa. xliv. 28.) "When Cyrus read this, having an earnest desire to fulfill what was so written, he called for the most eminent Jews that were in Babylon, and gave them leave to go back to their own country, and to rebuild their city Jerusalem." (*Jose. Ant.* b. xi. c. i. s. 2.) For, said he, "the Lord God of heaven hath . . . charged me to build him a house at Jerusalem," which could not be done until the city was built; for "all the houses of Jerusalem" had been "burnt with fire." (2 Kings xxv. 9.) This proves that we must supply the word "build" in Ezra i. 3, and read the text thus: "Let him go up to *build* Jerusalem, which *was* in Judah;" for they could not go up to that which did not exist; and in Ezra iv. 12, we find the Jews employed in building this city. The commandment, as given by "the Lord God of heaven" through his "shepherd" Cyrus, "even saying to Jerusalem, Thou shall be built," was the only one ever given "to restore and build Jerusalem." Since the Lord hath declared, saying, Cyrus "shall perform all my pleasure" concerning the commandment to build Jerusalem, "even saying to Jerusalem, Thou shalt be built" (Isa. xliv. 28), we can commence the sixty-nine weeks from the going forth of a commandment as given by no king under heaven save that of Cyrus. From the time the Jews left Egypt to the ruin of their city by the Romans, we are unable to find either in sacred or profane history another commandment for the restoration of Jerusalem; but had there been many, the following would yet restrict us to this as the one alluded to by the angel Gabriel. Jerusalem was lying desolate, and the Jews were in Babylon near the close of their captivity. Daniel, having understood by "books" that the Lord "would accomplish seventy years in the desolation of Jerusalem" (Dan. ix. 2), was engaged in prayer for that restoration of his people which had been foretold by Jeremiah saying, "O Lord, according to all thy righteousness, I beseech thee let thine anger and thy fury be turned away from thy city Jerusalem" (Dan. ix. 16);

and while thus praying for this restoration, as foretold by Jeremiah, an angel "being caused to fly swiftly, touched" him (Dan. ix. 21), and "informed" him, saying, "from the going forth of the commandment to restore and to build Jerusalem." (Dan. ix. 25.) What commandment? Daniel knew of but the one which the Lord was to give to his "shepherd" Cyrus, the going forth of which he expected at the end of seventy years from the beginning of the captivity; for he had just "understood by books" that the Lord "would accomplish seventy years in the desolation of Jerusalem" (Dan. ix. 2); hence, we need no longer conjecture as to the epoch from which the sixty-nine weeks of Daniel are to be dated; for it is this or none. (See p. 54.) If we subtract 483 from 488, 5 remains. This gives us B.C. 5 for the appearing of Christ.

B.C. 488. THE THIRD YEAR OF CYRUS.—Though "Darius, the Median, took the kingdom" at the time of the death of Belshazzar (Dan. v. 31), it had been revealed to Daniel that the "kingdom" was "divided and given to the Medes and Persians" (Dan. v. 28); so he reckons the reign both of Cyrus and Darius from the time of the death of Belshazzar; hence, what Daniel calls the "third year of Cyrus, King of Persia" (Dan. x. 1), is, by the author of ver. 21 of the first chapter of Daniel, called "the first year of King Cyrus." Daniel "prospered in the reign of Darius and in the reign of Cyrus the Persian" (Dan. vi. 28); but he died "the first year of King Cyrus" (Dan. i. 21), reckoning from the death of Darius, which was, by Daniel, called "the third year of Cyrus, King of Persia." (Dan. x. 1; xii. 13.)

B.C. 488. DANIEL'S "TIME, TIMES, AND A HALF."—"In the four and twentieth day of the first month" (Dan. x. 4),—Sunday, May 2, B.C. 488,—in answer to "How long shall it be to the end of these wonders?" (Dan. xii. 6), as seen in the vision of Daniel, the angel answered: "It shall be for a time, times, and a half; and when he shall have accomplished to scatter the power of the holy people, all these things shall be finished." (Dan. xii. 7.) Our God having declared that "The wise shall understand" (Dan. xii. 10), his word is here involved: therefore, no prophetic period can claim a more prayerful and untiring anxiety to comprehend than this. The most careful research is required to disclose these "times and a half;" for they are so involved in mystery that Daniel himself did not understand the period thus pointed out. "I heard, but I understood not." (Dan. xii. 8.) This period is of great importance; for within its limits all of those things as seen by Daniel in his visions are to be accomplished. (Dan. xii. 6.) So necessary is it for us to be fully satisfied as to its truthfulness, or exact accomplishment, that one of the glorious host of heaven was sent to ratify it with an oath: "When he held up his right hand and his left hand unto heaven, he sware by him that liveth forever, that it shall be for a *time, times, and a half.*" (Dan. xii. 7.) A superficial view of Revelations xii. has given rise to the almost universal supposition that this is a period of 1260 years (see A.D. 26); but we shall prove by three reasons that this is erroneous.

First. A "time, times, and a half" cannot be less than three years and a half; therefore, to make them consist of 1260 days we must allow 360 days to the year. But such a year was unknown to the Jews; for their shortest year consisted of 354, their longest of 384, days; while three and a half of their shortest years contained 1269 days, the same number of their longest consisted of 1299, and their average year of 365, days. In three and a half average years there were 1277 days; hence, it is impossible to make three and a half Jewish years consist of only 1260 days. The year, as regulated by Romulus, consisted of 304 days. This being changed by Pompilius, the Roman year contained 355 days; which, when reformed by Julius Cæsar, consisted of 365 days and 6 hours. The Turks, "Chaldeans, Egyptians, Armenians, Persians, and the principal Oriental nations, from the earliest times," used the year of 365 days. The ancient Grecian year consisted of only 354 days; but we know of no people whose year consisted of just 360 days.* Then, where is the authority for saying that three years and a half is to be understood as a period of just 1260 days?

Second. When Daniel inquired what period was meant by "a time, times, and a half," he was informed that this was not to be understood until 1290 days "from the time the daily sacrifice shall be taken away, and the abomination that maketh desolate set up" (Dan. xii. 11); and since our fathers, long before the end of the 1290 days, understood this to be a period of 1260 years, this is a clear proof of its incorrectness.

---

* By comparing Genesis vii. 11 with viii. 3, 4, some conclude that the antediluvian year consisted of 360 days; but if within the 150 days, Noah was unable to see the moon, their supposition is without foundation; for it is well known that in case the moon could not be seen on the 29th day, the month always consisted of thirty days.

Third. 1260 years would end in A.D. 773; but Daniel was informed that they were to reach to the accomplishing "to scatter the power of the holy people" (Dan. xii. 7),—a period within the limits of which all those things in Daniel's vision were to be fulfilled. To obviate this difficulty, it has been supposed that they were to be dated from the setting up of the abomination that maketh desolate; but not a shadow of authority is to be found for this in the book of Daniel. The question asked is, "How long shall it be to the end of these wonders?"—that is, how long from the 24th of the first month," B.C. 488.

But suppose we had authority for dating the 1260 years from the setting up of "the abomination that maketh desolate." We would yet want 75 years to reach the end of the 1335 years. The epoch from which the "time, times, and a half" are to be dated is clear. They are to be commenced on the 24th "of the first month, in the third year of Cyrus." (Dan. x. 1.) The only point of controversy is as to what length of time is meant. As "times" means years, the length of time would also be known had the number of "times" been given; but, since in the wisdom of God this was to be sealed up until the time of the end, the expression, "times" is used, which conveys to the mind no definite number; hence, says Daniel, "I heard, but I understood not." (Dan. xii. 8.) But when he had "inquired and searched diligently, . . . searching what, or what manner of time" this expression, "times, . . . did signify" (1 Pet. i. 10, 11), "he understood the thing, and had understanding of the vision" (Dan. x. 1); and since "unto the prophets it was revealed that not unto themselves, but unto us they did minister" (1 Pet. i. 12), his understanding this could not have been for his own individual benefit; hence, must be the key by which we, to whom he ministered, are to disclose, and, like him, have understanding of, the vision. Using this, then, as the key or rule by which we shall be governed in establishing the correct time, let us inquire as to how Daniel, who was required to "consider the vision," understood the matter, after he had "sought for the meaning." (Dan. viii. 15.) When he had ascertained the truth, he saw that it was a long period of time. But how did he discover this? A clue to this inquiry may be found by reference to Daniel xii. 12; for though he knew not when "the abomination that maketh desolate" would be "set up," he could learn from this that it must be a period longer than 1335 years; for it spans them. We shall gather more light on this subject by noticing that the angel had not promised to give Daniel any thing new, but simply to "show him that which was already noted in his scripture of truth." In answer to "How long the vision?" the angel had said "unto two thousand and three hundred days" (Dan. viii. 13, 14); and it is again asked, "How long shall it be to the end of these wonders?" (Dan. xii. 6.) Having answered this before, it is now confirmed with an oath. He "swore by him that liveth forever, that it shall be for a time, times, and a half" (Dan. xii. 7); hence, the heavenly instructor could not have meant a period less than 2300 years. So "the thing was true," being confirmed and ratified by an oath, "but the time appointed was long."

We now observe a shade of difference in the questions. The first was, "How long the vision?" which, being concerning that which was yet future, Daniel had just been informed would not begin its course until after "three kings" from that time—or four, including Cyrus—shall have stood "up in Persia" (Dan. xi. 2); while the second was, "How long shall it be to the end of these wonders?" from that present moment; hence, while Daniel discovered that "the time appointed was long," as it did span the 2300 years, he also saw that it must be even longer than that; and when he had "inquired and searched diligently, . . . searching what, or what manner of time" (1 Pet. i. 10, 11), or how long a period the angel meant, he not only discovered that "the time appointed was long," but "he understood the thing and had understanding of the vision." (Dan. x. 1.) There must, therefore, be some other rule by which Daniel was enabled to get the exact time. Then let us examine the matter again, remembering that those who lived under the typical dispensation were lost. Why? "Because" they knew "not the time of" their visitation." (Luke xix. 44.) Disregarding, then, those who say "The days are prolonged and every vision faileth" (Ezek. xii. 22), let us "search the Scriptures, . . . which are able to make" us "wise unto salvation through faith which is in Christ Jesus,"—that is, "if thou criest after knowledge, and liftest up thy voice for understanding; if thou seekest her as silver, and searchest for her as for hid treasures; then shalt thou understand." (Prov. ii. 3–5.)

It is declared that "the wise shall understand." But understand what? "Understand" that which Daniel "heard, but understood not" (Dan. xii. 8),—that is, the length of time revealed by the expression, "a time, times, and a half;" for the "wise man's heart discerneth both time and judgment." (Eccles. viii. 5.) Having now "sought for the meaning" (Dan. viii. 15), having "understood by books" that "the time appointed was long," we find that the angel has indeed given us a rule by which we can ascertain the definite length of time. "When he shall have accomplished to scatter the power of the holy people all these things shall be finished." (Dan. xii. 7.) We are now enabled to see how Daniel, who, having "heard, . . . understood not," by considering "the vision," finally "understood the thing; for Daniel knew that "the power of the holy people" was to be scattered seven times. "And I, even I, will chastise you seven times for your sins." Daniel knew that the epoch at which this scattering commenced was in the sixth year of Hezekiah; and he had seen seven times accomplished in seven Chaldean years (Dan. iv. 34), or in 2555 days. As 193 years had passed since Israel had been driven from their home, he saw that this "seven-times" chastisement must be according to the day-year system; and when Daniel subtracted 193 from 2555, he had 2362; he thus learned that when 2362 years more shall have passed away the Lord will "have accomplished to scatter the power of the holy people," and then "all these things shall be finished" (Dan. xii. 7); hence, Daniel, who first says, "I heard, but I understood not," could now say "he understood the thing and had understanding of the vision."

Having now found the governing rule, we discover that by "a time, times, and a half," as used in Daniel xii. 7, we are to understand "a time," five "times and a half," which, if found to agree with this rule,—that is, if a time," five "times and a half" proves to be just 2362 years,—then we may know that we are correct; but if found to be a single year more or less, it will thus prove that we have not yet discovered the truth.

At B.C. 1571 we observed that "seven times" is a period of 2555 days; for Moses was writing for those who had been accustomed to that method of reckoning time. For the same reason—that is, as Daniel had been accustomed to the use of sacred time—we here use it; for a revelation is always addressed to man in his own language. But the Jewish year being unequal, it becomes necessary to ascertain the epoch from which the "times" are to be reckoned before we can know the length of the year to be used.

The date as given by Daniel is the 24th of the first month "in the third year of Cyrus, King of Persia,"—that is, B.C. 488. The 24th of the first month in that year fell on May 2; therefore, the following year consisted of 354 days. Had the third year of Cyrus synchronized with B.C. 489, then the first year after would have consisted of 383 days, which at once shows the indispensable importance of knowing the particular epoch from which to reckon when we use sacred time; and having now learned what kind of time to use, we have no further difficulty; for all who are acquainted with sacred time are aware that the following six and a half Jewish years stand thus:—

Years.		Days.		Hours.		Minutes.		Seconds.
First	....	354	....	8	....	48	....	36
Second	....	354	....	8	....	48	....	36
Third	....	383	....	21	....	32	....	40
Fourth	....	354	....	8	....	48	....	36
Fifth	....	383	....	21	....	32	....	40
Sixth	....	354	....	8	....	48	....	36
Half-year	....	177	....	4	....	24	....	18
Total	....	2362	....	10	....	44	....	2

The foregoing table shows that six times and a half, or "a time," five "times and a half" is 2362 days; and each day for a year (Ezek. iv. 6) gives us 2362 years, which is the exact number, as demonstrated by the angel's rule; and proves that we now have the truth. B.C. 488 is A.M. 3638, to which, if we add 2362, we will have 6000; from which we learn that this definite period ends with the beginning of the great Sabbath of rest in A.D. 1875. In this same year Moses's "seven times" end; "and when he shall have accomplished to scatter the power of the holy people, all these things shall be finished." (Dan. xii. 7.)

That no doubt may rest upon the mind of any as to the correctness of our exposition of the matter,—that by a "time, times, and a half" we are here to understand a period of 2362 years,—call to mind,—

1. The question "How long shall it be to the end of these wonders?" (Dan. xii. 6) was as to the definite time; and Daniel, when he "understood the thing," said, "the time appointed was long" (Dan. x. 1); hence, a definite period.

2. It is certain that we are to understand a period reaching from "the twenty-fourth day of the first month . . . in the third year of Cyrus" (Dan. x. 1, 4) to "the end of these wonders" (Dan. xii. 6) as revealed in Daniel's vision,—that is, to the end of the world." (Dan. xii. 2.)

3. According to the rule, as delivered by the heavenly messenger, from which we are not to depart in disclosing the matter

we can make neither more nor less than six "times and a half" of the "time, times, and a half" as used, which is 2362 years.

4. The question asked being as to the definite time, it follows that the answer must be such as conveys to the mind a definite period of time; but the mere expression, "a time, times, and a half," when severed from the rule as given by the angel, conveys to the mind nothing definite as to the number of times; hence, says Daniel, "I heard, but I understood not." (Dan. xii. 8.) Yet, when he had "duly considered the vision," and "understood the thing," he discovered the definite period of time; hence, says, "the time appointed was long."

5. Though Daniel does not mention how he first ascertained the definite time, we observe that it was in a way which did not only satisfy him that it was a definite "appointed . . . time," and "long," but enabled him to testify that "the thing was true." (Dan. x. 1.) And we can readily perceive how he could, by the use of the rule given, know its truthfulness; for he could see that from that time 2362 years were wanting to accomplish "to scatter the power of the holy people;" and he knew that in "a time," five "times, and a half" there would be 2362 years; but if in "a time," five "times and a half" there had been 2361, or 2363, years, then he could not have testified to the correctness of what the angel had said; for the "time, times, and a half" could not be made to correspond with the rule.

6. As the 1335 years end at the resurrection (Dan. xii. 13), the "time, times, and a half" must reach beyond it; for there must be an interval—"a time of trouble"—between the resurrection and "the end of the wonders." And Daniel's time of trouble being the same with Ezekiel's seven-years war (Ezek. xxxix. 9), all the wonders in Daniel's vision will be finished seven years after the end of the 1335 years; and the "time," five "times and a half" ends seven years later than the 1335.

7. The 2300 days span the length of the vision from beginning to the end; and as the "time, times, and a half" were given in answer to "How long shall it be to the end of these wonders" (the end of the vision), the "time," five "times and a half" and the 2300 years must end together.

8. Divine authority warrants us in believing that the "time," five "times and a half" will end with Moses's "seven times;" for "when he shall have accomplished to scatter the power of the holy people, all these things shall be finished;" and according to our exposition of the matter, they do end together.

9. We are informed that from the setting up of the "abomination that maketh desolate," there shall be 1290 days before even the "wise shall understand" what length of time was meant by the "time, times and a half;" hence, whatever may have been the previous opinion of men, we have this authority for pronouncing it incorrect. But our exposition of the matter was never thought of before the end of the 1290 days, or A.D. 1823. And though the time we were enabled to remove the "seal" so as to discover the truth was of a later date, remarkable it is that at the end of the 1290 days, that moving cause, which has now disclosed the matter, first began; for the light was shining in a dark place until the day dawned and the day-star arose (2 Pet. i. 19), which, "as the shining light that shineth more and more unto the perfect day" (Prov. iv. 18), has dispelled the darkness, removed the "seal," and opened "the book" of Daniel.

10. Though none were to understand this period until after the end of the 1290 days, it was declared that after their expiration the "wise shall understand." But understand what? Clearly the length of time meant by "a time, times, and a half" as used in this place. Then have we not the authority of Him whose word cannot fail for saying, "the wise shall understand" what "the man clothed in linen which was upon the waters of the river" meant by the expression, "a time, times, and a half;" and if our exposition be the only way possible for man ever to make intelligible time of it, is not the promise that we "shall understand" equivalent to saying that we now have the truth?

11. That this was not to be understood immediately after the expiration of the 1290 days will appear from Revelation x.; for though the "little book" was from the time of the end of 1290 days declared to be "open," he who was to "prophesy again before many people and nations, and tongues, and kings," did not "eat it up" until after the "rainbow" angel had "cried with a loud voice as when a lion roareth," which answers to the movement of 1842–44, when the voice went throughout the land proclaiming, by the authority of "Him that liveth forever," that, according to their understanding, "there shall be time no longer" (Rev. x. 6); hence, the time for the Church to "eat" or understand the contents of the "little book" was not until after A.D. 1844. As it was since that time we discovered the truth, we have this additional evidence of the correctness of our view.

Some of those who have resolved not to understand these things say they are not to be understood until the "end of the world." As this charges our God with sending an angel from heaven to confirm with an oath that which is of no importance, it is unworthy of reply. Yet we will say this much: It is not said that these words are closed up and sealed until the end of the world; but "till the time of the end." (Dan. xii. 9.) While this expression is never used in the Bible in reference to the end of the world, it is certain that it is used in Daniel xi. 40, in allusion to a period before the end of this age. It is clear that the angel did not mean the end of the world when he said "the words are closed up and sealed till the time of the end; for the "wise" were to "understand" after the 1290 days, while the end of the world is not until after the 1335 days. "The time of the end" is a period at which "none of the wicked shall understand" when the end of the world will be, as made known by "time, times, and a half;" but when the end of the world comes, the wicked will know it as well as the wise.

However much our carnal inclinations may dispose us to close our eyes and ears to the truth, we must admit that he who did confirm the truthfulness of these things with an oath declared, saying: "the words are closed up and sealed till the time of the end." And we are compelled to admit that of all we have ever seen written on this subject, we have never yet met with an author who, writing before the expiration of the 1290 days, was able to explain the "time, times, and a half" in a way so as to make sense; for neither those who have understood it to mean only three years and a half, nor those who say it denotes a period "of 1260 years," pretend to date the beginning according to the question asked, "How long shall it be to the end of these wonders?" So this much we must admit has been fulfilled to the letter: that is, that "the words were closed up and sealed." We must also admit that this same author who declared that "the words" were "closed up and sealed till the time of the end," did also declare, saying, "the wise shall understand",—that is, after the expiration of the 1290 days. If our explanation be the only way we can ever make a definite "appointed" "time" of the "time, times, and a half," then we are certainly correct; for our God has said that this shall be understood.

B.C. 488. DANIEL'S VISION.—In the third year of Cyrus, on the 24th of the first month, Sunday, May 2, B.C. 488, Daniel saw his last vision, which was explanatory of his former one,—"I will show thee that which is noted in the Scripture of truth" (Dan. x. 21), and reveal that which "shall befall" God's "people in the latter days: for yet the vision is for many days." (Dan. x. 14.) After informing Daniel that he "stood to confirm and to strengthen Michael in the first year of Darius, the Mede" (Dan. xi. 1), he adds, "And now will I show thee the truth. Behold, there shall stand up yet three kings in Persia." (Dan. xi. 2.) The word of Michael was the 2300 days which Gabriel did greatly "confirm and strengthen" by showing that "seventy weeks are determined," or "cut off" from the 2300 days" (Dan. ix. 24); but Daniel had not been informed as to when the 2300 days should begin, hence, the angel added: "And now will I show thee the truth," or I will inform you as to the time from which your vision shall commence:— "Behold, there shall stand up yet three kings in Persia" before the beginning of the "pushing" of "the ram" as seen in the vision. (Dan. viii. 4.) These three kings were Cambyses, Darius, and Xerxes; for the impostor, the Magi, was not a Persian king, but a Mede. It is further added that this third king from Cyrus—or the fourth, including Cyrus—"shall be far richer than they all, and by his strength through his riches he shall stir up all against the realm of Grecia." This is well known to be Xerxes; therefore, until after the day of his reign, Daniel's vision, as seen "in the third year of Belshazzar" (Dan. viii. 1), does not commence. The Jews, not observing this, supposed that Gabriel meant that but four kings were to stand up in the kingdom of Persia. But the object here was to point out the time at which the pushing of the ram would commence, and not the number of kings that should stand up in Persia. The apparent omission between vers. 2 and 3 of Chap. xi. is supplied from ver. 4 of Chap. viii.: "I saw the ram pushing westward and northward and southward, so that no" soul "might stand before him; neither was there any that could deliver out of his hand;" which ram was "the kingdoms of Media and Persia." (Dan. viii. 20.) The pushing of the ram is not against the kingdoms of the world, but against Daniel's people: "I am come to make thee understand, not that which concerns the kingdoms of this world, but, what shall befall thy people." (Dan. x. 14.) The pushing could not be against other kingdoms; for the ram was not as the goat running over "the face of the whole earth;" but standing quietly "before the river "Ulai," showing that the powers of Persia was not at that time invading other kingdoms, "but was "at Shushan in the palace, which is in the province of Elam" (Dan. viii. 2); and before the pushing commenced, Daniel expressly declares that "the two horns were high" (Dan. viii. 3); hence, the pushing was not the means by which they became high. He adds: "I saw the ram pushing westward and northward and southward;" but the Persian power was never exerted in these several directions against other kingdoms, and yet at the same time remaining quietly "at Shushan in the palace;" for in their expeditions, the king accompanied the army. Daniel says further that none of those against whom he saw the rams pushing "might stand before him;" which cannot be the kingdoms of the earth; for so far from the kingdom of Grecia being unable to stand before the Persian power, he tells us that "there was no power in the ram to stand before" the goat (Dan. viii. 7), or "the kingdom of Grecia" (Dan. viii. 21): "Neither was there any that could deliver out of his hand" those against whom the ram was pushing; but those nations which had been conquered by the Persians were by the Greeks delivered out of the Persian power. Such was the power the ram possessed over those against whom he pushed, he "did according to his will." (Dan. vii. 14.) But, in regard to the surrounding nations, Persia was never able to do according to its will. In the expedition of Cyrus, the first Persian king, against the Queen of Massagetæ the greater part of his army was slain. (*Herod.* b. i. c. 214.) Cambyses, the second king, was not only compelled to abandon "his design on the Ethiopians" (*Herod.* b. iii. c. 25), but was even dethroned and lost his kingdom by an impostor. (*Herod.* b. iii. c. 61.) Darius, the third king, when he undertook his expedition against the Scythians, "was obliged to return, having lost numbers of his best troops." (*Herod.* vii. c. 10.) As for Xerxes, the fourth king, no one ever met with a more shameful defeat than he did in his great expedition against Greece; and as from this may be dated the decline and fall of the Persian Empire, it is useless to trace the subject farther. No Persian king was able to do to other kingdoms according to his will.

This pushing, therefore, was against Daniel's people, and not other nations: "I am come to make thee understand what shall befall thy people" (Dan. x. 14); and as Gabriel informed Daniel that after the reign of Cyrus there should "stand up yet three kings in Persia" before the beginning of the pushing against his "people," it could not have commenced until after the reign of Xerxes, the third king from Cyrus, nor before the seventh of Artaxerxes, at which time the kingdom of Persia, having ceased from war, "he made a release to the provinces" (Est. ii. 18); for the ram at the time the pushing occurred was standing quietly "before the river Ulai," thus representing the kingdom in a peaceable state at that period. The seventh of Artaxerxes was a time of "perfect peace" (Ezra vii. 12); hence, the way now opened for the pushing, which commenced in the twelfth year of his reign —even for the slaughter of the whole nation of Daniel's people (Esther iii. 12),—which when he saw he "fainted and was sick certain days."

The pushing could not have been that of war with other kingdoms; for all of the Persian wars in which the Jews were much concerned took place before what he calls the third year of Cyrus, at which time he was informed that this pushing had not yet commenced; for yet the vision is for many days" (Dan. x. 14); "and now will I show thee the truth: behold,"—mark this,—"there shall stand up yet three kings in Persia" (Dan. xi. 2), before the time of this pushing, to "devour much flesh" (Dan. vii. 5); which, being that of Daniel's people, it is certain that the decree which was issued for the slaughter of all the Jews in one day was the pushing of the Persian power as seen in the vision. We can find nothing else in the history of Persia that will answer to the expression, "They said thus unto it, Arise, devour much flesh." Though he is thus told "to devour much flesh," it is not said that he did this; "but he did according to his will," which was to rescue Daniel's people from the impending ruin with which that bloodthirsty voice, "Arise, devour much flesh," has threatened them.

It is further added that he "became great,"—not that Persia waxed greater in power; for "the two horns" of the ram were at that time "high," and there is nothing said as to their rising higher; neither was there any addition to the bear's dominion; but "dominion was given to the "leopard;" for it had not reached the height of its power when Daniel first saw it.

As the vision is concerning the Jews, the rams becoming great must be the exercise of a great power towards them, either favorable or the reverse. And since the "exceeding great" power of Antichrist is not a national greatness, but consists alone in the power wielded over the people of God, why may not the greatness of the Persian power, as alluded to here, have reference to a power as exercised towards the Jews.

The vision is concerning Daniel's people; and the King of Persia became "great" towards them, in acts of kindness; and made Mordecai "great among the Jews." (Est. x. 3.)

Daniel was further informed that after this pushing, which fills up the interval between vers. 2 and 3 of Chap. xi., that "a mighty king shall stand up that shall rule with great dominion, and do according to his will." (Dan. xi. 3.) This was Alexander the Great who did "rule with great dominion;" and in regard to the Jews he did "according to his will." (*Jose. Ant.* b. xi. c. viii. s. 5.)

Ver. 4. "And when he shall stand up, his kingdom shall be broken,"—that is, the kingdom of Greece. Therefore, from this epoch we have no more to do with that kingdom.

Ver. 4. "And shall be divided toward the four winds of heaven;" hence, the four horns are not to be found in Greece, but "towards the four winds of heaven."

Ver. 4. "And not to his posterity,"—that is, they are not to be of the Alexandrian family.

Ver. 4. "Nor according to his dominion which he ruled,"—that is, the four horns are not all to be found within the empire over which Alexander ruled, and neither of them in "the kingdom of Grecia;" the goat's original dominion for the "four kingdoms shall stand up out of the nation, but not in his power" (Dan. viii. 22),—that is, not in the power of the goat's first horn which was "the kingdom of Grecia." The northern horn was the kingdom of Syria,—the royal palace being at Antioch (1 Mac. iii. 37). The southern was the kingdom of Egypt (Dan. xi. 8); the eastern, the Parthian empire, under which the Jews suffered calamities "greater than any upon record before" (*Jose. Ant.* b. xviii. c. ix. s. 1); the western was Rome, for that was the only western power bearing rule over the Jews, which was not "according to" the goat's "dominion which he ruled." All agree that one of the four horns was Syria, and another, Egypt. The other two are said to be Thrace and Macedonia; but these being northwestern kingdoms, leaves none in the east. To obviate this difficulty, the kingdom of Syria has been called the eastern; but how absurd, since the royal palace being at Antioch, north of Jerusalem, Syria was always called "the king of the north." (Dan. xi. 6.) The only reason offered for supposing that Thrace and Macedonia were two of the four horns is, that this was the division into which Alexander's kingdom was divided. But this is a proof that they are not; "for his kingdom shall be plucked up even for others besides these" (Dan. xi. 4): the "four kingdoms" were to "stand up out of the nation, but not in his power" (Dan. viii. 22), while Thrace and Macedonia were in the seat of his power.

It is clear from the book of Daniel that the northern horn was the kingdom of Syria; the southern, Egypt; and that the other two were Rome and Parthia. Notice that the horns were "four notable ones towards the four winds of heaven" (Dan. viii. 8); and these are the only two "notable" kingdoms in those opposite directions in which the Jews were much concerned. That Rome was one of the four horns we thus know: the leopard had but four heads, one of which must answer to "the great horn" which "was broken,"— that is, to the kingdom of Greece (Dan. viii. 8); so on the leopard we have but three heads answering to the four horns of the goat: this proves that the "fourth beast" (Dan. vii. 7) answers to the fourth horn on the goat, which "fourth beast" all admit to be Rome.

The four heads of the leopard are Greece, Syria, Parthia, and Egypt,—the "fourth beast" answering to Rome; for Greece must not be left without a head. As an additional proof that Parthia and Rome are two of the "four notable" horns of the goat, notice that at the time they came up "the great horn," which answered to the "kingdom of Grecia," was "broken" off; hence, we must not expect the four horns to rise in that kingdom; for, leaving Greece, the goat had now come "from the west on the face of the whole earth." (Dan. viii. 5.) "Therefore, the he-goat waxed very great;" for his four horns embraced Egypt, Syria, and the Roman and Parthian empires. But at the time of Alexander's death, the goat had not yet "waxed very great;" for "when he was" only "strong, the great horn was broken."

Ver. 5. "And the king of the south shall be strong." For a continuation of the comment between this and ver. 14, see Dr. A. Clark.

Ver. 14. "And in those times there shall many stand up against the kings of the south." This "was fully verified by the leaguing of the Kings of Macedon and Syria together against" the King of Egypt "to seize all his dominion and divide it between them." Many even of his own people stood up against him, inasmuch as he was put to death by them.

Ver. 14. "Also the robbers of thy people." The "robbers of" Daniel's "people" were the Samaritans, and those wicked Jews (1 Mac. i. 11) who, revolting from the God of their fathers (1 Mac. i. 13, 15), robbed their brethren (2 Mac. iv. 32, 42, 50) even of the religion of their fathers (2 Mac. iv. 13, 14); but the chief robber— he who reduced Daniel's people to ruin—was Antiochus Epiphanes. He "took away the golden altar and the candlesticks of light and all the vessels thereof;" "and the golden ornaments that were before the temple he pulled off. He took also the silver and the gold and the precious vessels: also he took the hidden treasures which he found" (1 Mac. i. 21–23); "yea, he robbed them of the privilege of worshiping God according to the law of their fathers." (1 Mac. i. 45.)

Ver. 14. "Shall exalt themselves to establish the vision,"—that is the vision of Daniel; for this was the subject at issue. According to his vision, "the city and the sanctuary" were to be "destroyed; the sacrifice and oblation cease." (Dan. ix. 26, 27.) And those robbers, as above-mentioned, did exalt themselves "to establish the vision" by putting an end to the Mosaic dispensation." (2 Mac. iv. 10, 13.) By them "the city was sore defaced and ready to be made even with the ground." (2 Mac. viii. 3.) Her sanctuary was laid waste like a wilderness; her feasts were turned to mourning; her sabbaths into reproach; her honor into contempt." (1 Mac. i. 39.) They came, indeed, so near establishing "the vision" that those who have given the subject only a superficial view have been led to believe that the vision really received its fulfillment here.

Ver. 14. "But they shall fall,"—that is, they shall fail (Dan. xi. 35) "to establish the vision," or fulfill the prophecy of Daniel; for to accomplish it, "the place of his sanctuary" must be "cast down" (Dan. viii. 11),—that is, the little horn "shall destroy the city and the sanctuary." (Dan. ix. 26.) Antiochus had resolved to do this. "He was going in haste to lay the holy city even with the ground, and to make it a common burying-place" (2 Mac. ix. 14); but death prevented: so it is literally true that he failed "to establish the vision." According to the vision, "the sanctuary and the host" must "be trodden under foot two thousand three hundred days" (Dan. viii. 13, 14), which they did for only 1103 days. (1 Mac. iv. 54.) They here fell 1197 short of the 2300. The little horn "shall also stand up against the Prince of princes" (Dan. viii. 25); but Antiochus died 160 years before "the Prince of princes" was born. Those who contend that the vision was fulfilled, say he stood up against Onias, the high-priest; but he was not "the Prince of princes. Neither did Antiochus stand up against Onias; for he was slain by Andronicus in the absence of Antiochus, who, so far from having done this himself, knew nothing of it; and when he was informed of the cruel deed, "he was heartily sorry, and moved to pity, and wept." (2 Mac. iv. 37.) He was so grieved that he slew the murderer, although he was his most highly-favored friend, and next to him in the kingdom. (2 Mac. iv. 38.) So Antiochus stood up neither against the Jewish high-priest, nor against "the Prince of princes. For further proof that Antiochus failed "to establish the vision," see B.C. 425.

Ver. 15. "So the king of the north shall come." Antiochus, as the chief leader of that band of "robbers" who "shall exalt themselves to establish the vision," went to Jerusalem to destroy the Jews, he "entered proudly into the sanctuary." (1 Mac. i. 21.)

Ver. 15. "And cast up a mount." To "cast up a mount" is to form a breastwork or fortress. (Ezek. xvii. 17.) And this Antiochus did. "Finding that the King of Egypt was not well-affected to his affairs," in order to "provide for his own safety," he went "to Joppe, and from thence to Jerusalem" (2 Mac. iv. 21), "to take a view of the frontier towards Egypt, and to put them in a thorough posture of defence against any attempts which the Egyptians might make upon them." "He put the frontiers in a condition to serve as a barrier, and to check the utmost efforts the Egyptians might make to recover these provinces." (*Rollin,* 194.) And thus he cast up a mount for his defence.

Ver. 15. "And take the most fenced cities." Antiochus took 'the strong cities in the land of Egypt." (1 Mac. i. 19.) He took indeed, all the cities of "Egypt except Alexandria, which alone held out against him." (*Rol.* 194.) He also took the cities of Israel,—"insomuch that the inhabitants of Jerusalem fled because of them; whereupon the city was made the habitation of strangers, and became strange to those that were born in her, and her own children left her." (1 Mac. i. 38.)

Ver. 15. "And the arms of the south shall not withstand." The King of the South being only fifteen or sixteen years of age when Antiochus made his expedition against Egypt, was incapable of acting as king; he "always kept as far as possible from danger, and had not even shown himself to those who fought for him." (*Rol.* 194.) Hence, instead of the king of the south, the Eastern power at that time was properly "the arms of the south;" and they did not stand; for they were "afraid of him, and fled, and many were wounded to death." (1 Mac. i. 18.)

Ver. 15. "Neither his chosen people." By this expression we are to understand the chosen people of the king of the north. And the Jews, whom he had selected as a protection against the Egyptians, fell before his oppressive power: even "Andronicus, a man" whom he had chosen "for his deputy, a man in authority," was unable to stand before him. (2 Mac. iv. 38.)

Ver. 15. "Neither shall there be any strength to withstand." The military power of Egypt, and the ambassadors from "the Grecian states," were of no avail; neither could the favor or kindness, as manifested on the part of the Jews (2 Mac. iv. 22), secure their peace. "The inhabitants of Jerusalem fled" (1 Mac. i. 38); the Egyptians "were afraid of him, and fled" also.

Ver. 16. "But he that cometh against him shall do according to his own will." "Him" cannot apply to the "arms of the south," but has reference to the last person mentioned,—the king of the north; and he that came against Antiochus was the western kingdom, or Rome. The will of Rome was that Antiochus "let that country alone;" and he—that is, Rome—"did according to his will;" for, by "the declaration of the Romans," Antiochus "was driven out of all Egypt." (*Jose. Ant.* b. xii. c. v. s. 2.) "He obeyed the commands of the Roman ambassadors as strictly as if they had been sent from the gods." (*Rol.* 196.)

Ver. 16. "And none shall stand before him,"—that is, before the Romans. "From that instant every thing gave way before them, and the Roman name grew formidable to all princes and nations." (*Rol.* 196.)

Ver. 16. "And he shall stand in the glorious land." The land of Israel had long been tributary to different kingdoms, but this was never called a standing in the land; and as Syria never so placed the seat of authority in Judea as to answer to the expression, "shall stand in the glorious land," this must be a continuation of the history concerning the western king; and when Rome placed her authority in Judea by making Herod King of the Jews, it could properly be said that "he," the Roman power, did "stand in the glorious land;" and this was more fully accomplished when Palestine was reduced to a Roman province.

Ver. 16. "Which by his hand shall be consumed." The once "glorious land" of Israel was "consumed" by the Romans; insomuch it never has been, nor never will again be, the home of the Hebrews; for their city "shall never be built." (Isa. xxv. 2.) In order to make it appear that Antiochus Epiphanes was the little horn, some say the prophecy, as recorded in this verse, was accomplished by Antiochus the Great; but this is incorrect; for it is here emphatically declared: "He that cometh against him shall do according to his own will," which Antiochus did not; for his avowed intention was to subdue Egypt; and in order to do so, he had entered into a league with Philip, King of Macedon; but after all his preparations, he was unable to carry out his design; for he was prevented by the Romans from invading the kingdom of Egypt." (*Prid.*, B.C. 201.)

Again: it is said that "none shall stand before him;" and it is well known that many did stand before the king of the north. It is added: "and he shall stand in the glorious land, which by his hand shall be consumed;" but so far from having been consumed by Antiochus, the Great, no king, from the day of Artaxerxes, the husband of Esther, had ever conferred such large favors upon the Jews as he did. (*Jose. Ant.* b. xii. c. iii. s. 3, 4.) While the historical facts during the reign of Antiochus the Great are the reverse of what is mentioned in ver. 16, our commentators have to make it a mere repetition of what was mentioned in ver. 15, in order to find a place for it during the reign of that king.

Ver. 17. "He shall also set his face to enter with the strength of his whole kingdom." As it is unreasonable to suppose that with "the strength of his whole kingdom" he would set his face to enter" a land already consumed, the inspired historian has now returned to the thread of his prophetic history, or to the continuation of the history concerning the Syrian king. As in ver. 15 we have that which relates alone to the western kingdom, ver. 17, in order to continue the history concerning the king of the north, is as properly connected with ver. 15, as if ver. 16 had been omitted. In ver. 15 it is said: "So the king of the north shall come;" and here it is added: "He shall also set his face to enter with the strength of his whole kingdom;" which Antiochus did. "Breathing out fire in his rage against the Jews," he set his face to "come to Jerusalem, and make it a common burying-place of the Jews." (2 Mac. ix. 4, 7.) To this end "he sent and gathered together all the forces of his realm, even a very strong army." (1 Mac. iii. 27.) As he here gathered "*all the forces of his realm*," he had "set his face to enter with the strength of his whole kingdom" to "destroy and root out the strength of Israel and the remnant of Jerusalem, and to take away their memorial from that place." (1 Mac. iii. 35.) Those who understand Antiochus to be the hero of Daniel's prophecy, tell us that this was also accomplished during the reign of Antiochus the Great; but since so far from any historian mentioning the circumstance of Antiochus the Great having again "set his face to enter" Egypt, we know, from the prohibition of the Romans, that he never did. Thus, they have been forced to call that "friendship and league," as made by Antiochus "with Ptolemy" when he "gave him his daughter Cleopatra to wife," the setting of "his face to enter with the strength of his whole kingdom;" and in order to make it appear that this was what the prophet meant by entering "with the strength of his whole kingdom," they have to suppose that the object of Antiochus in thus giving his daughter was only a fraud, thinking by this means he would be enabled to get the kingdom of Egypt into his power. But the prohibition of the Romans is a clear proof that he had no such design,—it forbidding his imposing upon that people in any way.

Ver. 17. "And upright ones with him." Some translate this thus: "And Israelites with him." Those wicked Israelites who, revolting from the religion of their fathers, united with Antiochus, did more than all the heathen for the ruin of the Jewish nation.

Ver. 17. "Thus shall he do." In the first clause of this verse it is said: "He shall also set his face to enter;" and here it is added: "thus shall he do,"—that is, he shall enter. In order to do this, he "gathered together all his friends, and the captains of his army;" and, as if the "strength of his whole kingdom" was not enough, "there came also unto him from other kingdoms, and from isles of the sea, bands of hired soldiers." (1 Mac. vi. 28, 29.) So he entered "with the strength of his whole kingdom."

Ver. 17. "And he shall give him the daughter of women." The king of the south gave his daughter to the king of the north. (1 Mac. x. 58.)

Ver. 17. "Corrupting her." As Ptolemy, the king of the south, "imagined wicked counsels against Alexander," the king of the north, and only gave him his daughter because he was desirous of his kingdom," and thus "went about through deceit to get Alexander's kingdom and join it to his own" (1 Mac. xi. 1, 8, 11), his object was not that she might be his bosom companion, but that by this means he might set "two crowns upon his head, the crowns of Asia and of Egypt." (1 Mac. xi. 13.) And if ever a woman was truly corrupted by the wicked designs of a father, surely she was; for she occasioned "the death of two of her husbands; and as to her children, she had murdered one with her own hands by plunging a dagger into his breast, and prepared a poisonous draught for another." (*Rol.* 260.)

Ver. 17. "But she shall not stand." The giving of his daughter was "a league of amity" to bind the two kingdoms together in ties of friendship (1 Mac. x. 54), which did not stand; for "he took his daughter from him, and forsook Alexander, so that their hatred was openly known." (1 Mac. xi. 12.)

Ver. 17. "Neither be for him." Though by thus corrupting his daughter, the king of the south had placed "the crown of Asia" upon his head, this crown was not for the kingdom of the south; for "King Ptolemy also died the third day after;" and "by this means Demetrius" obtained the crown of the north. (1 Mac. xi. 18, 19.) So she was neither for the king of the south, nor the means by which the kingdom of the south came in possession of the king of the north.

Ver. 18. "After this shall he turn his face unto the isles,"—that is, "the isles of the Gentiles" (Gen. x. 5), or heathen.

Ver. 18. "And shall take many." Demetrius, who then headed the kingdom of the north, "gathered from the isles of the heathen bands of strangers; wherefore all the forces of his father hated him," and went from him, forsaking him. (1 Mac. xi. 38, 43.)

Ver. 18. "But a prince for his own behalf shall cause the reproach offered by him to cease." Demetrius, by "gathering bands of strangers" to fill the place of those who belonged to the Syrian kingdom, thus brought upon himself "the reproach" of his own kingdom, "wherefore all the forces of his fathers hated him." "But a prince for his own behalf"—that is, "young Antiochus"—caused the reproach offered by Demetrius towards the northern kingdom "to cease." "Then there gathered unto him all the men of war whom Demetrius had put away." (1 Mac. xi. 55.)

Ver. 18. "Without his own reproach he shall cause it to turn upon him." Though Antiochus had himself given no cause of reproach, the confidence he placed in Tryphon caused this "reproach," which Demetrius had brought upon the kingdom, so to turn upon him as to be the cause of his death; for "Tryphon dealt deceitfully with the young king Antiochus, and slew him." (1 Mac. xiii. 31.)

Ver. 19. "Then he shall turn his face toward the fort of his own land." Tryphon having slain Antiochus, "crowned himself King of Asia" (1 Mac. xiii. 32); and thus the kingdom passed from the family of Antiochus. Therefore, to "turn his face toward the fort of his own land" would be for the Antiochian family to return and again take possession of the kingdom. From ver. 18 we learn that the way he left or lost the kingdom was by "turning his face unto the isles:" so the next time we hear from this Antiochian family, they are coming from the isles to recover the kingdom. (1 Mac. xv. 1–37.) The Parthians had also taken possession of a large portion of the country which Antiochus recovered: so he turned "his face toward the fortress of his own land by again "coming in full possession of the Syrian empire." (*Rol.* 258.)

Ver. 19. "But he shall stumble." Though Antiochus recovered the Syrian empire, he made a great blunder in the excess of luxury; and for the want of discretion and good judgment, his large army was "cut in pieces, or made captives, so that there scarce returned a man into Syria of all this vast number to carry thither the doleful news of this terrible overthrow." (*Prid.* B.C. 130.)

Ver. 19. "And fall." As far as the Jews were concerned, this dates the fall of the Syrian kingdom. From this time they "wholly freed themselves from all" servitude or subjection to the kingdom of Syria. (*Prid.* B.C. 130.) Yet that kingdom lingered on the decline before it fell to ruin in B.C. 65. "Here ended the empire of the Selewcidæ in Asia, after it had there lasted two hundred and fifty-eight years." (*Prid.* B.C. 65.) But the kingdom of the south "shall continue more years than the king of the north" (Dan. xi. 8),—that is, thirty-five years more; for the kingdom of Egypt reached its end B.C. 30, when it had "continued 293 years." (*Rol.* 244.)

Ver. 19. "And not be found." In B.C. 57 Prideaux dates the end of "the whole race of Selewcus; and none of them," says he, "were any more left to survive the loss of that empire which they once possessed." But he seems to have forgotten that a portion of this family was in Parthia. In B.C. 37 the King of Parthia "caused all his brothers whom his father had by the daughter of Antiochus, King of Syria, to be murdered." (*Rol.* 286.) So from this epoch, B.C. 37, the kingdom of Syria can "not be found." He stumbled in B.C. 130, fell B.C. 65, and was lost B.C. 37.

Ver. 20. "Then shall stand up." This expression dates the rise of another kingdom at the same epoch at which the kingdom of Syria was lost; and the next one in succession which ruled over Daniel's people rose that very year; for in B.C. 37 "Herod was put in thorough possession of the kingdom of Judah." (*Prid.* B.C. 37.)

Ver. 20. "In his estate." The "estate," or "place" of the kingdom of Syria, as connected with the Jews, was that of oppression and cruelty; and in this sense Herod stood up in "his estate." "The Jews had borne more calamities from Herod in a few years than had their fathers during all that interval of time that had passed since they had come out of Babylon, and returned home in the reign of Xerxes." (*Jose.*)

Ver. 20. "A raiser of taxes." We are unable to see how a better description of the character of Herod can be given in fewer words than these,—"a raiser of taxes." So heavy was the burden of taxation imposed on the Jews by him, that whenever he wished "to recover their good-will, all that was necessary on his part was only to relieve them of a part of their taxes." (*Jose. Ant.* b. xv. c. x. s. 4.

Ver. 20. "In the glory of the kingdom." As Rome was introduced in ver. 16, which Gabriel dropped in order to carry out the history of the kingdom of the north, this is an allusion to it; for next to the kingdom of Syria, which, according to the inspired historian, had now passed away, Rome was the last-mentioned; and since we are here informed that he was to stand up in the kingdom, we must understand some subordinate kingdom, and not that of Rome; for we cannot, properly speaking, say the Roman kingdom stood up in the kingdom of Rome. But Herod's kingdom did properly stand up in that kingdom, being himself subject to the Romans; and it was during the "glory of that kingdom;" for at that time "the Roman empire extended itself farther than ever before or since; so that it was then called the empire of the whole earth." (Matt. Henry on Luke ii. 1.)

Ver. 20. "But within fewer days he shall be destroyed." As Herod reigned but thirty-four years, this was but a few days in comparison to the 258 years, during which the kingdom of the north, and the 293 years during which the kingdom of the south, had continued.

Ver. 20. "Neither in anger, nor in battle." At the death of Herod his kingdom reverted to the Romans. "The power of disposing of it belonged to Cæsar," who "destroyed" Herod's kingdom not "in battle, neither in anger," but by cutting it up into small provinces, over which governors ruled, and not kings. (*Jose. Ant.* b. xvii. c. xi. s. 2, 4.)

Ver. 21. "In his estate." Herod's "estate," or "place," was that of an oppressive king,* using that "uncontrollable authority which

* The reader will bear in mind that so far we have shown how every "jot" and "tittle" of this prophetic history has been accomplished, while those who make Antiochus the hero of Daniel's prophecy have to "confess there may be some doubtful and obscure terms which may be differently explained and are variously interpreted by commentators." (*Rol.* p. 174.) The avowed object of this prophetic history was "to make" Daniel "understand what shall befall" his "people in the latter day;" and if the reader will examine the history through which we have passed in noticing the accomplishment of this prophecy, he will find that every word which fell from the lips of the prophet was in reference to that in which the people of Israel were concerned. But while those who make Antiochus the hero of Daniel's prophecy have been unable to make any sense of a large portion of this prophecy, much of that which they make appear plausible, according to their explanation of the matter, in no way concerns Daniel's people.

tyrants exercise over their subjects; and made use of that authority for the destruction of the Jews." (*Jose. Ant.* b. xvii. c. xi. s. 2.)

In the latter portion of his life his "estate" was that of standing up against "the Prince of princes," being "exceeding wroth," even exalting himself to "slay the Son of the living God." (Matt. ii. 16.) And in this sense, Antichrist, the "prince of the power of the air" (Eph. ii. 2), who "sitteth in the temple of God" (2 Thess. ii. 4), is now standing up in the estate of Herod, using his tyrannical authority over the people of God, even casting "down some of the host" "of heaven" and of the "stars to the ground, and" stamping "upon them; yea, he magnified himself even to the Prince of the host." (Dan. viii. 10.)

Ver. 21. "Shall stand up a vile person,"—that is the "man of sin," that son of perdition, who opposeth and exalteth himself above all that is called God." (2 Thess. ii. 3.) As Antichrist is that spirit "that denieth that Jesus is the Christ" (1 John ii. 22), this "man of sin" could not have been in the world before the birth of Christ; and he first made his appearance in the bosom of Herod, who "was exceeding wroth, and sent forth and slew all the children that were in Bethlehem and in the coasts thereof." (Matt. ii. 16.)

We have remarked that Rome was one of the "four notable" horns; and as Herod's kingdom was in the Roman Empire, Rome was the one out of which "the little horn" arose, which, at its first appearance, was so small as to be concealed in the bosom of Herod under the false pretence that he desired to "come and worship" the newborn babe. (Matt. ii. 8.) But he has now "waxed" so "exceeding great" as to stamp all the earth beneath his heavy tread. His course was first "towards the south" (Dan. viii. 9); for as the Babe of Bethlehem was taken "into Egypt" (Matt. ii. 14), the Egyptians were the first people after Herod and the Jews to deny that he was the Christ. His next course was "towards the east;" for when the wise men of the east "departed into their own country" (Matt. ii. 12), and there published what they had seen, those who "confessed not that Jesus Christ is come into the flesh" were immediately transformed into the image of this "deceiver and antichrist." (2 John vii.) It then went "towards the pleasant" ways of all the paths of peace (Prov. iii. 17) as opened on earth by the Son of God; and is even to the present day oppressing the people of God.

Ver. 21. "To whom they shall not give the honor of the kingdom." Antichrist, "the prince of the power of the air," being that "spirit" which "worketh in the children of disobedience" (Eph. ii. 2) has from its rise ever reigned as king over the sons of men; yet, true to the letter it is, they never have, nor never will give him "the honor of the kingdom."

Ver. 21. "But he shall come in peaceably and obtain the kingdom by flatteries." Antichrist being "a vile person," "that man of sin," "the son of perdition," commenced from the first venting the fury of his wrath against the saints; but so far from this, his war with them, being the means by which he obtained his seat "in the temple of God," this, his tyrannical fury, was the very thing that restrained and prevented his taking his seat there. (2 Thess. ii. 6.) But when the persecuting power of Antichrist was by Constantine "taken out of the way" (2 Thess. ii. 7), and the religion of Jesus became honorable, then, assuming the cloak of deception, he came "in peaceably and obtained the kingdom by flatteries." And this is the means by which that "vile person" yet "sitteth in the temple of God;" for as he has never yet received "the honor of the kingdom," as none of the professed followers of Christ will acknowledge allegiance to him, these his "flatteries" are the only means by which he can retain his seat in "the temple of God."

Ver. 22. "And with the arms of a flood shall they be overflown from before him,"—that is, "the people of the Prince that shall come"—those in whose hearts this "man of sin" has taken up his abode—"shall destroy the city and the sanctuary, and the end thereof shall be with a flood." (Dan. ix. 26.) It is literally true Jerusalem was destroyed by Antichrist,—by those wicked Jews "who confess not that Jesus Christ is come into the flesh" (2 John vii;) for though the Roman army was the "hand" by which it was "consumed" (Dan. xi. 16), they cannot be charged with its ruin, as Titus not only did all he could to save the city, but even "spreading out his hands to heaven, called God to witness that this was not his doing." (*Jose. Wars*, b. v. c. xii. s. 4.)

Ver. 22. "And shall be broken." During the Seven-years War at Jerusalem, "the sacrifice and the oblation" did forever "cease" (Dan. ix. 27): hence, the Mosaic dispensation passed away, and the Jewish people as a nation united under their own laws was "broken."

Ver. 22. "Yea, also the Prince of the covenant." Some say this little horn, which "magnified himself even to the Prince of the host" (Dan. viii. 11), and stood "up against the Prince of princes" (Dan. viii. 25) was Rome; and it is true our Lord was crucified upon a Roman cross; but Peter, who witnessed the cruel deed, charges Antichrist—those who "denied the Holy One and the Just"—with having "killed the Prince of life." (Acts iii. 15; iv. 10; v. 30.) This "vile person"* had already pronounced the sentence "of death" (Matt. xxvi. 66) before he was brought into the presence of "Pontius Pilate, the Governor;" and by "washing his hands before the multitude, saying, I am innocent of the blood of this just person" (Matt. xxvii. 24), he cleared the Romans of this charge which Antichrist himself acknowledged, saying, "His blood be upon us and on our children." (Matt. xxvii. 25.)

Ver. 23. "And after the league made with him he shall work deceitfully." "The league made with "Antichrist could not have been formed by any nation of earth, as the formation of such a league would immediately transform them into Antichrist; hence, there was but one people with whom such a league could be formed,—the so-called Christian. And the only way the Church could form a league with Antichrist was by means of transgression (Dan. viii. 12); for while they confess Christ, they must by works deny him, in order to be united or leagued with Antichrist; and this is the way the league was formed: "a host was given him by reason of transgression." (Dan. viii. 12.) This league was formed by Constantine, the Emperor of Rome, in A.D. 312, at which time he "took the religion of Christ to the unhallowed embrace of

---

* Our commentators say this "vile person," as mentioned in Daniel (xi. 21), was Antiochus Epiphanes. We will here pause a moment and expose the absurdity of such an opinion.

1. This was "a vile person" before he ascended the throne; and as every word must be in reference to that in which Daniel's people are concerned, he must exhibit his tyrannical sway towards that people before he received his kingdom, which Antiochus did not.

2. He must be one "to whom they shall not give the honor of the kingdom;" but Antiochus did have the honor of the kingdom of Syria.

3. It was declared: "he shall come in peaceably, and obtain the kingdom by flatteries;" but Antiochus, using no "flatteries," came in with open hostilities, and obtained the kingdom by force of arms.

4. "With the arms of a flood they were to be overflown from before him and broken." Some say the kingdom of Syria; others say Egypt: but neither Egypt, Syria, nor the Jewish nation, was broken before Antiochus.

5. "Also the Prince of the covenant." This, we are told, was Onias, the high-priest. But we have already noticed that so far from Antiochus having slain Onias, he slew that wretch who was guilty of the cruel deed. Had the heavenly teacher used the expression, "a prince," there might have been no objection to supposing one of the Jewish high-priests was meant; but since he uses the expression, "the Prince of the covenant," we are restricted alone to the God-man Christ Jesus; for none but God can be "the Prince of the covenant" of God.

State; assumed to unite in his own person the civil and ecclesiastical dominion;" and from this time Antichrist began to "work deceitfully." The profession of the religion of Jesus now becoming popular, many professed Christ only from unhallowed motives.

Ver. 23. "For he shall come up, and shall become strong with a small people,"—that is, "come up" into the Church, or "the temple of God." (2 Thess. ii. 4.) The hand of persecution being now "taken out of the way" (2 Thess. ii. 7), Antichrist, in its transgressive form entered the Church, and "became strong with a small people," or a few true Christians.

Ver. 24. "He shall enter peaceably even upon the fattest places of the province." This "vile person," laying aside that tyrannical fury which he had exhibited even towards "the Prince of the covenant," now, clad in "sheep's clothing," "entered peaceably" into all the privileges of the Church. The Emperors of Rome richly endowed the churches over which they presided with wealth and worldly honors, and thus Antichrist entered "even upon the fattest places of the province."

Ver. 24. "And he shall do that which his fathers have not done, nor his fathers' fathers." The idolatrous worship of saints was now introduced into the Church; they also assumed the privilege of changing the ordinances of Heaven: neither of which their "fathers," since the opening of the Christian dispensation, nor their "fathers' fathers," under the Mosaic dispensation, had dared to do. But our object was not to write a commentary upon the book of Daniel, but only to show the rise of Antichrist.*

B.C. 488. NEHEMIAH.—The first we hear of Nehemiah was when he returned from Babylon. As at that time he was a distinguished

---

* As our Lord was crucified upon a Roman cross, by the little horn some understand the Roman empire; but, as we have before remarked, it was Antichrist, and not Rome, that stood up "against the Prince of princes."

2. This was "a little horn" following in succession to the "four notable ones" (Dan. viii. 23); but Rome was great before the rise of the other three kingdoms.

3. This horn, though "little at first, "waxed exceeding great;" but Rome, having reached its height at the time it came in connection with Daniel's people, did not wax any greater.

4. It was said his "power shall be mighty, but not by his own power;" while all the power Rome possessed was properly its own. But the power of Antichrist, which is greater than that of Rome, is not his "own power." The great secret of the power of Antichrist is obtained by assuming the name of Christ.

5. "He shall be broken without hands;" but Rome has long since been broken with hands.

character, holding an important office over the returning Jews (Ezra. ii. 2), he must have been at least twenty years old; and if so, he was eighty-nine in the twentieth of Artaxerxes. As this would make Nehemiah one hundred and forty-seven years old in the fifteenth of Darius Nothus, when the advocates of Ptolemy's canon end "the first seven of the seventy weeks of Daniel's prophecy," they are reduced to the necessity of trying to make it appear that this was not the same Nehemiah. But their conjectures cannot outweigh positive authority. That this was the same Nehemiah as found in office when they returned from captivity, observe that the same person who in Ezra ii. 63 is called "the Tirshatha," is in 1 Esdras v. 40, called Nehemiah; and in Neh. x. 1; viii. 9, we are told positively that Nehemiah was "the Tirshatha." This is another proof of the incorrectness of Ptolemy's canon.

B.C. 485. CAMBYSES'S FIRST YEAR.—According to Herodotus, Cambyses reigned "seven years and five months" (*Herod.* b. iii. c. 66); but the beginning of his reign dates not from the death of his father, but from the time Cyrus commenced the Scythian war; for, says Herodotus: "Cyrus then formally delegated his authority to his son Cambyses." Herodotus is correct in this, as will appear from Xenophon; for instead of Cyrus at the time of his death appointing Cambyses as his successor, he speaks of him as having been before appointed,—thus: "Do you, therefore, Cambyses, hold the kingdom as allotted you by the gods, and by me." (*Xen.* p. 148.) As to when the Scythian war commenced, from which epoch the reign of Cambyses is to be dated, Herodotus does not inform us. He says, among the "many other and different relations" concerning "the end of Cyrus," that he was slain in a battle against the Scythians (*Her.* b. i. c. 214); but this is admitted to be incorrect; for, according to Xenophon, he died peaceably in his bed." (*Xen.* p. 150.) Though Xenophon does not say how long this was after the Scythian war, he says: "Immediately on Cyrus's death his sons fell into dissension; cities and nations revolted; every thing tended to ruin." (*Xen.* 150.) And we learn from Herodotus that this happened a short time before the death of Cambyses; hence, Cambyses did not long survive his father, which we can prove again from the history of his life. According to Polyænus, "Nitetius, who was in reality the daughter of Apries, lived a long time with Cyrus as the daughter of Amasis. After having many children by Cyrus, she disclosed to him who she really was; for, though Amasis was dead, she wished to revenge herself on his son Psammenitus. Cyrus acceded to her wishes;

but died in the midst of his preparations for an Egyptian war. Cambyses was persuaded by his mother to undertake this, and revenge on the Egyptians the cause of the family of Apries;" hence, Psammenitus was King of Egypt before the death of Cyrus, and had reigned only six months when Cambyses subdued Egypt; and as he died before he reached home, surely he could not have lived over one or two years after the death of his father. He was associated with his father in the kingdom in the twenty-sixth year of Cyrus, which we prove,—

1. By the seventy-years "indignation." (See B.C. 477.)

2. By the seventy-years "fast." (See B.C. 475.)

3. By the eclipse of the moon "in the seventh year of Cambyses." (See B.C. 479.)

4. By the eclipse of the moon "followed by the death of Cambyses." (See B.C. 479.)

According to Clemens Alexandrinus, Cambyses reigned "ten years." This may be reconciled with Herodotus by supposing that Cyrus made Cambyses successor to Darius over the province of Babylon; for it was just about ten years from the time of the death of "Darius, the Median" to the death of Cambyses. Ptolemy, not observing that Herodotus dated the beginning of the reign of Cambyses from the time of the Scythian war, places the beginning of his reign at the time of his father's death; but this would make Cambyses remain in Egypt about seven years; for, "as soon as he succeeded to the throne he commenced hostilities against Egypt." (*Herod.* b. iii. c. 3.) Since it is unreasonable to suppose that Cambyses remained seven years in Egypt, the advocates of Ptolemy's canon place the time he went there about the beginning of his fifth year; which not only contradicts Polyænus, as quoted above, but is at variance with all the historical accounts we have yet met with.

B.C. 485. YEAR OF JUBILEE.—"The commandment to restore and to build Jerusalem" went forth on the 10th of the fifth month, B.C. 488. If from that time we allow the Jews about three years in which to return home and build their cities, we will have B.C. 485 as the period at which "all Israel" were "in their cities." (Ezra ii. 70.) Ezra ii. is only a register containing the genealogy of the children of Israel that went up from Babylon. Hence, Chap. iii. commencing with ver. 2 is as properly a continuation of the first chapter as if the second was entirely omitted. And since the cities of Israel had been destroyed, the time they were "dwelling in their cities," as mentioned in Ezra ii. 70, could not have been before they had rebuilt those cities. Ezra says: "And when the seventh month was come, and the children of Israel were in the cities,"—not when they had just returned from Babylon, but when they were "in the cities,"—"the people gathered themselves together as one man to Jerusalem." (Ezra iii. 1.) As to why they thus assembled at Jerusalem, Ezra does not inform us; but we have the continuation of this history in Nehemiah, from which it appears that this was their year of jubilee, or at least the sabbatical year, during which "all Israel" were required by law "to appear before the Lord," and at which time they were required, saying, "Thou shalt read this law before all Israel in their hearing" (Deut. xxxi. 11); for "Ezra the scribe stood upon a pulpit," and read in "the book of the law of Moses" that which the Lord had commanded to Israel." (Neh. viii. 1, 4.) From ver. 6 Chap. vii. to ver. 36 Chap. x. of Nehemiah was copied from some other author; and by comparing Nehemiah vii. 73 with Ezra ii. 70, we learn that this in chronological order properly belongs there; for it was written after they "were come again out of the captivity" (Neh. viii. 17), and when the temple was building (Neh. xi. 12), which house was finished in the sixth of Darius. (Ezra vi. 15.)

B.C. 481. CAMBYSES'S FIFTH YEAR.—In the fifth year of Cambyses, reckoning from the Scythian war, Cyrus died; and soon after his death Cambyses commenced his "expedition against Egypt." (*Herod.* b. ii. c. 1.) According to Josephus, this king, whom the Greeks called Cambyses, was the same one called Artaxerxes by Ezra (iv. 11.) That Josephus is correct in this, we prove thus: Herodotus says this Cambyses of the Greeks was the son of Cyrus; and the Artaxerxes of Ezra was the son of Cyrus. (Ezra iv. 15: 1 Esdras vi. 21.) As the name Ahasuerus is mentioned before that of Artaxerxes, some conclude that Cambyses was the Ahasuerus, and the Magi called Artaxerxes. But this is clearly incorrect; for while this Artaxerxes was the son of Cyrus, the Magi was not even of the Persian nation. If reference be made to Ezra (iv. 5), we find that Darius was the last name mentioned; and from this Ezra runs back, as he had run down from Cyrus; and in going back from Darius, the Magi, who is by Ezra called Ahasuerus, comes before that of Cambyses, whom he calls Artaxerxes.

Cyrus dying "in the midst of his preparation for an Egyptian war," his son Cambyses commenced the "expedition against Egypt." The adversaries of the Jews, availing themselves of this favorable opportunity of prevailing with the king to cause them to cease to build Jerusalem and the temple, wrote to Cambyses concerning the matter (Ezra iv. 11); in answer to which he wrote to them, saying, "Give ye now commandment to cause these men to cease, and that the city be not built until another commandment shall be given from me" (Ezra iv. 21),—that is, until he return from the Egyptian war; and on his return, he passed through the land of Judea, and granted the Jews the privilege of resuming their work (Ezra vi. 14); but before they were ready to commence, "Cambyses died at Damascus;" and the adversaries of the Jews, writing immediately to the Magi called Ahasuerus, prevented the work: "so it ceased unto the second year of the reign of Darius, King of Persia." (Ezra iv. 24.)

B.C. 479. ECLIPSE OF THE MOON.—According to Ptolemy there was an eclipse of the moon during "the seventh of Cambyses;" and by calculation there was a total eclipse at Babylon on March 14, at 32m. after five in the morning, B.C. 479.

B.C. 479. ECLIPSE OF THE MOON.—Says Ferguson: "An eclipse of the moon was followed by the death of Cambyses;" and by calculation there was a total eclipse of the moon at Babylon on September 7, at 15m. after nine in the afternoon, B.C. 479; from which we conclude that Cambyses died about the 8th of September, B.C. 479; and if to this we add "seven years and five months," we have April, B.C., 486, for the beginning of his reign.

B.C. 479. THE REIGN OF THE MAGI.—"After the death of Cambyses, the Magus, by the favor of his name, pretending to be Smerdias, the son of Cyrus, reigned in security during the seven months which completed the eighth of the reign of Cambyses." (*Herod.* b. iii. c. 67.)

B.C. 478. DARIUS'S FIRST YEAR.—"The seven months" the Magi had a peaceable possession of the kingdom from the "death of Cambyses,"—that is, from September 8, B.C. 479,—will give us April 8, B.C. 478; and if from the time the imposition was detected, we allow about one month for the interval, we will have May, B.C. 478 for the beginning of the reign of Darius. But concerning the duration of his reign there is an apparent difficulty; for while we can prove by clear astronomical demonstration that his reign continued only about twenty years after the time of the slaughtering of the Magi, Ptolemy, who dates the beginning of his reign at that time, says he reigned thirty-six years, which thirty-six years he found in the book of Herodotus. In order to reconcile this, we must make inquiry as to the way Herodotus was in the habit of making out the number of years he allowed for the reign of kings. He says "Cyaxares died after he had reigned forty years;"

and yet, according to his own statement, Cyaxares was really in possession of the kingdom but twelve years. Again: he tells us that Cyrus reigned twenty-nine years; but, according to Xenophon, Cyrus was really in possession of the kingdom only about seven years. And he tells us that Cambyses reigned "seven years and five months;" yet, as we have before noticed, Cambyses survived his father only about two or three years. This gives us a clue to the inquiry as to how he made out the thirty-six years he allowed Darius. That which appears to be the most plausible is this: Darius at twenty years of age having married "Atossa, daughter of Cyrus," was made Governor of Persia, in B.C. 495; about ten years after, Cyrus had a "dream in which he thought he saw Darius having wings on his shoulders, one of which overshadowed Asia, the other Europe; from which" he concluded that Darius, his son-in-law and Governor of Persia, was "plotting against" him, or "forming designs" to dispossess him of his empire. He, therefore, sent Hystaspes, the father of Darius, to dispossess Darius of his office as governor, saying: "Do you, therefore, go back to Persia with all speed, and take care that when I have conquered those people, and return home, you bring your son before me to be examined;" and from this, Hystaspes continued Governor of Persia until Darius received the kingdom. (*Herod.* b. iii. c. 70.) The circumstance of Darius vowing "to the King of Heaven" "to build Jerusalem in the day" when he shall receive the "kingdom" (1 Esdras iv. 43, 46), shows that, after the death of Cambyses, he was the next heir; and the only way we are enabled to account for his being heir to the throne is upon the supposition that he had before that time married the daughter of Cyrus; hence, Herodotus was mistaken in supposing that Cambyses married his sister Atossa.

From the time Darius was made Governor of the province of Persia, he was in authority exercising all the power of a subordinate king; therefore, if those who informed Herodotus of the duration of his reign wished to include the whole time he was in authority, they must date from the commencement of his authority as governor, which is more plausible than to allow the reign of Cyrus to include the time he was only acting as a general over the armies of his father. That which proves that Herodotus did in the thirty-six years include this time in which he exercised the authority of a subordinate king, is the expression, "in all;" for if the thirty-six years be reckoned from the time he came in full possession of the kingdom, we are unable to see why he said that

Darius "reigned thirty-six years in all." This Darius, that obtained the kingdom after the slaughter of the Magi, was, says Herodotus, "the son of Hystaspes;" and Josephus informs us that he was the one in whose reign the temple was completed. Herod, the King of the Jews, declares the same thing. The expression, "even until the reign of Darius, King of Persia," as used by Ezra (iv. 5), is equivalent to Darius, the first King of Persia; for if up to the time Ezra wrote, there had been more than one Persian king by this name, had he wished to inform us what king he meant, he would have said Darius the second, or third, King of Persia. Ezra used the expression, "King of Persia," to distinguish him from Darius the Mede, who was the first of that name who reigned over the Jews. (Dan. v. 31.)

B.C. 477. THE SECOND YEAR OF DARIUS.—On Sunday the first day of the week, September 26, B.C. 477, which was the 24th "day of the sixth month, in the second year of Darius the King," the Jews again commenced the building of the temple. (Hag. i. 15.) This was before they had obtained permission from Darius to do so; for it was not until the intrusion of their enemies compelled, that they applied for one. Cambyses, the Artaxerxes of Ezra, who had, during his expedition against Egypt, prohibited the Jews from going on with their work "until another commandment should be given from" him (Ezra iv. 21), had, on his return from Egypt, as he passed through the land of Judea, granted them the privilege of continuing their work. (Ezra vi. 14.) But Cambyses dying "at Damascus," the adversaries of the Jews, writing immediately to "Ahasuerus an accusation against the inhabitants of Judea and Jerusalem" (Ezra iv. 6), deterred them in this. But Cambyses, when, on his dying bed, he admonished the Persians to wrest the kingdom again from the usurper, had made Darius take an oath, saying, "Build Jerusalem in the day when thou comest to thy kingdom." (1 Esdras iv. 43.) Darius having thus "vowed to the King of Heaven" that he would grant the Jews the privilege of building their house, as soon as the impostor was slain, and things in Persia had quieted down again, the prophets Haggai and Zachariah commenced stirring up the people to a preparation for the work; and by the 24th "day of the sixth month in the second year of Darius" they were ready, "and began to build the house." (Ezra v. 2.) But their enemies, the Governor Tatnai and others, learning that they had no permission from Darius, desired to oppose them; hence, wrote to the king concerning the matter, after which he ordered a search for the decree of Cyrus (Ezra vi. 1);

and about this time his feast came off, at which time Zerubbabel obtained his permission to build the house. (1 Esdras iv. 47.)

B.C. 477. END OF THE SEVENTY-YEARS INDIGNATION. The Indignation commenced with the ruin of the city and the burning of the temple, in the fifth month, B.C. 547; and seventy years from that time ends with the fifth month, B.C. 477. From Zachariah we learn that the seventieth year of the Indignation reached its end "in the second year of Darius." (Zach. i. 12.) This proves that we have the reign of Cambyses properly arranged.

B.C. 475. THE SEVENTY-YEARS FASTING AND MOURNING.—Jerusalem was burned on the 10th of the fifth month (Jer. lii. 12), and Gedaliah slain "in the seventh month" (2 Kings xxv. 25), B.C. 547: hence, the earliest time at which the Jews could have commenced to "fast and mourn in the fifth and seventh months," was in B.C. 546; from which, if we subtract seventy years, we have B.C. 476. But "the commandment to restore and to build Jerusalem" going forth on the 10th of the fifth month in B.C. 488, there could have been no fasting and mourning at that time. "The fast of the fifth month" was on that day exchanged for "joy and gladness." (Zach. viii. 19.) Neither could there have been fasting and mourning in the seventh month; for they were then rejoicing at Jerusalem. (Ezra iii. 6.) But before the time of the fast in the following year, they were again molested by their enemies (Ezra iii. 8; iv. 1); hence, the fasting and mourning of the fifth and seventh months, commencing again, continued to the fourth year of the reign of Darius. (Zach. vii. 1–5.) With the omission of the fasting in the fifth and seventh months of B.C. 488, the seventy years ends in the fourth year of Darius, B.C. 475. Another proof of the correctness of our arrangement of the reigns of Cambyses and Darius.

B.C. 475. DARIUS'S TWENTIETH YEAR.—It is said there was an eclipse of the moon in the "twentieth of Darius Hystaspes;" and by calculation, there was a total eclipse in the twentieth year of Darius, reckoning from the time he was made governor in Persia, which was the fourth year from the acquisition of his kingdom. This eclipse occurred on June 26, at 13m. after eight in the afternoon on the meridian of Babylon.

B.C. 472. THE TEMPLE COMPLETED.—On Sunday, February 15, "the third day of the month Adar, which was in the sixth year of the reign of Darius the King," the temple "was finished." (Ezra vi. 15.)

B.C. 465. THE BATTLE OF MARATHON.—Struyk has an eclipse of the moon about the time of the battle of Marathon,—that is, according to Ptolemy's canon. This battle was fought B.C. 465; and by calculation there was a total eclipse of the moon at Athens, on June 6, at 25m. after twelve A.M. in that year. According to Herodotus, Darius died in the sixth year after the battle of Marathon. Six from B.C. 465 leaves B.C. 459 for the time of his death. Thus we prove by three eclipses of the moon that Ptolemy was mistaken in supposing that Darius lived thirty-six years after the death of Cambyses; and that Herodotus is correct in saying that he reigned thirty-six years "in all,"—that is, including his subordinate reign.

B.C. 464. DARIUS'S THIRTY-FIRST YEAR.—It is said there was an eclipse of the moon in the "thirty-first of Darius Hystaspes;" and by calculatiou there was one at Babylon on November 19, at 35m. after twelve A.M.. in B.C. 464,—the quantity eclipsed 9¼ digits. And according to our table of chronology B.C. 464 was the thirty-first year of Darius, reckoning from the time he was appointed Governor of Persia, which was the fifteenth year from the time he came in full possession of the kingdom.

B.C. 461. EGYPT REVOLTED FROM DARIUS.—"In the fourth" year after "the battle of Marathon," "the Egyptians, who had been reduced by Cambyses, revolted from the Persians." In this year Darius "appointed Xerxes to be king over the Persians; from which epoch Herodotus commences his reign; but he does not say how long it continued.

B.C. 458. XERXES'S FIRST YEAR.—Ptolemy begins the reign of Xerxes at the death of his father; and gives him twenty-one years.

B.C. 457. XERXES'S EXPEDITION AGAINST GREECE.—After the battle of Marathon, Darius spent "three years in making preparations to invade Greece." "In the fourth year, Egypt revolted; and in this year, "Darius appointed Xerxes to be king over the Persians." "In the year after the revolt of Egypt, Darius died;" and "in the year which followed his death, Xerxes commenced the war with Egypt." Having spent "four whole years in assembling his forces and providing things necessary for the expedition," he commenced his march to invade Greece, "in the course of the fifth year" of his reign, reckoning from the time he was associated with his father in the kingdom, which was the second after the death of Darius. In the next year, which was "the tenth year after the battle of Marathon," Xerxes entered Greece. (*Thu.* b. i. c. 18.)

B.C. 457. ECLIPSE OF THE SUN.—When Xerxes was on his march to Greece, there happened a total eclipse of the sun, which Herodotus describes thus:—"The sun, quitting his seat in the heavens, disappeared, though there were no clouds, and the air was perfectly serene; and night ensued in the place of day." As "the sun .... disappeared" when "there were no clouds," this was a total eclipse. The sun appeared to have "quit its place in the heavens;" therefore, the smallest particle could not have been visible; and as "night ensued in the place of day," it was not only a total, but a dark eclipse, such as can only happen when the moon is in its perigee. Some translate it: "The darkest night succeeded." On p. 44 we have observed that this eclipse occurred when Xerxes was in Celænæ, in Phrygia. Xerxes was then on his way to Sardis, where he spent the winter; hence, it was late in the autumn; and as the Greeks were celebrating the Olympic games when he reached Greece in the following summer, this eclipse was in the fourth year of "the Olympic games," and in the fifth year of Xerxes, reckoning from the time he was made King of Persia by his father; or the second of his reign, reckoning from the death of Darius,—that is, B.C. 457. Since we are able to point out with such precision the time and place at which this total eclipse of the sun occurred, it is the most important one to be found in profane history for establishing the true chronology.

By calculation, there was a total eclipse of the sun at Celænæ, Phrygia, on December 16, at 15m. after nine, in B.C. 457,—the moon was at that time in her perigee; hence, a very dark eclipse. Herodotus mentions that this eclipse happened when Xerxes "was on the point of setting out;" or, as some translate it, "at the moment of their departure." We would hardly suppose that they would at that season have left before eight o'clock in the morning; and this eclipse began to be visible about 10 or 15m. after eight: so it answers in every particular to the description of Herodotus.

No one at all acquainted with ancient history can believe Xerxes invaded Greece before B.C. 754, nor later than B.C. 431; and from the former to the latter, we have examined the fourth year of each Olympiad, by which we find that this is the only eclipse that answers to the description, the time, quantity, and place, as mentioned by Herodotus; hence we must admit that this settles to a certainty the time at which Xerxes invaded Greece.

B.C. 455. ECLIPSE OF THE SUN.—According to Herodotus, there was another "eclipse of the sun" during the spring of the second year of the Persian War, which was in the first year of the Olympic games. B.C. 455 was the second of the Persian War; and by calculation, there was an eclipse of 7½ digits at the isthmus in Greece, at 30m after nine A.M., May 31, B.C. 455. This being in connection with the total eclipse of B.C. 457, points out the year Xerxes invaded Greece; thus putting it beyond all doubt that our chronology is the correct one.

B.C. 455. ECLIPSE OF THE SUN.—In S. Bliss's catalogue of eclipses, as copied from Dr. Hales, he has one dated: "Feb. 13, aft. 2, dig. 11½,—year after the Persian War." As to where this was seen, or what historian has mentioned it, we know not; but by calculation, a total eclipse of the sun passed central through Asia, on May 31, B.C. 455, which was the year after Xerxes, having been defeated at Salamis, fled from Grecia.

B.C. 446. ARTAXERXES ASSOCIATED WITH HIS FATHER.—"The ill success of Xerxes in his expedition against the Greeks, and which continued afterwards, at length discouraged him" so much that, giving up all public affairs of the kingdom to Artaxerxes, he "abandoned himself entirely to luxury and ease, and was studious of nothing but his pleasure." (*Rol.*)

Says Thucydides:—"Themistocles fled to King Artaxerxes, the son of Xerxes, who was lately come to the throne." (b. i. c. 137.) "Strabo, Plutarch, Diodorus, Siculus, Africanus, Eusebius, and all others that write of these times, fix this incident under Xerxes," which is positive proof that the reign of Artaxerxes began before the death of Xerxes. Prideaux, not noticing that Xerxes had thus associated his son with him in the kingdom, first says: "according to Thucydides, Xerxes was dead;" and then enters into an argument to prove that he was mistaken. Had Prideaux received the express language of Thucydides, without supposing he meant more than he said, his argument here would have been uncalled for; for Thucydides does not say that he was dead: he only says that "Artaxerxes, the son of Xerxes, was lately come to the throne." (*Thu.* b. i. c. 137.) Usher, Rollin, and others, who admit that the flight of Themistocles was in the reign of Artaxerxes, commence his reign at the end of the twelfth year of Xerxes; and in this they are correct. But, in supposing that Xerxes died at that time, they were mistaken; for "Ptolemy, Diodorus, Siculus, Plutarch, Africanus, and Eusebius, all say that Xerxes reigned twenty-one years;" "Petavius supposes that Xerxes, nine years before his death, admitted his son Artaxerxes to reign in copartnership with him;" and from the time Xerxes associated his son with him in the kingdom is to be reckoned the forty-one years during which Artaxerxes reigned.

B.C. 438. ARTAXERXES'S FIRST YEAR.—Ezra, Nehemiah, and others, in reckoning by the reign of Artaxerxes, date the beginning of his reign from the time of his father's death; and from this epoch he reigned about thirty-two years (Neh. xiii. 6); for his thirty-second year from the death of Xerxes, ends with the forty-first year from the time he was associated with his father. His reign commenced as early as the ninth month in B.C. 438. (Neh. i. 1.)

B.C. 431. ESTHER TAKEN TO THE KING.—"Esther was taken unto the King Ahasuerus, into his house royal, in the tenth month, which is the month Tebeth, in the seventh year of his reign" (Est. ii. 16),—that is, about the first of January, B.C. 431. In profane history we find no king called Ahasuerus; but in the Bible we have three called by that name. The first was that King of the Medes, who was by the Greeks called Astyages; the second, was the impostor "Smerdis the Magian," who reigned after Cambyses; and the third, was the husband of Esther. He is distinguished from the two who reigned before him by being called the "Ahasuerus which reigned from India even unto Ethiopia over an hundred and seven and twenty provinces. (Est. i. 1.)

All that is now necessary in order to learn what King of Persia this was, is to ascertain the name by which he was called among the Greeks; and this we can easily do, since we have a history of Esther, which was originally written in Greek. Those authors who wrote in Greek called the Kings of Media and Persia by the same name which the Greeks call them; for example: the king who was called Ahasuerus, in that portion of the book of Daniel which was written in Hebrew, was in that written in Greek, called Astyages. (Compare Dan. ix. i. with the history of "Bel and the Dragon," i. 1.) And so with the book of Esther: in that portion which was written in Hebrew, the husband of Esther is called Ahasuerus; but the Greek copy has the same name by which he was known among the Greeks,—that is, Artaxerxes. Thus we prove that the Ahasuerus of Esther was the Artaxerxes of the Greeks. The first king thus called by the Greeks was the son of Xerxes. As this Artaxerxes reigned "from India even unto Ethiopia over a hundred and seven and twenty provinces," this language forbids our looking for any other after him; hence, proves that the son of Xerxes was the husband of Esther. Says Josephus:—"The son of Xerxes," whom the "Greeks called Artaxerxes," was the husband of Esther; and the Septuagint, throughout the whole book of Esther wherever the Hebrew text hath Ahasuerus, translates Artaxerxes;" for the Ahasuerus of the Romans and the Artaxerxes of the Greeks are the same.

B.C. 431. EZRA WENT UP TO JERUSALEM.—Xerxes, the fourth King of Persia, having stirred "up all against the realm of Grecia" (Dan. xi. 2), the Jews were thus "led into Persia" (2 Mac. i. 19), to accompany him in his expedition against Greece; and such was the shock his kingdom received at that time by the Greeks, he too much needed their service to suffer them to return home during his life. But in the seventh year of the reign of his son Artaxerxes, the Greeks, who had threatened his kingdom with ruin, having commenced a war among themselves, he had no further cause of fear ; hence, "made a release to the provinces" (Esther ii. 18), granting the soldiers the privilege of returning home. This release was made in the tenth month in the seventh year of Artaxerxes,—that is, January, B.C. 431; and by the "first day of the first month," Sunday, April 12, N.S., B.C. 431, the Jews were ready to leave Babylon; and on "the first day of the fifth month," Friday, July 31, N.S., they reached "Jerusalem." (Ezra vii. 9.) Ezra does not attribute the privilege of thus returning home to any act of kindness on the part of Artaxerxes; but gives all the praise to his God, saying, "Blessed be the Lord God of our fathers which hath put such a thing as this in the king's heart." (Ezra vii. 27.) But as to the means used by the Lord, he does not inform us. A clew to this inquiry may be gathered from the words of Artaxerxes himself. He says: "Why should there be wrath against the realm of the king and his sons?" (Ezra vii. 23.) From this it is clear that there was then some visible mark of the displeasure of Heaven, or at least something which Artaxerxes supposed to have been a manifestation of the "wrath" of Heaven against "the realm of" his kingdom,—which was not that of war, for it was a time of "perfect peace" (Ezra vii. 12); but was this: About that "time there broke out a most grievous pestilence, which . . . spread itself throughout the whole Persian Empire." It was a very fatal disease,—"so that they either died in most cases on the ninth or seventh day, through the internal burning, while they had still some degree of strength; or, if they escaped that stage of the disorder, "the greater part were afterward carried off through the weakness occasioned by it." (*Thu.* b. ii. c. 49.) Artaxerxes considering this "most grievous pestilence" a manifestation of the "wrath" of God "against the realm of" his kingdom, was in anxiety to have things "done speedily" (Ezra vii. 21), —that is, that Ezra, going in haste to Jerusalem, "buy speedily" those things necessary in order to offer sacrifice. (Ezra vii. 17.) As the time this "most grievous pestilence" thus "spread itself throughout the whole Persian Empire" was about B.C. 431, this is an additional proof that this was the year Ezra went up to Jerusalem.

B.C. 431. ECLIPSE OF THE SUN.—(See p. 48.)

B.C. 431. THE INTERVAL.—According to our English copy of the book of Thucydides, there was an interval of fifty years between the expedition of Xerxes against Greece and the time of the Peloponnesian War. We have only about twenty-five years;* yet, since a different punctuation would give a different construction, this can hardly be considered as clashing with Thucydides; for the arrangement of the punctuation is not his, but one of a modern date. The difficulty is removed by punctuating it thus: "All these things the Greeks performed against one another and the barbarian, occurred in about fifty years." Thus, placing a full stop at "fifty years," we will commence a new sentence for the time "the Athenians established their empire on a firmer footing." Indeed this is the only way we can punctuate it so as to reconcile Thucydides with himself; for he tells us positively,—not that a part, but, emphatically,—"All these things the Greeks performed"—not only against one another, but also against "the barbarian—occurred in about fifty years." (*Thu.* b. i. c. 118.) And in another place he tells us that the war with "the barbarian" commenced ten years before the exedition of Xerxes. (*Thu.* b. i. c. 18.)

B.C. 426. THE TWENTY-THREE HUNDRED DAYS. — As these "twenty-three hundred days" were given in answer to "How long the vision?"—not a part, but the whole of the vision; both that of "the daily, and the transgression of desolation, to give both the sanctuary and the host to be trodden under foot" (Dan. viii. 13), —the "two thousand three hundred" must measure the whole duration of the vision commencing with the "pushing" of the the ram; hence, all that is necessary in order to learn the epoch from which they are to be dated, is to find the time at which the kingdom of Persia commenced that "pushing" as seen by Daniel in his vision. We have already at B.C. 488 observed that this "pushing" cannot be against kingdoms; for the ram was not as the goat running over the face of "the whole earth," but standing quietly "before the river Ulai;" and from the rise to the fall of the Persian Empire, there was no epoch at which the Persian power

* While those who follow Ptolemy's canon are reduced to the necessity, in so many ways, to contradict authors both sacred and profane, this is the first place that our chronology appears to come in contact with any author of that age.

was pushing against three different nations "westward, and northward, and southward," and at the same time standing quietly "at Shushan in the palace, which is in the province of Elam." (Dan. viii. 2–4.) The wars with other nations is something in which Daniel's people were but little concerned; but the "pushing" of the "ram" was against Daniel's people,—"I am come to make thee understand what shall befall thy people." From the expression, "Arise, devour much flesh" (Dan. vii. 5), it is evident this "pushing" was no ordinary expedition against other kingdoms; for the object of war is not to "devour much flesh," but to conquer with the loss of as few men as possible. In all the expeditions of the Persians against other kingdoms, the voice to do this came from the council of war; hence, from the Persian power; but the bloodthirsty voice which said, "Arise, devour much flesh," came not from the bear, but from the "three ribs in the mouth of it, between the teeth of it." (Dan. vii. 5.) Three ribs are but parts of a skeleton: so the voice must have come from the remains of some already ruined people who were at that time "between the teeth," ready to be crushed by the Persian power. From the book of Esther we learn that a voice for the slaughter of the whole Jewish nation, came from Haman (Est. iii. 9), who was but a skeleton, or the last of those Amalekites (*Jose. Ant.* b. xi. c. vi. s. 5), which had been "utterly destroyed" by Saul. (1 Sam. xv. 20.) As these ribs were between the teeth, we understand that they were crushed by the bear, and "they hanged Haman on the gallows." This is the last we hear of the Amalekites. "Amalek was the first of the nations, but his latter end shall be that he perish forever." (Num. xxiv. 20.) The time these "ribs"—the skeleton or remains of the already "utterly destroyed" Amalekites—"said thus unto it, Arise, devour much flesh," was after the bear had "raised up itself on one side," which is explained to mean that Persia "shall stir up all against the realm of Grecia." (Dan. xi. 2.) From this we leaan that the time the ribs said unto the bear, "Arise, devour much flesh," was after the expedition of Xerxes against Greece; hence, in the third year of Cyrus, Daniel's vision was in the future: "for yet the vision is for many days." (Dan. x. 14.) After this, Gabriel gave him the definite time, or told him the exact number of kings that should yet stand up in Persia before the time of the pushing of the ram: "And now will I show thee the truth. Behold" (notice this), "there shall stand up yet three kings in Persia" before the pushing as seen in the vision; hence, the pushing of the ram could not commence until after the death of Xerxes; and since from the reign of Cyrus there were but three kings to stand up before the beginning of the vision, the pushing must commence some time during the reign of Artaxerxes, the son of Xerxes; and it did not commence before "the seventh year of his reign;" for at the time Daniel saw the vision, the ram was standing quietly "before the river," which shows that this "pushing" occurred at a time when, the Persians having ceased from war, the king was "at Shushan in the palace which is in the province of Elam" (Dan. viii. 2); and it was not until "the seventh year of his reign" that "he made a release to the provinces" (Est. ii. 18), or, ceasing from war, suffered the soldiers to return to their several homes,—this was a time of "perfect peace" (Ezra vii. 12); and about five years after this,—that is, "in the twelfth year of King Ahasuerus,"—this pushing commenced for the slaughter of the whole Jewish nation.

For the covenience of the reader we here place the vision and interpretations in opposite columns:—

THE VISION.	THE INTERPRETATION.
The bear "raised up itself on one side."	"He shall stir up all against the realm of Grecia."
"There stood before the river a ram."	"Perfect peace; and at such a time" the king "made a release to the provinces."
The bear had "three ribs in the mouth of it, between the teeth of it."	Haman, who was but a skeleton, or the last remains of "the Amalekites," was in the Persian power.
As these ribs were "between the teeth," we understand that they were crushed.	"They hanged Haman on the gallows."
"And they" (the ribs) "said thus unto it, Arise, devour much flesh."	"And Haman said unto King Ahasuerus," "Let it be written that they may be destroyed."

"I saw the ram pushing westward, and northward, and southward; so that no soul might stand before him."

"The post went out, being hastened by the king's commandment," "into all the king's provinces, to destroy, to kill, and to cause to perish all Jews, both young and old, little children and women in one day."

"Neither was there any that could deliver out of his hand."

Even Esther the queen in the king's palace was not exempt.

"And it came to pass when I saw" *the ram*, "that I" *saw him* "at Shushan the palace, which is in the province of Elam."

"And the decree was given in Shushan the palace."

"But he did according to his will."

Which will was to save Daniel's people from pending ruin. "Write ye also for the Jews."

"And became great."

"Great among the Jews."

Some commence the twenty-three hundred days in the seventh year of Artaxerxes; but the powers of Persia were at that time pushing neither against the Jews, nor other nations; for the king had just made a release to the provinces; hence, war had then ceased in Persia; and so far from pushing against Daniel's people, Artaxerxes granted them a great favor, even that of returning to their homes. Since the twenty-three hundred days were given in answer to the question, "How long the vision?"—"the daily" or "continual heathen persecution" "and the transgression of desolation,"—how unreasonable to suppose that they are to commence with the very reverse of this, or with the time the Jews were delivered from heathen oppression, when "all they of the people of Israel" were granted the privilege of returning home and enjoying their former privilege of all things "whatsoever is commanded by the God of heaven." (Ezra vii. 13.) Others date the beginning of the twenty-three hundred days from the time of the expedition of Xerxes against Greece,—the incorrectness of which is evident from the following reasons:—

1. The ram, at the time Daniel saw him "pushing," "stood before the river Ulai; from which we learn the king was at that time "at Shushan in the palace." But at the time of the expedition, Xerxes, he, having left Shushan, was in Greece.

2. The ram was not pushing at the goat; but "pushing westward, and northward, and southward."

3. Daniel did not see the goat until, the ram having ceased its pushing, he "was considering the matter."

4. The ram did not leave the river and go towards the goat; but the goat came to the ram.

5. The ram was "pushing westward, and northward, and southward;" but the expedition against Greece was only a "westward" pushing.

6. Against the pushing, Daniel saw "no soul might stand before;" but the Greeks stood before Xerxes, and he was shamefully defeated; and Daniel declares that "the rough goat," which "is the kingdom of Grecia," not only stood before the ram, but did "break his two horns, and there was no power in the ram to stand before him." This proves that the expedition of Xerxes against Greece was not the pushing of the ram. At B.C. 488 we have remarked that among all the Kings of Persia there was not one before whom some nation was not enabled to stand; hence, this pushing cannot mean an expedition against kingdoms, but was against Daniel's people.

7. If the "pushing" of the ram was against kingdoms, then the pushing must be the means by which the ram became "great;" but so far from the Persian Empire becoming great by Xerxes's expedition against Greece, this dates its decline and fall.

Whether by the expression, "pushing," we understand only an ordinary expedition against the kingdoms of earth, or that most awful pushing for the slaughter of all God's chosen people, which was the greatest effort ever made on earth to frustrate and over turn the purposes of Heaven, one thing is certain,—the twenty-three hundred days are to be dated from the beginning of the "pushing;" for the question was: "How long the vision?"—not a part, but the whole vision; if, therefore, the pushing is against kingdoms, the twenty-three hundred days must be reckoned from the rise of the kingdom of the Medes; but they cannot be dated from the beginning of that kingdom; for the vision was concerning that which was in the future, while the rise of the kingdom of the Medes was one hundred and sixty-four years before Daniel saw the vision. "The ram which Daniel saw was the Kings of

Media and Persia" (Dan. viii. 20), and "the reign of the Kings of Persia" did not begin until after the fall of Babylon (2 Chron. xxxvi. 20); hence, the pushing, as seen by Daniel, did not take place before the end of that kingdom; and from the time of the ruin of Babylon there was no "pushing" of the Medes and Persians against other kingdoms that can answer to the description as given by Daniel: "I saw the ram pushing westward, and northward, and southward, so that no beast might stand before him, neither was there any that could deliver out of his hand; but he did according to his will, and became great." The first pushing after the fall of Babylon, which was after the rise of the second horn, or the beginning of "the reign of the Kings of Persia" (2 Chron. xxxvi. 20), was that of Cyrus against the Scythians; and so far from this nation being unable to stand before the ram, the greater part of the Persians were slain. And "immediately on Cyrus's death, his sons fell into dissension; cities and nations revolted; every thing tended to ruin." (*Xen.* p. 150.) If "cities and nations revolted," then there were some that "could deliver out of his hand;" and if "every thing tended to ruin," the Persian power did not in a national sense "become great." So far from becoming "great," Cambyses lost his kingdom by an impostor, at which time it passed out of the family of Cyrus into the hands of the Magi. After the slaughter of the Magi, Darius, the son of Hystaspes, obtained the kingdom. The first pushing worthy of notice during his reign, was that of his expedition against the Scythians; and so far from their being unable to "stand before him," but for the favor of "Histiacus, tyrant of Miletus," this "would have been an end of the Persian" kingdom. (*Herod.* b. vii. c. 10.) As this aid came not from the Persians, we here discover the ram so completely overpowered, that he must have been slain but for foreign aid. The Persians said: "It is painful to repeat, and afflicting to remember, that the safety of our prince and his dominion depended on a single man." (*Herod.* b. vii. c. 10.) But for foreign aid the ram could have had no power to deliver himself out of the hand of the Scythians, —just the reverse of what Daniel saw. After this, Darius undertook an expedition against the Greeks, who were not only able to "stand before him," but they drove him out of Greece with the loss of "six thousand and four hundred men." On the death of Darius his son Xerxes ascended the throne. He invaded Greece with the largest army the world has ever known; but even against this effort, embracing the entire strength of Persia, the little band of Greeks stood so boldly that the ram received that fatal blow from which he never recovered. The exalted pride of the Persians was completely humbled, insomuch that their king fled from Greece, and, "renouncing all thoughts of war and conquest, abandoned himself entirely to luxury and ease" (*Rol.*), which epoch dates the decline and fall of the Persian kingdom.

We have, in the first place, proven that the pushing, as seen by Daniel, could not have taken place before the fall of Babylon; and, in the second place, that since that time there has been no pushing of the Persian power against other kingdoms that can answer to that seen by Daniel. So we are now compelled to admit with Gabriel that the pushing which Daniel saw was something concerning his people: "I am come to make thee understand what shall befall thy people;" and the only pushing of the power of Persia against the Jews which in every particular answers to his description, was that of the pushing of the authority of Persia for the slaughter of the whole Jewish nation. In this Daniel's people were more concerned than in all the wars or pushing against nations since the creation of the world. In commemoration of that awful event, an annual festival was enjoined, "that these days should be remembered and kept throughout every generation" (Est. ix. 28), which festival is observed by the Jews even to the present day.

Those heralds which thus went pushing throughout all the Persian Empire for the slaughter of Daniel's people were even by the Persians considered as more worthy of regard than their most prominent warriors. "Homer more than once calls them the sacred ministers of God and man." "The functions they were to perform were the most important possible: and they were on all occasions regarded as sacred." "They denounce war and proclaim peace." Such was the so-considered sacred authority with which they were invested, they even passed among the armed troops of Cambyses, that most cruel King of Persia, "ordering them to obey Smerdis, the son of Cyrus alone," which "orders were everywhere obeyed." (*Herod.* b. iii. c. 61.) Daniel may well have called these Persian heralds a "pushing;" for, says Herodotus, they "travel with a velocity which nothing human can equal." The proper meaning of the original Hebrew, which our translators have rendered, "no beast might stand before him," is that "no soul could stand before him;" and this place should have been thus translated. To say "no beast might stand before him," is to contradict ver. 7; for the goat did stand before him. And according to this, the correct translation, the "pushing" of the ram will answer to nothing but the decree for the slaughter of the whole Jewish nation; for in all the pushing of the Persians against any people, this was the only time at which "no soul could stand," or at which the decree was for the slaughter of every individual. On this occasion it was literally true "no soul could stand;" every individual was to be destroyed, "both young and old, little children and women,"—even unto the queen; for it was said: "Thou shalt not escape in the king's house." (Est. iv. 13.) "Neither was there any that could deliver them out of his hand." But though it had thus been said to him, "Arise, devour much flesh," "he did according to his will," in that he destroyed them not. As "the decree was given in Shushan the palace," the ram was therefore properly standing "before the river Ulai, pushing westward, and northward, and southward, so that no soul could stand before him." There being no Jews east of Persia, nothing is said about any pushing in that direction. Hence, in this decree for the slaughter of the Jews, every "jot" and "tittle" was literally accomplished.

And now "were the king's scribes called on the thirteenth day of the first month," "in the the twelfth year of King Ahasuerus" (Est. iii. 7, 12),—that is, on Saturday, March 27, B.C. 426. If we allow them one full day to write out the king's orders "to the governors" and "rulers" in the "hundred and seven and twenty provinces," we will have Monday the 15th of the first month for the day on which this pushing commenced; and that this is strictly correct to the very day, we prove thus: Daniel was informed that "seventy weeks are determined;" or, if properly translated, "cut off" of the 2300 days. In 70 weeks there are 490 years; and if to 426 we add 65 diminished by 1, we will have 490; so the 70 weeks cut off of the 2300, ends on the 15th of the first month, A.D. 65,—the time at which the Seven-years War commenced at Jerusalem. And now "the prince that shall come shall destroy the city and the sanctuary;" "and he shall confirm the covenant"—that is, covenant of vengeance (Dan. ix. 12)—"with many for one week" (Dan. ix. 27), or 7 years; this 7 years added to 65 gives the 15th of the first month, A.D. 72 for the end of the seven-years covenant of wrath. According to Josephus, this was the day and year in which the war ended at Jerusalem, which proves that we have the correct epoch,—not only as to the year, but the very day on which the 2300 days are to be commenced,—that is, on the 15th "day of the first month," Monday, March 29, B.C. 426, or A.M. 3700, to which, if we add 2300, we have 6000; hence, the great Sabbath of rest begins as soon as the sanctuary is duly cleansed. As some have supposed that the "seventy weeks" of Daniel ix. 24 end at the time of the crucifixion, it is necessary to meet this error. 1. The "seventy-weeks are determined" or "cut off" "upon" Daniel's "people;" and they continued as a people, having the privilege of observing their own laws until the destruction of Jerusalem by the Romans. 2. The "seventy weeks" were also to measure the length of time as "determined," or "cut off" "upon" Daniel's "holy city," which city was not destroyed until about forty years after the crucifixion. This makes it clear that the "seventy weeks" did not end before the beginning of the war, which was in A.D. 65.

Gabriel informed Daniel that "in the first year of Darius" he "stood to confirm and to strengthen" Michael (Dan. xi. 1; x. 21); and the word of Michael, which Gabriel did "confirm and strengthen," was the 2300 days. This he confirmed and strengthened by adding an additional number of "seventy weeks," or 490 years, ending with the destruction of the "holy city" and ruin of Daniel's "people." This greatly strengthens and confirms the correctness of the 2300 days, by showing that when the "holy city" shall be destroyed, 490 years of the 2300 days will have been "cut off," or passed away; hence, from that time there remains but 1810 to be accomplished; and since he "shall confirm the covenant with many for one week" in the Seven-years War, the 70 weeks must end with the beginning of the one week in A.D. 65. The following diagram will make it clear to the reader how the "seventy weeks" confirm and strengthen the 2300 days.

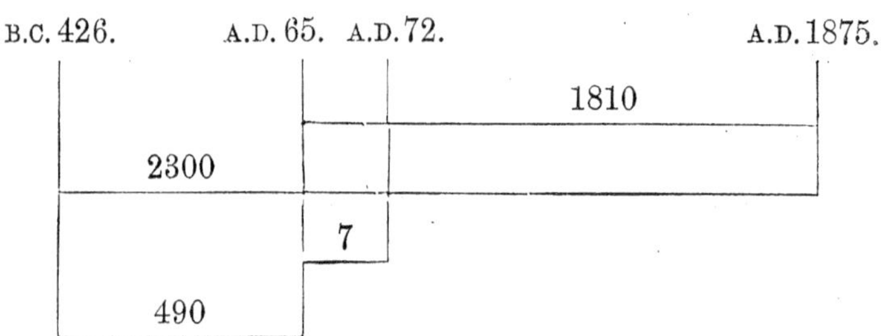

The above diagram is too plain to need any explanation. The reader will notice that in A.D. 65 the 490 years were cut off of the 2300; from which time there remains but 1810 to be accomplished. While the book of Daniel was yet sealed, it was supposed that the seventy weeks commenced with "the going forth of the commandment to restore and to build Jerusalem;" but

Daniel was informed that the "seventy weeks are cut off" of the 2300 days; hence, they commence with the 2300; and as the days measure the length of the vision, they cannot commence until the time the vision began, which "vision," "in the third year of Cyrus," was "yet" "many days" in the future. "The word which is translated 'determined,' is found only in Daniel ix. 24. Not another instance of its use can be traced in the Hebrew Testament. It has the single signification of *cutting*, or *cutting off*." (*Hale.*)

B.C. 425. THE DAY-YEAR SYSTEM.—Some of those who have paid but little attention to prophetic dates are not yet satisfied as to the authority for believing that each day in Daniel's vision signifies so many years, which makes it necessary to establish this.

The weeks as mentioned in Daniel (ix. 24, 25) are by all—both Jew and Gentile—admitted to be weeks of years; but if they are years, why not the days? In the same way that they are proven to be weeks of years, we can prove the days to signify years. For example, it is said: "the days." But of what kind? "The days of the years." Here each one represented a year; for "the days of the years" were "a hundred threescore and fifteen years." (Gen. xxv. 7.) Pharaoh said unto Jacob, "How many are the days of the years of thy life?" (Heb.) "And Jacob said unto Pharaoh, the days of the years of my pilgrimage are a hundred and thirty years." (Gen. xlvii. 8, 9.) In prophecy, each day was taken for a year, thus: "After the number of the days in which ye searched the land, even forty days, each day for a year, shall ye bear your iniquities, even forty years." (Num. xiv. 34.) It is said in Ezekiel: "Thou shalt bear the iniquity of the house of Judah forty days. I have appointed thee each day for a year" (Ezek. iv, 6); and in Genesis (vi. 3), "His days shall be an hundred and twenty years." This is sufficient to prove that days were sometimes used to signify years.

Daniel's vision is given in symbolic language; hence, those days which measure the length of the vision are symbols representing years. If "the ten horns" represent "ten kings," the 2300 days must be so many years, or they would bear no resemblance to the vision with which they are connected. It is morally impossible that they can be literal days, for they were to span the whole duration of Daniel's vision. "How long the vision?" "Unto two thousand and three hundred days." King James's translators have obscured the force of this argument by supplying two words, "concerning" and "sacrifice." The only argument that can favor the literal day system, is the supposition that those translators were justifiable in this; but we shall now proceed to prove that hese words should not have been supplied.

1. The question asked was concerning that which Daniel had seen in his vision; and he had seen nothing concerning the Jewish sacrifice.

2. Though it is true the Jews offered a sacrifice, morning and evening, "day by day, continually" (Ex. xxix. 38), the expression "daily sacrifice," is not found in the Bible; nor is the term expressive of the Jewish sacrifices and offerings in general; for it restricts us to that sacrifice which was offered daily; but the larger portion of the Jewish sacrifices and offerings were not made daily. Had reference here been made to the Jewish sacrifice, the simple expression, "sacrifice and oblation," as in Daniel ix. 27, with the omission of the word, "daily," would have been much clearer.

3. Since, in the more than four hundred times that reference is made in the Bible to sacrifices and offerings, the express word is in every case used, is it not strange that it is here not only omitted, but a word used five times (Dan. viii. 11–13; xi. 31; xii. 11) which, if placed in connection with the word, "sacrifice," would so limit its meaning that it could no more embrace the Jewish sacrifices?

4. This marking the epoch from which such an important period is to be reckoned, there is not another place in the Bible where it was so necessary to have used the word, if the Jewish sacrifice was meant; yet "sacrifice" is not only omitted here, but a term is used in each instance which cannot apply to their sacrifices. If allusion was here made to the Jewish sacrifice, we must admit with the Church of Rome, that Antiochus was the hero of Daniel's vision, and that the 2300 days, during which the sanctuary lay desolate, transpired during his reign. With this admission, the ques- asked would stand thus: "How long shall be the vision concerning the daily sacrifice and the transgression of desolation to give both the sanctuary and the host to be trodden under foot? Hence, the 2300 days must begin with the ceasing to offer the "daily sacrifice," which was on "the fifteenth day of the month Chasleu in the hundred and forty-fifth year" (1 Mac. i. 54),—December 17, B.C. 168. The sanctuary was cleansed "on the twenty-fifth day of the" same month "in the hundred and forty-eighth year" (1 Mac. iv. 52),—December 24, B.C. 165. The interval is 1103 days, wanting 1197 of making out the 2300. Colver in attempting to solve this difficulty, supposed that the 2300 days may be reckoned from the time some of the Jews, forsaking the religion of their fathers, fell

into heathen idolatry (1 Mac. i. 11); but he is here at variance with himself. He tells us in the first place to "Mark well this inquiry. It is not how long shall be the time for every thing that Daniel saw in the vision, but 'How long shall be the vision concerning the daily sacrifice?'" The reason which he gives for supposing the 2300 are literal days, necessarily restricts him to the time they ceased to offer the sacrifice for their beginning. All who suppose the 2300 to be literal days, understand Antiochus to be the "little horn" of Daniel's prophecy; and since "by him the daily sacrifice was taken away" (Dan. viii. 11), we cannot begin the 2300 days before he commenced the war with the Jews; for it was by force of arms that he was to "take away the daily sacrifice." (Dan. xi. 31.) Antiochus commenced the war with the Jews "in the hundred and forty-third year" (1 Mac. i. 20), which begins with September, B.C. 170; and the sanctuary was cleansed December 24, B.C. 165. In this interval there were 1940 days, which is all we can get even upon the supposition that Antiochus, leaving Egypt upon the first of the one hundred and forty-third year, reached Jerusalem, and, on the same day caused "the daily sacrifice" to cease. This, the utmost limit to which we can go, yet wants 360 days to make out the 2300. Can this be received as a literal fulfillment of the word of God? We have only given this extreme view to show the impossibility of accomplishing the 2300 days here. By referring to Maccabees, it will be seen that Antiochus commenced the war with the Jews "in the hundred and forty-third year,"—that is, between September, B.C. 170, and September, B.C. 169; "and after two years fully expired, he sent his chief collector of tribute unto the cities of Judah, who came unto Jerusalem with a great multitude, and caused the sacrifice to cease on the fifteenth day of" the ninth month; "for the kings had sent letters by messengers unto Jerusalem and the cities of Judah that they should follow the strange laws of the heathen, and forbid burnt-offerings, and sacrifices, and drink-offerings, in the temple." (1 Mac. i. 45). Hence, they ceased to offer sacrifices for only 1103 days. The 2300 days having never been fulfilled in literal days, it is certain they must be in so many years. Again, it is said: "From the time the daily sacrifice shall be taken away, and the abomination that maketh desolate set up, there shall be twelve hundred and ninety days." Antiochus "set up the abomination of desolation" in the "fifteenth day of the month Chasleu, in the hundred and forty-fifth year" (1 Mac. i. 54), December 17, B.C. 168; and the sanctuary was cleansed "on the twenty-fifth day of the ninth month," "in the hundred and forty-eighth year,"—December 24, B.C. 165,—an interval of only 1103 days. We here want 187 days to complete the 1290, and lack 232 of the 1335 days. Those who contend that the vision of Daniel was fulfilled here, are restricted to 1103 days,—*first* for the accomplishment of Daniel's 2300 days; *second*, for his 1290 days; *third*, for his 1335 days; *fourth*, for his "time, times, and a half," which cannot be less than 1269 days. Out of the four prophetic periods there is not one that can be accomplished within the limits of 1103 days. If rejecting the authority of Josephus and Maccabees as to dates, it is contended that the days in Daniel's vision are to be understood as such, we will here prove that they never have been, nor never can be, accomplished in literal days. If rejecting what has been supplied by man, we adhere alone to the word of God, the 2300 days must span, not a part, but the whole duration of the vision; hence, must be 2300 years. But since some prefer being governed more by that which was supplied by man, we will try that. "And from the time the daily sacrifice shall be taken away," "there shall be a thousand two hundred and ninety days;" but in answer to "How long the vision?" concerning the daily sacrifice, it was said, "unto two thousand three hundred days." As it is impossible to reconcile these two dates without the omission of the words, "concerning" and "sacrifice," it is clear they never should have been added; and with their omission we are compelled to admit that the 2300 days represent 2300 years. And since Daniel is not yet standing in the lot of his inheritance, it is certain that the 1335 days are to be understood as years. Colver supposes that they were to reach the death of Antiochus, just 45 days after the end of the 1290, though, says he, "The precise date of the death of Antiochus, we have not the means of knowing." It is true that the exact day of his death is not given, but the year is,—"King Antiochus died in the hundred and forty-ninth year." (1 Mac. vi. 16.) From the 25th of the month Chasleu, in the 148th year to the beginning of the 149th, there were 250 days. If Antiochus had died in the 1st of the 149th year, the time of his death would yet be 205 days over the 45 which, Colver says, reaches the time of his death. His death, however, was more of a curse than a blessing to the Jews; for in his affliction he "vowed unto the Lord that the holy city he would set at liberty, and the holy temple he would garnish with goodly gifts, and restore all of the holy vessels, with many more, and out of his own revenue defray the charges belonging to the sacrifices; yea, and that also he would become a Jew himself, and go through all the world that was inhabited and declare the power of God." (2 Mac. ix. 13–17.) After his death, the Jews complained of more hardships, or "a greater affliction" (1 Mac. ix. 27); the largest army that had ever invaded the land of Israel then came; and Nicanor, "a man that bare a deadly hatred unto Israel," was sent "with commandment to destroy the people" of Israel; (2 Mac. vii. 26), who "sware in his wrath," saying, "I will burn up this house,"—that is, the temple. Instead of the calamities which at that time befell the Jews, ceasing at the end of 1335 days, they continued 27 years. (Compare 1 Mac. i. 20 with xiii. 41.)

But even if at the end of the 45 days from the time the sanctuary was cleansed the Jews had enjoyed a time of the greatest prosperity and happiness ever known on earth, the fact that Daniel is not yet standing in "the lot of his inheritance" (Ps. cv. 11) would prove that we have not reached the end of the 1335 days.

We will now show that Antiochus was not the hero of Daniel's prophecy:—

1. The "little horn" came "out of one of "the "four notable" horns (Dan. viii. 9); hence, was a fifth horn or kingdom. But Antiochus constituted no new kingdom; for his continued to be one of the four,—that is, the Syrian kingdom.

2. This was at first a "little horn which waxed exceeding great" (Dan. viii. 9); but Antiochus "did not enlarge" his kingdom.

3. The little horn was to arise "in the latter time of" the kingdom of the four horns (Dan. viii. 23); but Antiochus was not in the latter time of these kingdoms; for he was "the eighth in the Syrian line of kings," which numbered twenty-five.

4. The little horn was to arise "when the transgressors are come to the full" (Dan. viii. 23); and the space of time as allowed "to finish the transgression" (Dan. ix. 24), did not end until about 228 years after the death of Antiochus.

5. It is said of this horn: "his power shall be mighty." (Dan. viii. 24.) Antiochus, being "tributary to the Romans," had no mighty power.

6. Though his power was mighty, it "was not by his own power" (Dan. viii. 24.) But what power Antiochus had was properly his own; for he had no aid from other nations.

7. "And he shall destroy wonderfully." (Dan. viii. 24.) It is said that Antiochus destroyed "about eighty thousand Jews;" but Rome, in a single siege, destroyed 1,100,000.

8. And he "shall prosper and practice" (Dan. viii. 24); but such was the reverse of prosperity with Antiochus: "He was astonished

and moved; whereupon he laid him down upon his bed, and fell sick for grief because it had not befallen him as he looked for." (1 Mac. vi. 8.)

9. He "shall destroy the mighty and the holy people" (Dan. viii. 24); which people were not destroyed under 230 years after the death of Antiochus.

10. "And by peace shall destroy many." (Dan. viii. 25.) Antiochus destroyed none "by peace."

11. "He shall also stand up against the Prince of princes" (Dan. viii. 25); but Antiochus died 158 years before the Prince of princes was born.

12. By this horn, "the place of the sanctuary was cast down." (Dan. viii. 11.) Antiochus left it standing.

13. "The people" of the prince were to "cast down the place of the sanctuary" at the end of the "seventy weeks" (Dan. ix. 24–26), which was more than 230 years after the death of Antiochus.

14. "And the king shall do according to his will." (Dan. xi. 36.) When he made an expedition against Egypt because he had a desire to gain it, "he was driven out of all Egypt by the declaration of the Romans, who charged him to let that country alone" (*Jose. Ant.* b. xii. c. v. s. 2); and when he desired to rob the city "Elymaius, in the country of Persia," they "rose up against him in battle; so he fled, and departed thence with great heaviness" (1 Mac. vi. 3, 44); also his "armies which went against the land of Judea were put to flight." (1 Mac. vi. 5.)

15. The kingdom of Persia which extended "from India even unto Ethiopia over a hundred and seven and twenty provinces" (Est. i. 1) is only called "*great*" (Dan. viii. 4); and Grecia, the "third kingdom" which bare rule over all the earth" (Dan. ii. 39), is called "VERY GREAT" (Dan. viii. 8); but this little horn "waxed EXCEEDING GREAT." (Dan. viii. 9.) Can Antiochus, the King of Syria, who was "tributary to the Romans all of his days," be considered greater than the kingdoms of Persia and Greece? So far from Antiochus having "waxed exceeding great toward the south, and toward the east, and toward the pleasant land" (Dan. viii. 9), the very reverse was the truth. He became so very weak "he feared that he should not be able to bare the charges any longer;" "wherefore, being greatly perplexed in his mind he determined to go into Persia, there to take the tribute of the countries, and to gather money" (1 Mac. iii. 30); "but he was not able, because they of the city" "rose up against him in battle; so he fled and departed thence with great heaviness, and returned to

Babylon" and there died, saying, "Behold, I perish through great grief in a strange land." And why? Only because of the extreme weakness to which his kingdom was reduced in that he was no longer able to carry out his ambitious designs against the Jews. Because of this, his weakness, he "fell sick for grief," saying, "I thought with myself into what tribulation am I come, and how great a flood of misery is it wherein now I am." (1 Mac. vi. 1–16.)

Since it is so very clear that Antiochus cannot be the hero of Daniel's vision, the opinion that the dates are to be understood as literal days is forever exploded; for none of those who understand them as literal days ever pretend to place their accomplishment anywhere else. That the abomination of desolation, as mentioned in Daniel, was something yet future, in the day of our Saviour's incarnation, see Matthew xxiv. 15.

B.C. 423. DARIUS NOTHUS.—The twentieth year of the Peloponnesian War commenced in the spring of B.C. 412; and according to Thucydides, "the thirteenth year of the reign of Darius" synchronized with the twentieth year of the war. (*Thu.* b. viii. c. 58.) This gives the spring of B.C. 424 for the beginning of the reign of Darius Nothus. According to Thucydides, his father Artaxerxes died during the winter of the seventh year of the war,—that is, B.C. 425; but since Thucydides lived more than 1800 miles from Persia, and this was during the war, at which time there was but little communication with other countries, it is possible he might have been mistaken in this, especially when we notice the source whence he received his information, which was from those who accompanied Artaphernes to Ephesus. Had those ambassadors gone to Susa, and there from good authority learned that Artaxerxes was dead, we would feel disposed to credit their statement; but when they frankly acknowledge that they only went "to Ephesus," and, "on hearing there that King Artaxerxes, son of Xerxes, was lately dead, they returned home" (*Thu.* b. iv. c. 50), we are under no obligation to credit that which was a mere rumor while we have overwhelming authority to the contrary. Let us, in the first place, inquire as to what gave rise to this rumor concerning the death of Artaxerxes. By reference to the book of Esther, we learn that "in the twelfth year of King" Artaxerxes,—that is, B.C. 426,—"letters were sent by post into all the king's provinces, to destroy, to kill, and to cause to perish all Jews, both young and old, little children and women, in one day,—even "upon the thirteenth day of the twelfth month,"—Tuesday, the 15th of February, B.C. 425; but though the law of the Medes and Persians was irrevocable, we find just the reverse of the thing carried out. "The king granted the Jews which were in every city to gather themselves together, and to stand for their life, to destroy, to slay, and to cause to perish, all the power of the people and province that would assault them;" and they "slew of their foes seventy-five thousand;" and since "the writing which is written in the king's name, and sealed with the king's ring, may no man reverse" (Est. viii. 8), had not the people throughout the Persian Empire a good reason for believing that the king, who issued the first decree for the slaughter of the whole Jewish nation, was now dead, and that this second edict to reverse the former was issued by another king? And as this happened only seven or eight months before those Athenians reached Ephesus who told Thucydides that Artaxerxes was dead, it was just about the time for such a rumor to be in circulation. But the truth is that, instead of Artaxerxes, it was Haman who was dead. As he was then in "great authority," as the business of the kingdom was transacted through him, we must suppose that he was the person who sent Artaphernes to Greece; and since Artaphernes was taken up "at Eion on the Strymon," in Macedonia (*Thu.* b. iv. c. 50), the natural inference is that the secret mission on which Haman had sent him into Macedonia, was to carry out his design "to have translated the kingdom of the Persians to the Macedonians." (Apoc. Est. xvi. 14.) This accounts for Artaphernes sending the Athenian ambassadors back as soon as he discovered that Haman's design was thwarted; but we are unable to see how the mere death of Artaxerxes could have been a sufficient reason for sending them back, as his son could have carried out the designs of his father.

Artaxerxes having preferred a retired life, in B.C. 424, associated his son Darius with him in the kingdom, to whom he committed its business affairs. It is possible, therefore, that not only the Greeks, but a large portion of the Persian Empire was under the impression that Artaxerxes was dead; for the Persian kings were but seldom seen in public. If the Magi could ascend the throne, and continue there seven months before the imposition was discovered even at Susa, surely there is no mystery in the Greeks belonging to another kingdom 1800 miles distant, supposing that Artaxerxes was dead, since, transferring the management of the kingdom into the hands of his son Darius, he had retired to Babylon to spend his days in a more private repose. (Neh. xiii. 6.) The true reason why the Greeks continued under the impression that Artaxerxes was dead, may be inferred from what Thucydides says:—"Men receive alike without examination from each other the reports of past events, even though they may have happened in their own country. For instance: the mass of the Athenians think that Hipparchus was tyrant when he was slain by Harmedius and Aristogiton, and do not know that Hippias held the government as being the eldest of the sons of Pisistratus." (*Thu.* b.i. c.20.) If the Greeks did not know their own king or tyrant, ought it to be considered strange that they supposed the King of Persia was dead from the fact that his own son had the management of the kingdom?

Having noticed the origin of the rumor as to the death of Artaxerxes, and the reason as to why the Greeks continued to believe that he was dead, we will now call attention to the fact that while we have pointed out so many places in which Ptolemy's canon contradicts not only profane, but sacred authors, this is the first place in which our chronology brings us in direct contact with any writer of that age; but in order to establish Ptolemy's canon, its supporters are forced to suppose that this same author was mistaken in another place, and concerning that in which it is much harder to believe that he could have been in error,—which is the flight of Themistocles, who was a renowned Athenian general; and it is hard to believe that Thucydides could have been mistaken as to that in which all the Greeks were so much concerned.

We admit that Ptolemy's method of arranging the Kings of Persia appears to be the most plausible, and the method we would all follow, had we no good reason for a different one; but a mere supposition ought not to outweigh a historical fact. It is impossible to reconcile Josephus with Nehemiah, but upon the supposition that Artaxerxes associated Darius with him in the kingdom; for while Nehemiah informs us that he "found a register" in which was "recorded" the "chief of the fathers, also the priests, to the reign of Darius the Persian," Josephus affirms that none of the sacred writings were written after the day of Artaxerxes. Again: to reconcile Nehemiah with Ptolemy, we must admit that Artaxerxes associated his son with him in the kingdom; for he returned to the "King of Babylon" in the thirty-second year of his reign: "and after certain days obtained I leave of the king, and I came to Jerusalem." (Neh. xiii. 6.) Hence, it was not later than the thirty-third year of Artaxerxes when he went the second time to Jerusalem;" and he speaks of "the reign of Darius the Persian" (Neh. xii. 22), as having commenced before that; but according to

Ptolemy, Artaxerxes reigned forty-one years. To make this agree with the opinion that Artaxerxes did not thus associate Darius with him, Prideaux says this "was never written by Nehemiah, but is an interpolation there inserted long after his death;" but this contradicts Josephus again, who, declaring that no part of the sacred canon was written after the day of Artaxerxes, says: "No one hath been so bold as either to add any thing" to the sacred writings or "to take any thing from them, or to make any change in them."

Nehemiah only claims to bring the history of the Levites down to the days of Eliashib. This catalogue is headed: "The Levites in the days of Eliashib." Their names are then added, which are, "Jehoiada, and Johanan, and Jadua." Nehemiah informs us that these three men were "recorded chief of the fathers in the days of Eliashib." He also mentions that they were "the priests,"—not high-priests, but "priests to," or in, "the reign of Darius the Persian." (Neh. xii. 22.) That Artaxerxes did associate his son with him, we can further prove by the age of Sanballat. Having had a daughter married as early as the thirty-second of Artaxerxes (Neh. xiii. 28), he must at that time have been at least thirty-six years old. Admitting that he was then only thirty-six, he would, according to Ptolemy's canon, have been one hundred and thirty-seven in B.C. 332, when, according to Josephus, he died. Hence, Ptolemy's advocates have here again to contradict Josephus, or to say, in the milder terms of Prideaux, "The true answer to this matter is Josephus was mistaken."

As this was not the first Darius who had reigned in Persia, there must be some reason for the expression, "Darius the Persian," which was this: Artaxerxes, having placed his son Darius on the throne, and having himself removed to Babylon, they were thus distinguished: "Darius, the Persian" (Neh. xii. 22), and "Artaxerxes, King of Babylon" (Neh. xiii. 6.) According to Ptolemy, Darius reigned nineteen years; this brings us to B.C. 405; from which epoch we have no further dispute with chronologists. Though beyond this period we have been compelled to come in direct contact with what was considered the settled opinion of the world, in so doing, we have strictly followed the best authorities on earth,—the Bible, Astronomy, and those historians who lived at the time the things happened of which they wrote. And thus our chronology is settled.

B.C. 418. NEHEMIAH WENT UP TO JERUSALEM.—In the twentieth year of Artaxerxes, Nehemiah was granted the privilege of building the wall of Jerusalem, which was finished in the twenty and fifth day of the month Elul, in fifty and two days" from the time they "returned every one unto his work" on "the wall" (Neh. iv. 15); for Nehemiah informs us that he "continued in the work of this wall from the twentieth year even unto the two and thirtieth year of Artaxerxes, the king; that is, twelve years." (Neh. v. 14, 16.)

B.C. 406. THE COMPLETION OF THE WALL.—At B.C. 418 we observed that the wall of Jerusalem "was finished in the twenty and fifth day of the month Elul" (Neh. vi. 15) in the thirty-second year of Artaxerxes,—that is, on Wednesday, August 28, B.C. 406. Daniel was informed that the "street shall be built again and the wall even in troublous times," which was literally true; for "they which builded on the wall, with one of his hands wrought in the work, and with the other hand held a weapon." (Neh. iv. 17.) He was also informed that "after threescore and two weeks" after the wall's completion, the "Messiah" would "be cut off." (Dan. ix. 26.) In "threescore and two weeks" there are 434 years. The Julian period for B.C. 406 is 4308, to which, if we add 434, we have 4742,—the Julian period for A.D. 29; hence, the "threescore and two weeks" end on the 25th of the sixth month, A.D. 29. Six months and eighteen days after this our Lord was crucified, which answers to the expression, "after threescore and two weeks."

B.C. 312. ERA OF THE SELEUCIDÆ.—This era dates from September 1, B.C. 312.

B.C. 163. SABBATICAL YEAR.—The one hundred and fiftieth year of the Seleucidæ was a sabbatical year. (See 1 Mac. vi. 20, 49, 53.

B.C. 135. SABBATICAL YEAR.—By comparing 1 Mac. xvi. 14 with *Jose. Ant.* xiii. c. viii. s. 1, it will be seen that the one hundred and seventy-eighth year of the Seleucidæ was a sabbatical year.

B.C. 41. HEROD: HIS FIRST YEAR.—"On the taking of Jerusalem, Hèrod was put in thorough possession of the kingdom of Judea." (*Prid.*) From this epoch, he reigned thirty-seven years. (*Jose. Ant.* b. xvii. c. viii. s. 1.)

B.C. 37. SABBATICAL YEAR.—According to Josephus, the third year of the one hundred and eighty-fifth Olympiad was a sabbatical year. (*Jose. Ant.* b. xiv. c. xvi. s. 4; b. xv. c. i. s. 2.)

B.C. 5. THE BIRTH OF CHRIST.—E. Robinson says:—"The birth of Christ cannot in any case be fixed later than the autumn of B.C. 5." If we may be allowed to adhere strictly to the language of inspiration, we can get not only the year, but the month and day of the birth of Christ,—thus: We have remarked that the Babylonish captivity commenced on the 10th of the fifth month, B.C. 558. And the Lord said: "After seventy years be accomplished at Babylon, I will visit you and perform my good word towards you in causing you to return to this place." (Jer. xxix. 10.) If to the day the word of God was strictly fulfilled, "the commandment to restore and to build Jerusalem" went forth on the 10th of the fifth month, B.C. 488. From this, "unto the Messiah the Prince, shall be seven weeks and threescore and two weeks," which end on the 10th of the fifth month, B.C. 5; and in that year the 10th of the fifth month fell on the 14th of August.

In proof of the correctness of this, Luke informs us that there were "shepherds abiding in the field, keeping watch over their flock" (Luke ii. 8) at the time of his birth, which shows that it could not have been earlier than April, nor later than September; for it "was a custom among the Jews to send out their sheep to the deserts about the passover, and bring them home at the commencement of the first rain."

No other prophetic dates in the Bible pointing out the time of "the Messiah, the Prince" by "the fullness of the time," Paul must have reference to these sixty-nine weeks of Daniel, which he ends at the time "the Messiah" was "made of a woman." (See p. 56.)

B.C. 4. ECLIPSE OF THE MOON.—According to Josephus, there was an eclipse of the moon at Jerusalem a short time before the death of Herod, which is found by calculation to have occurred on the 13th of March at 29m. after two in the morning. Herod's death is, therefore, rightly assigned to B.C. 4, which is confirmed from the duration of his reign; for Josephus states, "by the interest of Anthony, Herod was appointed king by the Roman Senate in the one hundred and eighty-fourth Olympiad, when Caius Domitius Calvinus, the second time, and Caius Asinius Pollis, were consuls; and that he was established in the kingdom by the death of his rival, Antigonus, who had. been set up by the Parthians, when Marcus Agrippa and Caninius Gallus were consuls." (*Antiq.* 14, 16, 4.) He adds, that Herod reigned thirty-seven years from his first appointment by the Senate, and thirty-four years from the death of Antigonus. (*Antiq.* 17, 8, 1.) "Such a critical conformity of astronomical and historical evidence, both furnished by an author the most competent to procure genuine information, establishes both, and decides that Herod's death was not later than B.C. 4. Christ's birth, therefore, could not have been earlier than B.C. 6, nor later than B.C. 5." (*Hales.*)

A.D. 11. THE FIRST YEAR OF TIBERIUS CÆSAR.—"On August 28, A.D. 11, Augustus associated Tiberius with himself in the full government of the empire, that he might have equal power with himself in all the provinces, and in all the armies of the empire." (*A. Clark.*)

A.D. 14. TIBERIUS CÆSAR.—"Augustus died, August 19, A.D 14." From which time, "Tiberius became sole Emperor;" and, according to Josephus, he reigned "twenty-two years, five months, and three days." (*Jose. Ant.* b. xviii. c. vi. s. 10.)

A.D. 14. ECLIPSE OF THE MOON.—One month and eight days "after the death of Augustus Cæsar," there was a total eclipse of the moon at Rome, on September 27, at 32m. after three in the morning. (*Tacitus.*) By this eclipse, the beginning of the reign "of Tiberius, reckoning from the death of Augustus, August 19," A.D. 14, "is indisputably fixed." (*Hales.*)

A.D. 26. THE BAPTISM OF CHRIST.—Our Lord was baptized "in the fifteenth year of the reign of Tiberius Cæsar" (Luke iii. 1), at which time he "began to be about thirty years of age." (Luke iii. 23.) If he was thirty years old to the very day, then he must have been baptized, August 12, A.D. 26; for the fifteenth year of Tiberius commenced on August 28, A.D. 25.

A.D. 26. THE BEGINNING OF CHRIST'S MINISTRY.—During the feast of tabernacles, which in A.D. 26 commenced on October 15, John the Baptist, having gone to the river Jordan, in order to baptize those who desired this at his hands (John i. 28), "the Jews sent priests and Levites from Jerusalem to ask him, Who art thou?" (John i. 19.) Our Lord was then at Jerusalem. (John i. 26.) "The next day," which was the 23d of the seventh month, "the feast of tabernacles being over, Jesus went down to the place where John was (John i. 29); and "the day after,"—that is, the 24th (John i. 35),—at "about the tenth hour" (John i. 39), our Lord's disciples commenced following him; this was Thursday, October 24, A.D. 26; and the time Christ died upon the cross was about the tenth hour on Thursday, April 6, A.D. 30. (Matt. xxvii. 46, 50.) Therefore, the duration of his ministry was 1260 days to the very hour. (Rev. xii. 6.)

Some understand these 1260 days to mean a period of 1260 years; but they were not the subject of prophecy at the time John wrote. This being then a matter of history, each day must be taken as such; for in history, days are never used for years. Those who say this was prophetic, tell us that "the man-child" is the dynasty of Christian emperors, beginning with Constantine's public acknowledgment of his belief in the divinity of the Christian religion; but this was more properly a transformation of the dragon into the woman, than a child born of the woman. The child must come out of the Church, as "the remnant of her seed" (Rev. xii. 17) was commanded to "come out of her" (Rev. xviii. 4); but Constantine was by birth one of the heads of the dragon, and instead of coming out of the Church, he entered into it. It is evident from Psalms ii. 9, that Christ is the "man-child who was to rule all nations with a rod of iron." "The great dragon" was "that old serpent called the devil and Satan which deceiveth the whole world" (Rev. xii. 9),—that is, "the old serpent" was to "the great dragon" what the soul or life of man is to the body; and those nations which stood up against the Church of God were "to the great dragon" what the body of man is to the soul; for they were prompted to action by the agency of "the old serpent called the devil."

The seven heads are the same seven kingdoms as seen by Daniel: 1, the Chaldean, commencing with the time they carried Israel away captive; 2, Persia; 3, Greece; 4, Egypt; 5, Syria; 6, Parthia: 7, Rome. The ten horns are the same ten divisions of the Roman Empire as alluded to in Daniel vii. 7.

In order "to devour the child as soon as it was born," the hand of the dragon "slew all the children that were in Bethlehem and in all the coasts thereof;" but her child was "caught up unto God and to his throne," and yet sitteth "on the right hand of the throne of the Majesty in the heavens" (Heb. viii. 1); and as "the kingdom of God cometh not with observation" (Luke xvii. 20), "the woman fled into the wilderness of the people" (Ezek. xx. 35), "where she hath a place prepared of God that they should feed her there a thousand two hundred and threescore days" (Rev. xii. 6), which place was prepared for her in the wilderness by the preaching of John the Baptist (Matt. iii. 1, 3). The 1260 days do not measure the period she continues in the wilderness, but the length of time she is fed in a supernatural way. The Church was thus fed by Christ both with the bread of life (Matt. iv. 4) and by a miraculous preservation of his apostles (Matt. x. 9), 1260 days to the very hour; which we prove thus: "In the fifteenth year of the reign of Tiberius Cæsar, on the tenth day of the fifth month,"—August 12, A.D. 26, our Lord "began to be about thirty years of age" (Luke iii. 1, 23), from which time he continued forty days in the wilderness,—that is, until the 20th of the sixth month. Nine days after this, the seventh month commenced; hence, Jesus went to Jerusalem to "the feast of ingathering" (Ex. xxiii. 16). The last day of this feast in that year was on October 22; therefore, he could not have left Jerusalem before the 23d. On this day, Wednesday, October 23, he went to Bethabara where "John was baptizing;" and "the day after," Thursday, October 24, "about the tenth hour" of the day, his disciples commenced following him. (John i. 39.) From which there was just 1260 days to the tenth hour of the same day on the 6th of April A.D. 30, at which time he died on the cross.

Not noticing the chronological order of things, some have supposed the "time, times, and half a time," as mentioned in Revelations xii. 14, covers the same period with that of the 1260 days in ver. 6. This, however, is incorrect; for in ver. 6, the woman, though in the wilderness, is without wings and in the presence of the dragon; for she is persecuted by him (Rev. xii. 13); but in ver. 14, the woman having received "two wings of a great eagle," leaves the presence of the dragon, and spends the "times and a half a time" far away "from the face of the serpent." By "a time and times and half a time" we cannot understand a period of less than three years and a half; and the shortest period of Jewish time that can be called three years and a half, is 1269 days,—which the 1260 cannot span. Hence, the long-cherished theory that "a time and times and half a time" is to be restricted to the limits of 1260 days, is thus proven to be erroneous.

A.D. 27. THE FIRST PASSOVER after the beginning of our Lord's ministry was on Thursday, April 10, A.D. 27, O.S., or April 8, N.S. At which time "Jesus went up to Jerusalem" (John ii. 13), and "John was not yet cast into prison." (John iii. 24.) John was imprisoned about November, A.D. 27; for it was at least "four months" before the following harvest. (John iv. 35.) The time of John's imprisonment dates a new era in our Saviour's ministry. "He left Judea, and departed again into Galilee" (John iv. 3) "preaching the gospel of the kingdom of God, and saying, The time is fulfilled, and the kingdom of God is at hand; repent ye, and believe the gospel." (Mark i. 15.) By the fulfillment of the time is to be understood that of John's ministry, during which he bare the people's sins. "John the Baptist was the link that connected Malachi with Christ." (*A. Clark.*) There being no succession of prophets during this interval to bear the sin of the people, the Lord required this at the hand of Ezekiel: "I have laid upon thee the years of their iniquity; according to the number of the days three hundred and ninety days, so shalt thou bear the iniquity of the house of Israel." (Ezek. iv. 5.) According to Josephus, Malachi could not have lived longer than to B.C. 405; and if from his death, or from B.C. 405, we commence the 390 days during which Ezekiel was to bear "their iniquity," they reach the completion of the temple by Herod in B.C. 15.* From this time Ezekiel was to "bear the iniquity of the house of Judah forty days" (Ezek. iv. 6), which brings us to the beginning of the ministry of John in A.D. 26. When he had borne the iniquity of the people rather more than one year, he was "cast into prison" (Matt. iv. 12); from which time the burden was placed on Christ; and he "came into Galilee preaching the gospel of the kingdom of God, and saying, The time is fulfilled."

A.D. 28. THE SECOND PASSOVER during our Lord's ministry fell on Monday, March 29, O.S., or 27, N.S. "And Jesus went up to Jerusalem." (John v. 1.) Whether by "a feast of the Jews" John meant the passover, pentecost, or the feast of tabernacles, the season of the year, as mentioned in chronological order between the two named passovers, compels us to throw in another here; for the time our Lord was in Samaria was only "four months" before the coming harvest (John iv. 35), when the last festival for that year had passed; hence, the next feast must have been that of the passover. John having placed this feast before the passover, as mentioned in Chap. vi. 4, necessarily brings in another passover here before we can reach that.

A.D. 29. THE THIRD PASSOVER during the ministry of Christ was on Sunday, April 17, O.S., or 15, N.S., A.D. 29. (John vi. 4.)

A.D. 30. THE FOURTH PASSOVER, and the last during our Lord's ministry, fell on Thursday, April 6, O.S., or April 4, N.S A.D. 30. (John xxii. 1.) The prevailing opinion that our Lord was crucified on Friday—which clashes with twenty-four texts of Scripture—shows how men are disposed to be controlled by custom. If, regardless of tradition, we believe that Christ and his apostles meant what they said, we are compelled to admit that he was crucified on Thursday. Says Moses:—"Six days shall work be done, but the seventh day is the sabbath of rest." (Lev. xxiii. 3.)

* Herod commenced building the temple "in the fifteenth year of his reign" (*Jose. Wars*, b. i. c. xxi. s. 1), reckoning from the death of Antigonus (*Jose. Ant.* b. xvii. c. viii. s. 1), which was the eighteenth year of his reign reckoning from the time "he had been declared king by the Romans" (*Jose. Ant.* b. xv. c. xi. s. 1),—that is, B.C. 23; and they were "eight years" in building (*Jose. Ant.* b. xv. c. xi. s. 5), which, subtracted from twenty-three, leaves B.C. 15 for the temple's completion.

Each day is here understood to be a period of twenty-four hours. This is termed the natural or solar day. "And God made" the sun to rule the day. (Gen. i. 16.) This is called the artificial day. It commenced at sunrise (Mark xvi. 2), and ended at sunset. (2 Sam. iii. 35.) Their artificial day was divided into twelve equal parts called hours: "Are there not twelve hours in the day?" (John xi. 9.) The hours were of an equal length with ours at the time of the equinox, but at no other; for they must necessarily vary according to the length of the day. Our Lord was crucified on April 6, A.D. 30, and we here give a table of the Jewish hours for that day:—

Hours.	Minutes.	Jewish Hours.		
5	36	12th hour, or sunrise.		
6	40	1st	"	
7	44	2d	"	
8	48	3d	"	(Mark xv. 25.)
9	52	4th	"	
10	56	5th	"	
12	0	6th	"	(Mark xv. 33.)
1	4	7th	"	(John iv. 52.)
2	8	8th	"	
3	12	9th	"	(Mark xv. 34.)
4	16	10th	"	(John i. 39.)
5	20	11th	"	(Matt. xx. 6.)
6	24	12th hour, or sunset. (2 Sam. iii. 35.)		

Mark says:—"Now it was the third hour when they crucified him." (Mark xv. 25.) By the preceding table it will be seen that the third hour for that day was 48m. after eight, A.M. "And when the sixth hour was come there was darkness over the whole land." (Mark xv. 33.) This was at twelve or noonday. And darkness continued until the ninth hour (Mark xv. 33), which was 12m. after three P.M. "And now when the evening was come" (Mark xv. 42), —the twelfth hour "when the sun did set" (Mark i. 32),—was 24m. after six P.M.

Our Lord rose from the dead on "the first day of the week" (Mark xvi. 9), or Sunday. Having one point thus established, we can readily find the day of the crucifixion. Thus, "that same day" (Luke xxiv. 13)—that of the resurrection—was "the third day since these things were done,"—that is, since "the chief priests and our rulers delivered him to be condemned to death, and crucified him." (Luke xxiv. 20.) As it is impossible that the day on which these things were done" can be the day after they were done, this rule of measuring time gives us Thursday for the day of the crucifixion. Thus, Friday was the first, Saturday the second, and Sunday the third day, since these things were done. Had our Lord been crucified on Friday, it would stand thus: Saturday the first, and Sunday the second "day, since these things were done."

From the following texts it is evident that the crucifixion took place on Thursday:—

1. "Three days and three nights." (Matt. xii. 40: Jonah i. 17.)
2. "After three days." (Mark viii. 31: Matt. xxvii 63.)
3. "In three days." (John ii. 19, 20: Matt. xxvi. 61; xxvii. 40: Mark xv. 29.)
4. "Within three days." (Mark xiv. 58.)
5. "The third day." (Matt. xvi. 21: xvii. 23; xx. 19: Mark ix. 31; x. 34: Luke ix. 22; xviii. 33; xxiv. 7, 46: Acts x. 40: 1 Cor. xv. 4: Gen. xxii. 4.)
6. "Third day since." (Luke xxiv. 21.)
7. "Until the third day." (Matt. xxvii. 64.)

Not one of these twenty-four passages can be reconciled with the supposition that our Lord was crucified on Friday.

1. "Three days and three nights in the heart of the earth." (Matt. xxii. 40.) He was to remain there the same period as that in which Jonah remained in the fish; which, to follow the literal reading of the Hebrew, was "three evenings and three mornings." (*A. Clark.*) Thursday evening was one; Friday evening, two; Saturday evening, three; Friday morning, one; Saturday morning, two; Sunday morning, three. Had the crucifixion taken place on Friday, there could have been but two evenings and two mornings.

2. "And after three days rise again." (Mark viii. 31.) By comparing this with the parallel passages in Matthew xvi. 21 and Luke ix. 22, it will appear that while our Lord foretold to his disciples that he would "be raised the third day" after his burial, he also informed them that this would be "after three days" from the time he was "betrayed into the hands of sinners" (Matt. xxvi. 35) "and the sheep of the flock scattered abroad" (Matt. xxvi. 31); for he not only informed them that he would "be raised the third day," but also "began to teach them that the Son of man must suffer many things and be rejected of the elders and of the chief priests and scribes." (Mark viii. 31.) This their "hour and the power of darkness" (Luke xxii. 53) commenced on Wednesday night at

least "one hour" before Thursday morning. (Luke xxii. 59, 66.) From one hour before day Thursday morning to the same hour Sunday morning is three days; and the time he arose from the grave was about daybreak. (Matt. xxviii. 1.) It is, therefore, strictly true that "after three days" from the beginning of the "hour and the power of darkness," he rose "again from beneath the power of all his enemies." "The keepers did shake and became as dead men." (Matt. xxviii. 4.) But if the crucifixion had been on Friday, it would be after two days; and yet five minutes under three days will not answer to the expression, "after three days."

3. "After three days I will rise again." (Matt. xxvii. 63.) On the night the Jews passed the sentence of death upon our Lord, he said unto them, "After three days I will rise again,"—that is, three days after he used these words. This was Wednesday night; and from Wednesday night to Sunday morning is "after three days."

4. "And the third day he shall rise again." (Matt. xx. 19.) These words were not delivered on the day of the crucifixion; but were a matter of prophecy, the object of which was to make known to his disciples the time he would remain in the grave; hence, two full days must pass before the third can begin (Hosea vi. 2.) In measuring time by the natural day according to the custom of the world, the beginning of the first day commences with his being placed in the tomb, which could not have been earlier than the ninth hour, or three o'clock in the evening; for at that time he was yet alive. (Matt. xxvii. 46.) From three o'clock Thursday to the same hour on Sunday, is three days; and as our Lord rose from the grave on Sunday morning, it was on the third day. Had he been crucified on Friday, it would have been on the second day. The general method of reconciling this with the received opinion that our Lord was crucified on Friday, is regardless of the fact that these words were delivered to the apostles many days before,—thus discovering to them the length of time our Lord would remain in the grave. They explain it the same way as if our Lord had said on the day of the crucifixion: I shall be buried to-day, remain in the grave to-morrow, and the third day rise again. But after all this forced and unnatural construction, it amounts to nothing; for he was not buried until the "even was come" (Matt. xxvii. 57),—that is, until the day ended (Lev. xxiii. 32) on which he was crucified; and he rose from the dead "while it was yet dark" (John xx. 1), which was about an hour before the commencement of the third artificial day.

5. "Thus it is written;" hence, "thus it behooved Christ to rise from the dead the third day." (Luke xxiv. 46.) This is written in Genesis xxii. 1, 12. In a literal sense, Isaac was not slain at all; in a moral sense he was slain the moment Abraham gained his consent to "offer him for a burnt-offering," and he was received in a figure" (Heb. xi. 19), or as a type of the resurrection of Christ on the third day from that time; for "Abraham rose up early in the morning, and went unto the place of which God had told him. Then on the third day Abraham lifted up his eyes and saw the place afar off." (Gen. xxii. 3, 4.) Here it is certain that two full days passed from the time Isaac was morally slain before the third day commenced on which he was, as "from the dead, received in a figure" of the resurrection of Christ. (Heb. xi. 19.) Paul declares that Christ "rose again on the third day according to the Scriptures" (1 Cor. xv. 4); and if so, then two days must have passed from the time of his death before the third day commenced.

6. "He was buried, and rose again the third day." (1 Cor. xv. 4.) This text is historical; and its history was "received" from Heaven. Two very important points are established by it: 1. It declares that which was prophetic has been fulfilled,—that the prediction of Christ, saying, "the third day he shall rise again" (Matt. xx. 19), has been literally accomplished. 2. That in order to reach the third day on which he rose from the dead, the first day is to be placed, not against the time of his death, but against that of his burial, which was not until after the day of his crucifixion.

The Jews divided the artificial day into twelve equal parts called hours. "Are there not twelve hours in the day?" (John xi. 9.) The division of these hours we have given in the foregoing table for the 6th of April. The twelfth hour of the artificial day they called evening (Mark i. 32), and the same hour of the night they called morning (Mark xvi. 2); that is, instead of saying the twelfth hour of the day, they would call it the evening: "When the evening was come" (Matt. viii. 16); and for the twelfth hour of the night, they would say morning, or "very early in the morning," which commenced "at the rising of the sun." (Mark xvi. 2.) Their evening was the same with the twelfth hour of the artificial day; for it was just "one hour" after "the eleventh hour" of their day. (Matt. xx.) The Jewish morning commenced with the rising of the sun (Mark xvi. 2: Judg. ix. 33: 2 Sam. xxiii. 4: 2 Kings iii. 22), and their evening with its going down. (Lev. xxii. 6, 7: Josh viii. 29; x. 26, 27: 2 Sam. iii. 35: Deut. xvi. 6.) That which in 1 Kings xxii. 35 is called "at evening" is in

2 Chronicles xviii. 34 called "the time of the sun's going down." The expression in Matthew viii. 16, "When the evening was come," Luke explains to mean "when the sun was setting" (Luke iv. 40); and according to Mark, the evening commenced "when the sun did set." (Mark i. 32.) And "When the even was come Joseph . . . went to Pilate and begged the body of Jesus" (Matt. xxvii. 57, 58: Mark xv. 42), which is the same expression as used in Matthew viii. 16, and explained by both Mark and Luke to mean, "when the sun did set;" and at sunset the day ended. (2 Sam. iii. 35.) It is, therefore, clear that the day on which our Lord was crucified had come to a close when Joseph went to Pilate; for "the even was come," which was one hour after the eleventh hour of the day. (Matt. xx. 8, 12.) As he was not buried until after that day had passed, no part of it can be reckoned in making out the third day on which he rose from the dead. If then our Lord had been crucified on Friday, he would have been buried after Friday had passed and Saturday the Jewish Sabbath had commenced (Lev. xxiii. 32); hence, the resurrection would have been on the second day, and the period he remained in the grave only one day and about ten hours, which cannot be reconciled with the historical fact as given us by Paul, saying, "that he rose again the third day;" but since the crucifixion was on Thursday, the resurrection was truly on the third day. Thus, Friday the first day, Saturday the second, and Sunday the third. It may be asked, Is it not clear from Mark xv. 42, that the crucifixion was on "the day before the sabbath?" To which we reply: By reference to Leviticus xxiii. 7, it will be seen that the day following the passover was always a sabbath, regardless of the day of the week on which it might fall: "Ye shall have a holy convocation: ye shall do no servile work therein." It is called the sabbath "from the morrow after the sabbath." (Lev. xxiii. 15. "No manner of work shall be done in it, save that every man must eat." (Ex. xii. 16.) The sabbath which followed the crucifixion was not an ordinary or weekly sabbath; "for that sabbath day was a high day." (John xix. 31.) Matthew also distinguisheth this from the weekly sabbath by calling it the "day that followed the day of the preparation." (Matt. xxvii. 62.) Had not two sabbaths here fallen together,* surely he would not have used such a term as this to point out the day to which he had reference, but would have said on "the Sabbath day;" for it was a day familiar

---

* **Two sabbaths thus fell together, B.C. 131. (*Jose. Ant.* b. xiii. c. viii. s. 4.)**

to all; while the day of the preparation was so little known that it was necessary to say, "that is the day before the Sabbath." (Mark xv. 42.) But since two sabbaths had here fallen together, it was requisite to make a distinction between them; and the expression, the "day that followed the day of the preparation," points out the one he meant. Mark informs us that "the preparation was the day before the Sabbath;" without saying what this preparation was for; but John tells us, "The preparation of the passover." (John xix. 14.) In A. Campbell's sixth edition of the New Testament the text reads: "Now it was the preparation of the Paschal sabbath about the sixth hour,"—that is, the "Sabbath" of the "fifteenth day," which was the first day "of unleavened bread" (Lev. xxiii. 15, 6); and "that sabbath day was a high day" (John xix. 31), being observed in commemoration of their rest from Egyptian bondage: "And ye shall observe the feast of unleavened bread; for in the self-same day have I brought your armies out of the land of Egypt: therefore, ye shall observe this day in your generation by an ordinance forever." (Ex. xii. 17.) The preparation of the Jewish seventh-day sabbath did not commence until "after the ninth hour" (*Josephus*), which by reference to the table on p. 185 will be found to answer to 12m. after three P.M. for that day, while six hours of the preparation of their Paschal sabbath had passed before the commencement of the third hour of the day (Mark xv. 25), or nine o'clock A.M. This was not the seventh-day sabbath; for it was "when the even was come" (Matt. xxvii. 57) that Joseph "went to Pilate," at which time the law enjoined it upon the people to commence the sabbath: "from even unto even shall ye commence your sabbath." (Lev. xxiii. 32.) As the Jews did not bury their dead on the sabbath, this proves that the crucifixion was not on Friday; for the seventh-day sabbath commenced with the going down of the sun. (Mark i. 32: Luke iv. 40: Matt. viii. 16.) It was the Paschal sabbath which followed the day of the crucifixion; for the evening had come, or the sun was down. The day on which our Lord was crucified had passed away; yet the sabbath had not fully commenced, but "the sabbath drew on." (Luke xxiii. 54.) For the sabbath that followed the passover was governed by the lunar month; and the first lunar sabbath by which all of the others were governed, could not commence until they could see "the new moon." (Ps. lxxxi. 3.)

Cruden says that "the Jewish sabbath was to begin immediately after the setting of the sun, or the rising of the stars." From this it would appear that while some of their sabbaths began with the setting of the sun, others commenced with the first appearance of the stars; and since it is certain that the seventh-day sabbath commenced with the setting of the sun, it follows that those which began with the appearance of the stars were such as belonged to particular days of the lunar months. From the setting of the sun to the appearance of the stars there is an interval of thirty or forty minutes. Joseph, therefore, had ample time to "take the body of Jesus," and lay it in a sepulchre which "was nigh at hand" (John xix. 42),—a work, perhaps, of not more than five or ten minutes; for it appears that he was laid there in haste "because of the Jews' preparation-day;" and "as yet they knew not the Scriptures that he must rise again from the dead." (John xx. 9.) It may have been their intention as soon as the sabbath had passed, to "take him away" (John xx. 15), embalm his body, (Luke xxiv. 1), and bury him at his native city, Nazareth. The sabbath which followed the day of the crucifixion could not have been the seventh-day sabbath; for the women remained at the sepulchre until they saw "how his body was laid," then "returned and prepared spices and ointments," after which they "rested the sabbath day." (Luke xxiii. 56.) If the body of Jesus had been buried on Friday evening, there would have been no time to prepare these spices; for they "rested the sabbath day." They returned from the sepulchre on Thursday evening, "and prepared spices and ointments" on Friday, "and rested the sabbath day" or Saturday. Since the "Jewish canon allowed all works necessary for the dead to be done even on the sabbath, such as washing and anointing, provided they move not a limb of the dead person" (*A. Clark*), and especially, since the disciples of our Lord had been taught that it was "lawful to do good on the sabbath" (Mark iii. 4), we may well suppose that, having thus "prepared spices and ointments," they went to the sepulchre on Friday to embalm the body of Jesus; but before they reached there, Pilate had made the sepulchre sure, sealing the stone and setting a watch." (Matt. xxvii. 66.) Hence, they returned "and rested the sabbath day,"—that is, Saturday. As the sabbath was over as soon as the sun was down on Saturday evening, surely they would have gone to the sepulchre at that time had they not, "according to the commandment of Pilate" (Luke xxiii. 56), which was, "that the sepulchre be made sure until the third day" (Matt. xxvii. 64), been forbidden to go earlier than Sunday morning,—this being the beginning of the third day.

7. "In three days I will raise it up." (John ii. 19.) This is a clear proof that when our Lord said, "the third day he shall be raised again" (Matt. xvii. 23), he meant that two full days must first pass from the time of his death before the third day could begin. It is true that the resurrection would have been within the limits of three days, if the crucifixion had been on Friday; but in this sense it was also within the limits of three years. And to say that when our Lord used the expression, "in three days," he meant a period within the limits of less than two days, is an inaccuracy with which we do not feel disposed to charge him. When the Jews understood him as having referred to the rebuilding of their temple, they were greatly surprised at this being done in the space of three days: "Forty and six years was this temple in building, and wilt thou rear it up in three days?" (John ii. 20.) Surely, they could not have understood our Saviour to have meant only about half of that time. If we place his death at "the ninth hour" (Mark xv. 34), or three o'clock P.M., Thursday, three full days will be accomplished at the same hour P.M., Sunday. His resurrection being on Sunday morning, it wanted only about ten hours of being three full days; but if Friday had been the day of the crucifixion, we would want ten hours to make two full days.

8. "To-day is the third day since these things were done." (Luke xxiv. 21.) This is another historical fact proving that the words of our Lord, who said, "the third day he shall rise again" (Matt. xx. 19), were literally accomplished. The passover was on the 14th of the first month, and on that day the "rulers delivered" Christ to be condemned to death and crucified him." (Luke xxiv. 20.) The 15th of the month was the day after; the 16th, the second; and the 17th "the third day since these things were done."

9. "Until the third day." (Matt. xxvii. 64.) This is a period of only two days; for the expression, "until the third day," limits the time to the commencement of the third day." (Ex. xii. 6.) These two days commenced with "the next day that followed the day of the preparation" (Matt. xxvii. 62), which was Friday morning; and from Friday morning to Sunday morning is just two days, ending at the beginning of the third day, or at sunrise on Sunday morning; hence, "according to the commandment" of Pilate (Luke xxiii. 56), "that the sepulchre be made sure until the third day" (Matt. xxvii. 64), the disciples could not have entered the sepulchre before "the first day of the week very early in the morning" (Luke xxiv. 1),—that is, "at the rising of the sun." (Mark xvi. 2.)

But had our Lord been crucified on Friday, the disciples could not have gone to the sepulchre until Monday morning.

10. The history of the Church also proves that the crucifixion took place on Thursday. "The day which was observed as the anniversary of Christ's death was called the Paschal day, because it was the same with that on which the Jews celebrated their passover,"—that is, the 14th of the first month, and three days after they commemorated the resurrection of the Redeemer." By adding 3 to 14, we have 17; therefore, the Church at that time "commemorated the resurrection" on the 17th of the Jewish first month, which in A.D. 30, fell on the first day of the week; hence, the crucifixion was on Thursday the 14th of the first month, and the resurrection on Sunday, which was the 17th.

11. Mary went to the sepulchre "when it was yet dark," but our Lord had risen before she reached it. (John xx. 1.) The resurrection, therefore, must have been at least one hour before sunrise, at which time the Jews commenced their artificial day; hence, upon the supposition that the crucifixion was on Friday, it is impossible to make out more than two days and two nights; for the resurrection being before the commencement of the first artificial day of the week, no part of Sunday can be counted as one of the three days. We are, then, compelled either to admit that the crucifixion was on Thursday, or deny the word of Christ: "So shall the Son of man be three days and three nights in the heart of the earth." (Matt. xii. 40.)

A.D. 30. THE YEAR OF THE CRUCIFIXION.—Our Lord was crucified on the day of the passover,—that is, the 14th of the first month, which in that year fell on the fifth day of the week. This enables us by the aid of astronomy to decide on the year of the crucifixion. Christ did not commence his ministry before "the fifteenth year of the reign of Tiberius Cæsar" (Luke iii. 1); hence, not before August 28, A.D. 25. During his ministry there were four passovers; the crucifixion, therefore, could not have been earlier than A.D. 29, nor later than A.D. 36; for it was during the government of Pontius Pilate, whose rule could not have continued later than the 28th of August, A.D. 26, as Luke informs us that Pilate was "Governor of Judea" during "the fifteenth year of Tiberius Cæsar," whose fifteenth year ended on August 28, A.D. 26; and according to Josephus, Pilate was governor but ten years, and lost his authority during the reign of Tiberius Cæsar, who died January 22, A.D. 37. We are consequently limited to eight years for the time of the crucifixion, which was on Thursday, the 14th of the first month, when, according to Josephus, the sun was in Aries.

The Paschal full moon, during these eight years, fell thus:—

A.D. 29	....	April 17	....	Sunday.
" 30	....	" 6	....	Thursday.
" 31	....	March 27	....	Tuesday.
" 32	....	April 14	....	Monday.
" 33	....	" 3	....	Friday.
" 34	....	March 23	....	Tuesday.
" 35	....	April 11	....	Monday.
" 36	....	March 31	....	Saturday.

From this table, it will be seen that the only Paschal full moon within the limits of these eight years that fell on Thursday, was in A.D 30. We thus prove that the crucifixion took place on April 6, A.D. 30.

We will now show that all the records of antiquity can only be reconciled upon the supposition of this being the day and year. The Roman calendar was divided into Calends, Nones, and Ides, by which they dated their transactions; but the Jews refusing to employ these terms,—by which the Romans pointed out the time of their heathen festivals,—used the calendar in the same way we do at the present day. In proof of this, the death-warrant of Christ is dated on March 27, instead of the 6th of the calendar of April. This being the custom of using the calendar in Judea, they dated the crucifixion on the 6th of the calendar of April instead of on the 8th of Ides, according to the Roman method. Others merely gave the date at which they were writing, without mentioning at what time the crucifixion took place; hence, one is dated on the 8th of the calendar of April, two days after the crucifixion; another on the 10th of April, four days after; another on the 13th of April, seven days after. Some of these records were dated on the nineteenth of Tiberius Cæsar, reckoning from the beginning of his reign as associated with Augustus; others, the seventeenth of Tiberius, computing from the death of Augustus. The nineteenth of Tiberius, reckoning from the first epoch, synchronizes with A.D. 30, which may be seen by reference to our Table of Chronology. According to Ptolemy's canon, the seventeenth of Tiberius, reckoning from the death of Augustus also answers to A.D. 30. (See Chronological Table.) Hence, there was but one opinion as to the time of the crucifixion until towards the end of the second century, when it was discovered that Tiberius's reign did not commence with January 1, but on August 19, A.D. 14; and reckoning from this, the passover of A.D. 31 was in the seventeenth of Tiberius. This circumstance originated a considerable difficulty; for the crucifixion was dated on the 6th of the calendar of April at the time of the passover, which always falls on the 14th of the first month; and they could easily discover by their lunar cycles that the 6th of April in A.D. 31 was on the 24th of the first month. As the Paschal full moon for that year fell on March 27, which was the 6th of the calends of April, it was but natural for them to suppose that those who had written on the subject had dated according to the Roman method. Therefore, that which was dated on the 6th of the calendar of April, they now understood to mean the 6th of the calends of April. This mistake was very easy to be made since calends was not written out in full, but only put thus: "cal," or "calend," which as properly stand for calends, as for calendar. At that time they had not learned to find the day of the week by the Dominical letter; hence, were unable to detect this error by discovering that March 27 of that year did not fall on Thursday. It therefore became the settled opinion that A.D. 31 was the year of the crucifixion. But the supposition that those authors who had dated according to the calendar of April meant the calends of April, caused great confusion; for their writings were thus thrown back before the day of the crucifixion. By this method those who wrote on the 8th of the calendar of April, two days after the crucifixion, were now supposed to date on the 8th of the calends of April, answering to March 25, two days before the Paschal full moon, which fell on March 27; those who had written on April 10, four days after the crucifixion, were thought to mean the 10th of the calends of April, which is March 23, four days before the full moon; and those who had written on April 13, which was seven days after the crucifixion, were supposed to mean the 13th of the calends of April,—the 20th of March, seven days before the Paschal full moon of A.D. 31. In the midst of this confusion the Council of Ephesus, in A.D. 196, settled upon the 8th of the calends of April,—March 25,—A.D. 31, as the date of the crucifixion; but after the establishment of the Christian era,—arranged by Dionysius in A.D. 527,—it was thought that by the fifteenth year of Tiberius, Luke meant the fifteenth of his reign, reckoning from the death of Augustus, which synchronizes with A.D. 29. As the ministry of Christ continued three years and a half, this gave them A.D. 33 for the time of the crucifixion; and having learned to tell the day of the week by the Dominical letter, Roger Bacon, in the thirteenth century, discovered that the Paschal full moon of that year fell on Friday. This led him then, and the larger portion of the Christian world since, to suppose that the crucifixion took place on Friday, which accounts for the want of decision at the present day as to the year of the crucifixion; for since it has been decided that Christ was born at least four years before the beginning of the Christian era, they cannot reach A.D. 33 without the absurdity of supposing that our Lord's ministry continued seven years. In addition to this, the Paschal full moon fell on Friday in no other year during which they can reasonably suppose our Lord was crucified; but having observed that the crucifixion took place on Thursday, we are now enabled to settle this much-disputed question by astronomy.

The sentence of death as passed on Jesus of Nazareth, which was found among the ruins of antiquity, in the kingdom of Naples, A.D. 1280, and which is considered of undoubted authority, dates the time of the crucifixion "in the year seventeen of the Emperor Tiberius Cæsar and the 27th day of March." If this and the corroborating testimony of all the early Christians who composed the Council of Ephesus in A.D. 196 can be received as authority, the controversy will thus be limited to but two years; for by the above-mentioned authority, the crucifixion must have been either in A.D. 30 or 31. If it was on Thursday, it could not have been in A.D. 31; for the Paschal full moon in that year fell on Tuesday, March 27; and since the Jews were so very strict in regard to the time of the passover that they would not commence the month until it was first declared on oath that the new moon was seen, this cannot be dated a single day higher. If cloudy, or they were unable to see the moon, they commenced their month on the next day; hence, we cannot go more than one day lower, which would be Wednesday. As it is well known that the crucifixion was neither on Tuesday nor Wednesday, it could not have been A.D. 31. Between these two years, then, we will have to take A.D. 30. We can again prove that our Lord was crucified in that year by the note at the end of the book of Nicodemus, dating it in "the nineteenth year of Tiberius Cæsar," which ended August 28, A.D. 30; hence, it could not have been later than A.D. 30; and as this same note dates the time of the crucifixion in the two hundred and second Olympiad, it cannot be before A.D. 30; for that Olympiad commenced July 11, A.D. 29. We are, therefore, restricted to A.D. 30 for the year of the crucifixion, though it was by others dated on the seventeenth of Tiberius, which, if reckoned from the death of Augustus, answers to A.D. 31. This is easily accounted for by observing that the seventeenth of Tiberius is here according to Ptolemy, who dates the reign of all from January 1, regardless of the day on which their reign commenced; and in order to reconcile this with the note we have alluded to, we must admit that they reckoned the reign of Tiberius from January 1, A.D. 14. The above-mentioned "death-warrant of Jesus Christ" was not taken to the "city of Aquilla, in the kingdom of Naples" before the gospel of our Lord was established there; hence, not earlier than the second century, when the Church was led to conclude that the crucifixion was A.D. 31. As by their lunar cycles they had then discovered that the Paschal full moon fell on March 27, in that year, which was the 6th of the calends of April, it was but natural for them to suppose that those who had dated the time of the crucifixion on the 6th of the calendar of April meant the 6th of the calends of April; for the 6th of the "*calend*" stood as properly for one as for the other; and it was only by finding the day on which the Paschal full moon fell that they were enabled to decide as to which was meant. Hence, as soon as by their lunar cycles they learned that the Paschal full moon in that year fell on March 27, it was but natural for them to conclude that by the 6th of the "*calend*" of April the 6th of the calends of April was meant, which was March 27; therefore, in translating this it was not considered altering the date to put it on March 27, but only to make it plainer so that all might understand. Upon the supposition that the crucifixion was on Thursday, April 6, A.D. 30, we can thus reconcile all who have written on the subject, while it is impossible to do so upon any other day or year. For example, suppose we say March 27, A.D. 31; then we must understand those who dated their writings the 13th of the "*calend*" of April to mean the 13th of the calends of April,—that is, March 20,—which places the date seven days before the crucifixion. But if we take April 6, A.D. 30, every difficulty is removed. Then we will understand those who have dated the 13th of the "*calend*" to mean the 13th of the calendar of April, which is seven days after the crucifixion; or suppose we admit that the crucifixion was on Friday, April 7, then we will be unable to reconcile those who dated the 6th of the "*calend*" of April; for if we understand them to mean the 6th of the calendar of April, it would date one day before the crucifixion; and if we understand them to mean the 6th of the calends of April, it would bear date on March 27, or eleven days before the crucifixion. Hence, to reconcile those authors we are compelled to fall back to Thursday, April 6, A.D. 30, on which day and year all may be reconciled, but on no other. The festival as observed by the early Christians, on Thursday until three o'clock in the afternoon in "remembrance of the sufferings of Christ," also shows that the crucifixion took place on Thursday.

The Jews were very strict in noticing the earliest appearance of the new moon; for it was a positive law: "In the beginning of your months ye shall blow with the trumpets" (Num. x. 10), and "offer a burnt-offering unto the Lord" (Num. xxviii. 11); and they were able to tell the very day on which the new moon could be seen. All that is necessary, therefore, in order to find a given day of their month, or year, is to learn the age of the moon at that time. As the passover was celebrated "on the 14th of the lunar month when the sun is in Aries" (*Jose. Ant.* b. iii. c. x. s. 5), the first new moon after March 7 must be the beginning of their year. In A.D. 30 there was a new moon on March 22, at 40m. after seven P.M. On March 23 the sun set at 3m. after six, at which time the moon was about one hour high; if clear, it may have been seen at about half-past six, or between that and seven in the afternoon, March 23; hence, March 24 was the first day of their month, commencing with the evening of March 23; and the 14th of their first month for that year fell on Thursday, April 6, commencing on Wednesday evening, April 5. A.D. 30 is thus astronomically proven to be the year in which the crucifixion took place. At B.C. 406, we observed that the wall as built by Nehemiah was completed on the 25th of the sixth month, B.C. 406. Daniel was informed that "after threescore and two weeks" from the completion of "the wall" "the Messiah the Prince" should "be cut off." (Dan. ix. 26.) In 62 weeks there are 434 years; and if to 406 we add 29 diminished by 1, we will have 434: hence, the 434 years from the completion of the wall ends on the 25th of the sixth month, A.D. 29, five months and eighteen days after that time "the Messiah the Prince" was "cut off."

A.D. 30. THE WOMAN IN THE WILDERNESS.—In B.C. 5, the Church "brought forth a man-child" who did not at that time, but was to, "rule all nations with a rod of iron;" hence, he "was caught up unto God and his throne," there to remain until the time appointed for him to take his seat upon the throne of his father David. Not yet having received his kingdom, his subjects, having no citizenship in the kingdoms of this world, "fled into the wilderness," there to remain until the "appearing and kingdom" of Christ. On the 10th of the first month, A.D. 30, he went to Jerusalem, as foretold, "saying, tell ye the daughter of Zion, Behold, thy King cometh unto thee" (Mal. xxi. 5); but he was rejected of that generation, because they knew not the time of their visitation. (Luke xix. 44.) Had he been received, "the kingdoms of this world" would have "become the kingdoms of our Lord and his Christ;" but the Shepherd being smitten, the sheep are scattered abroad. Having received the "wings of that spiritual law of" liberty wherewith Christ hath made us free from the obligation of the ceremonial law at Jerusalem, they left their father's house (Matt. xxiv. 2), their native land (Num. xv. 2), even their promised inheritance (Gal. xvii. 8); and the woman that once "fled into the wilderness," where she was fed in a supernatural way for 1260 days, could now even "fly into her place where she is nourished for a time and times and half a time from the face of the serpent" (Rev. xii. 14) until our King, having "put down all" opposing "authority and power," shall receive his kingdom.

The time, times and a half commenced with the 10th of the first month, and must therefore end on the 10th of the seventh month; but as to the number of times which fill up the interval, we must learn from other prophetic dates; for the expression, "times," conveys to the mind nothing definite as to their number, and there is no rule given here by which we can know the length of time. We know that it cannot be less than three times and a half, or 1269 days; hence, cannot be the same with 1260 days. From other prophetic dates we conclude that the times of the wilderness state of absence from the kingdom of Christ will end in the coming jubilee of 1868.

A.D. 65. END OF THE SEVENTY WEEKS OF DANIEL.—While Daniel was engaged in prayer for his people, the angel Gabriel "being caused to fly swiftly, touched" him "about the time of the evening oblation;" and he informed him saying, "Seventy weeks are cut off upon thy people and upon thy holy city" (Dan. ix. 24), —that is, "cut off" of the 2300 days (Dan. viii. 14); hence, with them the seventy weeks must begin. The object of these seventy weeks being to measure the length of time, as appointed for the continuation of Daniel's "people and" "holy city," they must end with the beginning of the ruin of that people. In 70 weeks there are 490 years; and the 2300 days commenced with the pushing of the ram on the 15th of the first month, B.C. 426. If to 426 we add 65 diminished by 1, we will have 490; hence, the 490 years which were cut off of the 2300 must end on the 15th of the first month, Wednesday, April 10, A.D. 65, at which time the Lord having given up the city to ruin, "the eastern gate of the inner court of the temple, which was of brass, and vastly heavy, and had been with difficulty shut by twenty men," "opened of its own accord about the sixth hour of the night,"—by which "the men of learning understood that the security of their holy house was dissolved of its own accord; that the signal foreshowed the desolation that was coming upon them." (*Jose. Wars,* b. vi. c. v. s. 3.) Florus, who "blew up the war into a flame," "had at that very time the purpose of showing his anger at the nation and procuring a war upon them" (*Jose. Wars,* b. ii. c. xiv. s. 3), which in the limits of only thirty days commenced with all of its terrors; for "except the Lord keep the city the watchmen waketh in vain." (Ps. cxxvii. 1.) The war commenced on the 16th of the second month,—Saturday, May 11, A.D. 65.

A.D. 69. ECLIPSE OF THE MOON.—Tacitus says there was an eclipse of the moon in "the year before the destruction of Jerusalem by Titus." By calculation, there was an eclipse of 9 digits at 25m. after eleven P.M. at Rome on October 18, A.D. 69; but none was visible in the Roman Empire, A.D. 70. That year is thus astronomically proven to be the one in which Jerusalem was destroyed.

A.D. 70. THE SACRIFICE AND THE OBLATION CEASE.—Daniel was informed that the "little horn," "the people of the Prince that shall come,"—that is, the people which constitute that prince called Antichrist (2 John 7) "shall confirm the covenant with many for one week, and in the midst of the week he shall cause the sacrifice and the oblation to cease." (Dan. ix. 27.) Josephus informs us that "the daily sacrifice" ceased on "the seventeenth day of Tamuz," Sunday, July 15, A.D. 70, which was in the midst of the week, or during the Seven-years War at Jerusalem. Some charge the Romans with having caused this; but Josephus declares that it was those "who confess not that Jesus Christ is come into the flesh." He charged them with having "deprived" God "of his everlasting worship" in thus causing the sacrifice to cease. The Romans did all they could "to have the Jewish laws observed," and almost compelled those sacrifices to be still offered to God which had by "the people of the prince that shall come" (Dan. ix. 26) "been intermitted." (*Jose. Wars,* b. vi. c. ii. s. 1.)

A.D. 70. THE BURNING OF THE TEMPLE occurred on "the tenth day of the month Ab," Monday, August 6; and the city was taken "on the eighth day of the month Elul," Monday, September 3, "in the second year of the reign of Vespasian," A.D. 70. The Romans are generally charged with having destroyed the city and temple; and it is true "by his hand"—that is, the hand of the Romans—the "land" was "consumed." (Dan. xi. 16.) Yet Antichrist was the actuating cause of its ruin. "The little horn," "the people of the prince that shall come," compelled the Romans to do this; for they would not venture to "set the sanctuary on fire but under the most pressing necessity," saying, "We will endeavor to preserve you your holy house whether you will or no." (*Jose. Wars,* b. vi. c. ii. s. 4.)

A.D. 72. END OF THE "ONE-WEEK COVENANT."—According to Josephus, the war with the Jews terminated "in the fourth year of the reign of Vespasian, on the fifteenth day of the month Nisan,"—that is, on Tuesday, March 24, A.D. 72. At A.D. 65, we observed that the seventy weeks which were to be "cut off" of the 2300 days ended on the 15th of the first month (Nisan), A.D. 65, at which time the "one-week covenant" commenced. This was therefore accomplished in seven years.

A.D. 533. THE ABOMINATION THAT MAKETH DESOLATE SET UP.—Since there is but one power on earth that can make either Jew or Gentile "desolate" under the gospel dispensation, we need not be in doubt as to what is meant by "the abomination that maketh desolate." What in all creation but "Antichrist," that "deceiver," "who confesses not that Jesus Christ is come into the flesh" (1 John 7) can make us so desolate as to "separate us from the love of Christ? Shall tribulation, or distress, or persecution, or famine, or nakedness, or peril, or sword?" "I," says the Apostle Paul, "am persuaded that neither death, nor life, nor angels, nor principalities, nor powers, nor things present, nor things to come, nor height, nor depth, nor any other creature, shall be able to separate us from the love of God which is in Christ Jesus our Lord." (Rom. viii. 38, 39.)

By comparing Matthew xxiv. 15 with Luke xxi. 20, some suppose that by "abomination that maketh desolate" we are to understand the Roman army; but Luke says nothing about the Romans: he only says, "armies,"—not the Roman armies; for they were to "stand in the holy place" (Matt. xxiv. 15), which, if they entered at all, it was not until about five years after the Christians—for whom the sign was intended—had left Jerusalem. It appears from Josephus that the Christians understood our Lord to mean the armies of Antichrist,—those wicked Jews "who confess not that Jesus is come into the flesh;" for after the Christians had seen these armies entering "into the temple," they "swarmed away from the city as from a ship when it was going to sink."

Rome was not called an abomination by the Jews; for they considered it a great honor to be a Roman citizen. (Acts xxii. 28.) Neither did the Christians understand Rome to be "the abomination of desolation," but to be that which prevented the revelation of "that man of sin." (2 Thess. ii. 3.) So far from Rome being "the abomination that maketh desolate," it was a power "ordained of God." (Rom. xiii. 1.) So "the abomination of desolation spoken of by Daniel the prophet" must be Antichrist, which was "standing where it ought not" (Mark xiii. 14) when the Jews revolted from and declared war against the Roman Empire. That power which stood "up against the Prince of princes" (Dan. viii. 25), and "destroyed the city and the sanctuary" (Dan. ix. 26; xi. 22), was Antichrist in its undisguised form,—or those who denied that Jesus was the Christ. (1 John ii. 22; Acts iii. 15.) But after that "league made with him" (Dan. xi. 23) "by reason of transgressions" (Dan. viii. 12),—that is, by "falling away" from Christ (2 Tim. ii. 3), he "worked deceitfully" (Dan. xi. 23); he made pretensions to that which was not real; and as his seat is in the Church, as "he sitteth in the temple of God" (2 Thess. ii. 4), we are here to understand Antichrist in its transgressive form,—those who with the mouth confess Christ, but by works deny him. The "little horn" which "came up among" the "ten horns" (Dan. vii. 8), though admitted to be Antichrist, cannot date the rise of Antichrist; for before the rise of the "ten horns" the whole Roman Empire (the true Christian Church excepted) had become Antichrist. In this sense, "the fourth beast was diverse from all the others, exceeding dreadful" (Dan. vii. 19); and since the coming up of the little horn among the ten cannot date the rise of Antichrist, it must date the revelation of the man of sin,—the time he received his kingly power,—or the setting up of "the abomination that maketh desolate;" for it is clear that the rise of this little horn among the ten dates some new epoch; and since he "sitteth in the temple of God," we must look within the pale of the Church, and nowhere else, for the rise of this new power called "the abomination of desolation;" hence, we have now only to inquire as to the epoch at which this new ruling power was set up in the Church of God. In A.D. 312, Constantine "took the religion of Christ to the unhallowed embrace of the state, assuming to unite in his own person the civil and ecclesiastical dominion." The open profession of the Christian religion then became popular: the hindering power that "withholdeth that he"—the man of sin—"might be revealed in his time," was then removed." (2 Thess. ii. 6.) From that epoch we may date the time the Church began to fall "away," and "by reason of transgression" (Dan. viii. 12) "the league" was made with Antichrist, from which time he did "work deceitfully; for he" came "up" into the Church, and "became strong with a small people." (Dan. xi. 23.) But this cannot date his seat there in his kingly authority; for that was not until after the division of Rome into ten kingdoms. (Dan. vii. 24.) Some date his seat in the Church from "the bestowment of the title of universal bishop by Phocus the tyrant," A.D. 606. But this cannot date the beginning of his kingly authority; for in the coming up of the "little horn,"—that is, in the rise of this new power,—there were "three of the first horns plucked up by the roots," which three divisions of the Roman Empire were plucked up seventy-three years before. To avoid mistake as to the correct date, bear in mind that while his coming up to take his seat "in the temple of God," "plucked up by the roots" three of the ten divisions of the Roman Empire (Dan. vii. 8), he was placed in the seat of his authority by force of arms. (Dan. xi. 31.)

At B.C. 488, we traced the history of Antichrist from its rise down to A.D. 312, when "this prince of the power of the air" came into the Church, and made "the league with him" "by reason of transgression," or by "falling away" from Christ. In continuation of that article we will here commence with Dan. xi. 31.

Ver. 31. "And arms shall stand on his part,"—that is, on the part of Antichrist in its transgressive form. Those northern arms that poured in like a flood upon the Roman Empire, stood on the part of that portion of the Church which "by reason of transgression" was transformed into Antichrist.

Ver. 31. "And they shall pollute the sanctuary of strength." Not the Jewish; for that was not "the sanctuary of strength," but "a worldly sanctuary" (Heb. ix. 1) "doomed to destruction." (Dan. ix. 26.) "The sanctuary of strength" is the Church,—"the true tabernacle which the Lord pitched, and not man" (Heb. viii. 2); hence, called "his sanctuary" in opposition to the Jewish. (Dan.

viii. 11.) Those northern powers which stood on the part of Antichrist in its transgressive form, by favoring and embracing at least the outward forms of the Christian religion, did greatly "pollute the sanctuary of strength" by introducing into the Christian Church the worship of pagan idols, or heathen gods. On the condition that they would "accept the Christian name, the Bishop of Rome and his clergy conformed as much as possible to their heathen rites and ceremonies;" and thus "the sanctuary of strength," or Church, was "polluted."

Ver. 31. "And shall take away the daily sacrifice." "Sacrifice" is in italic, showing that it was not in the original. At B.C. 425, we observed that "daily" does not mean those sacrifices as offered by the Jews; for so far from the word "sacrifice" being used, which is done in every case where the author has reference to it, we find a word which, even if placed in connection with "sacrifice," would so restrict its meaning that it could no longer apply to the Jewish sacrifices in general; for the larger number of them were not daily. Since in *every* case, whenever the author has reference to the Jewish sacrifice, the word itself is used, how absurd to suppose that Daniel meant the Jewish sacrifice, when, five times omitting that, he used the word, "daily;" and yet where it is certain that he had reference to the daily sacrifice, instead of "daily," he employed the word, "sacrifice."

Instead of "daily," some translate it "continual," which appears to be correct; for that which Daniel had seen in his vision was a continual succession of kingdoms bearing rule over the people of God. But if "daily" is preferred, this, like other prophetic dates, must be according to the day-year system.

Persia was the first kingdom called "the daily," which may be properly so called; for its ruling power was continued by an annual arrangement. "The king's son, his brother, or one of those they called the king's eye," took "a progress every year at the head of an army," to see that the king's orders were obeyed. Greece, the next kingdom, may be called "the daily," or an annual power; for the ephori continued in office but one year. The fourth kingdom was Rome, which, having its annual consuls, may also be called the "daily;" and the eastern division of the Roman Empire, which was one of "the ten horns out of this kingdom," was "plucked up by the roots," A.D. 533; for the ruling powers of a kingdom are the laws, which were destroyed when Justinian issued his new code, A.D. 533, and this new code of laws "became the civil and ecclesiastial constitution of the Roman Empire." They "were declared to be the legitimate system of civil jurisprudence; they alone were admitted in the tribunals; and they alone were taught in the academies of Rome." (*Gibbon.*)

Ver. 31. "And they shall place the abomination that maketh desolate." The placing of "the abomination" and the rise of the "little horn" are one and the same thing; and as we are informed that the little horn is a king (Dan. vii. 24), by its coming up we are to understand the rise of some new power in the Church; for he was diverse from the other ten kings. The Justinian code was properly the rise of a new power which came up in the Church; for its author not only claimed to be the "pious, fortunate, renowned, triumphant emperor;" but "his pride, under the mask of piety, ascribed the consummation of this great design to the support and inspiration of the Deity." (*Gibbon.*) Thus his so-called "eternal oracles" claimed the same divine origin with that of the Bible. One essential part of these "oracles" was that of constituting the Bishop of Rome head of all the churches,—"the true and effective corrector of heretics." Thus he received his seat of power and authority to make "war with the saints, and prevailed against them." This new code of laws by which the little horn was placed in its seat of authority, did as properly spring up in the Church as if it had been framed by the Pope himself; for the author was the chief head of the Church, being one of those Christian emperors to whom not only the Church, but the Bishop of Rome himself was subject. This "little horn" was unlike the other ten, as it claimed divine origin; and since these new laws constituted the Pope of Rome head of all the churches, it may properly be said to have "eyes like the eyes of a man, and a mouth speaking great things;" for the Pope has spoken many "great things," contrary to the word of God, and his eyes are ever over the Church.

Justinian also declared, "in the fullest and most unequivocal form," the Bishop of Rome the chief of the whole ecclesiastical body of the empire; hence, "that man of sin," who "sitteth in the temple of God," was placed there by him, A.D. 533. Although that horn, called "the Ostrogoths in Italy," did not fall off until March, A.D. 538, this may properly date the time it began to be "plucked up by the roots;" for Theodoric, King of the Ostrogoths, having "fixed his capital at Ravenna," the Pope was left "the only Prince of Rome." Such was "the power and influence" he had over those then in possession of the kingdom, that at his request they commenced exchanging their former laws for the new code; and the adoption of it by the Bishop of Rome, A.D. 533, dates the beginning of that work which, in March, A.D. 538, uprooted the remains of this horn. The third horn—"the kingdom of the Vandals in Africa"—was "plucked up on the eve of St. Cyprian, A.D. 533." Says Gibbon:—"One awful hour reversed the fortunes of the contending parties." This was a Catholic war, the object of which was to destroy those opposing powers, and place the Bishop of Rome on the throne of great authority in the Church, and lordship over the people of God; and as that "one awful hour" was the turning-point on which was pending the fate of the Vandals and Ostrigoths, it is the proper epoch from which to date the plucking up of the three horns, or taking "away the daily" and placing "the abomination that maketh desolate" by force of "arms" (Dan. xi. 31); for "the temple was now resigned to the Catholics, who loudly proclaimed the creed of Athanasius and Justinian, and he proceeded without delay to the full establishment of the Catholic Church." (*Gibbon.*) That new power, styled the "eternal oracles," being both the "civil and ecclesiastical constitution of the Roman Empire" "were proclaimed on solemn festivals at the doors of the churches." (*Gibbon.*) These oracles, having been substituted by the Church of Rome for the law of God, were thus transformed into "the abomination of desolation."

The eve of St. Cyprian was the 15th of September, which in A.D. 533 fell on the 10th of the Jewish seventh month: "And from the time the daily shall be taken away and the abomination that maketh desolate set up, there shall be twelve hundred and ninety days" before even "the wise shall understand" what was meant by the expression, "a time, times, and a half." If to A.D. 533 we add 1290 we have 1823,—the very time at which the Church commenced proclaiming that the "little book" was "opened." (Rev. x. ii.) From that date all who have been willing to examine the Bible concerning the second coming of our Lord are ready to acknowledge that it appears like a new book. If to the 10th of the seventh month, A.D. 533, we add 1335 years, we will have the 10th of the seventh month, A.D. 1868 for the time at which Daniel will stand in his lot in the year of jubilee; for "ye shall return every man unto his possession." (Lev. xxv. 9, 13.)

That we are correct in dating the beginning of the 1335 years from the day on which the Vandals fell before the arms of Justinian will again appear from the following reason. Though the emperor's letter, declaring the Pope of Rome "head of all the holy churches," must have been sent as early as March 25, A.D. 533, Justinian, as an individual, had not the power to place the Pope of

Rome in possession of this new kingly authority; his power being vested in his troops, "arms" must "place the abomination that maketh desolate" (Dan. xi. 31); hence, that hour which "reversed the fortunes of the contending parties" was the point of time at which the Catholic Church was established by force of "arms." When we call to mind that "arms shall stand on the part" of Antichrist, and, plucking "up by the roots" three divisions of the Roman Empire (Dan. vii. 8), shall at the same time "place the abomination that maketh desolate" (Dan. xi. 31), we find in all the history of the world but two epochs from which we can reasonably commence the 1335 days: the first, on the eve of St. Cyprian, A.D. 533, the other, March, A.D. 538, when the last remains of the third horn was "plucked up;" hence, the controversy as to the beginning of the 1335 days is clearly limited to these two dates. If the testimony of the Catholics themselves may be received, they date the title of "universal bishop," and their "earthly acknowledgment of her claim," "from the memorable year A.D. 533." It is evident that they are correct in this; for when "intelligence of the success of Belisarus in Africa reached the emperor, December 16, A.D. 533, impatient to abolish the temporal and spiritual tyranny of the Vandals, he proceeded without delay to the full establishment of the Catholic Church." (*Gibbon.*)

A.D. 538. THE SAINTS IN THE HANDS OF PAPAL ROME.—In A.D. 538, the 10th of the first month fell on March 27, about which time "the Pope was placed in quiet possession of the capital of Rome," from which epoch Daniel's "time, and times, and the dividing of time" commence. (Dan. vii. 25.) At B.C. 488, we observed that the expression, "a time, times, and a half," as used in Daniel xii. 7, meant "a time, five times and a half;" but in Daniel vii. 25 it cannot mean the same length of time; for the angel was here addressing himself directly to Daniel, and made him "know the interpretation of the thing." (Dan. vii. 16.) But in Chap. xii. Daniel only heard the conversation between two saints which he did not understand: "I heard, but I understood not." (Dan. xii. 8.) His understanding the former, and not the latter shows clearly that each cannot mean the same length of time. Daniel's having understood what time was signified, proves that the angel meant just what he said,—that is, "times," without any thing definite as to the number of times; for if he had meant two years as some suppose, or five times as in Chap. xii., it was impossible for Daniel to have known the number of times; for he did not here, as in Chap. xii., give a rule by which the number may be known; hence, all we can learn from this as to definite time is that if they commence on the 10th of the first month, they must end on the 10th of the seventh month. From Daniel xii. 12 we conclude that these "times and a half" will end on the 10th of the seventh month, A.D. 1868.

A.D. 629. THE HOLY CITY TRODDEN UNDER FOOT.—Those who are to tread "the holy city . . . under foot" are called Gentiles, and cannot, therefore, be Christians. Yet they must make some pretensions to the religion of Jesus; for they are in possession of "the court which is without the temple." (Rev. xi. 2.) To tread "the holy city" "under foot," they must use force of arms against the true worshippers of God; hence, we know of no people who answer to this description except the Mohammedans. It will not apply to the Pope of Rome, for his seat is not in the "court which is *without* the temple;" but he "sitteth *in* the temple of God." (2 Thess. ii. 4.)

Gibbon dates the flight of Mohammed A.D. 622; "and after an exile of seven years, the fugitive missionary was enthroned as the prince and prophet of his native country," A.D. 629; hence, this must date the epoch from which they shall "tread . . . the holy city . . . under foot forty and two months." (Rev. xi. 2.) In 42 months, according to the Jewish method of reckoning, there are 1239 days. If to A.D. 629, we add 1239, we will have A.D. 1868 for the time these Gentiles shall cease to tramp "the holy city under foot."

A.D. 1823. END OF THE TWELVE HUNDRED AND NINETY DAYS.—Daniel was informed that even the wise would be unable to understand what was meant by "a time, times, and a half" until 1290 days "from the time the daily shall be taken away and the abomination that maketh desolate set up." The abomination having been set up A.D. 533, the 1290 days end A.D. 1823, at which time the rainbow angel, though "clothed with a cloud" of obscurity, "had in his hand a little book opened;" and he "cried with a loud voice as when a lion roareth,"—for the midnight cry alarmed the kingdoms of the earth,—in affirming "by him that liveth forever and ever . . . that there shall be time no longer. But in the days of the voice of the seventh angel, when he shall begin to sound, the mystery of God shall be finished, as he hath declared to his servants the prophets." (Rev. x. 1–17.) Since which time the virgins, roused from slumber, have been trimming their lamps (Matt. xxv. 7), or eating the little book, which is indeed "sweet as honey," to those who delight to feast on the truths as now developed in God's sacred volume, but bitter to the carnal nature; for since "the little book" is eaten (Rev. x. 9), it is discovered that the end of all things is at hand. After "the little book" is eaten, the Church must prophesy again before many people, and nations, and tongues, and kings" (Rev. x. 11), "for yet a little while and he that shall come will come, and will not tarry." (Heb. x. 37.) Though since 1843, the Church has been eating the "little book," these things are not to be understood until 1864; for those who would understand must, with untiring wrestling in prayer with God, continue "mourning three full weeks," or twenty-one years, before we can have a full "understanding of the vision." (Dan. x. 2, 3.)

A.D. 1868. THE YEAR OF JUBILEE.—Those who pay but little attention to the types and shadows under the law, sometimes sing,

"The year of jubilee has come!
Return, ye ransomed sinners, home,"

as if they supposed that the gospel dispensation is the antitype of the jubilee. To such we propose a few questions:—

1. If the law was "a shadow of good things to come," ought not the shadow to bare some resemblance to that which is shadowed forth?

2. Did Israel leave Egypt in the year of jubilee, or was it not a Sabbath of sabbaths before the first jubilee?

3. Was the sojourning in the wilderness during the jubilee, or before the first jubilee?

4. Were sinners, Gentiles, or proselytes, received into the Jewish Church only in the year of jubilee, or at all times?

5. If the year of jubilee was "a shadow of good things to come," how can the reformation of sinners, who were coming to God more than two thousand years before the law, be that which was shadowed forth?

6. If the year of jubilee was a definite period of time, without which there was no jubilee, how can that be the antitype in which there is nothing definite as to time?

So far from there being any thing in the type resembling that of sinners returning to Christ, it was something pertaining alone to the people of God, to be observed "when ye come into the land which I give thee, saith the Lord." In the type they returned "every man unto his possessions" (Lev. xxv. 13); but the sinner has no possessions. They are "aliens from the commonwealth of Israel, and strangers from the covenant of promise having no hope." (Ephes. ii. 12.) Instead of returning to their possessions, they come saying, "Lord, make me as one of thy hired-servants." (Luke xv. 18). Hence, the year of jubilee could not have been a type of the reformation of sinners, but was "a figure for the time then present" (Heb. ix. 9) of the true Israel's returning to their everlasting possessions when "the great trumpet shall be blown;" for "the trumpet shall sound and the dead shall be raised." The type was a definite period of time at which not sinners, strangers, nor Gentiles, but the people of God, "shall return every man unto his possessions;" hence, it can only reach its antitype in the true Israel of God returning home to their everlasting possessions at a definite period of time. In the type, all of those who felt disposed to pay attention to that method of reckoning time, as enjoined by the God of Israel, knew when the year of jubilee would occur; hence, in the antitype, those who honor God so much as to seek to comprehend that which he has declared that "the wise shall understand," must know, when the year of jubilee will be proclaimed, they shall "see the day approaching." (Heb. x. 25.) By reference to our chronological tables, it will be seen that A.D. 1868 is the forty-ninth sabbatical year, in which, on the 10th of the seventh month, the year of jubilee begins. At B.C. 1563, we observed that "the land had enjoyed her sabbaths within the limits of seventy years; and if the law concerning the sabbatical rest of the land was fulfilled in the space of seventy years, then there can be but seventy jubilees; hence, with the beginning of the seventy-first jubilee the great antitype must commence; and on the Jewish sabbath, Saturday, the 10th of the seventh month, A.D. 1868, the seventy-first jubilee will begin, at which time the type,—"Then shalt thou cause the trumpet of the jubilee to sound on the tenth day of the seventh month,"—must reach its antitype in the proclamation of the great jubilee. As to the day and month of our time with which this synchronizes, we—omitting to mention—must leave for others to find out. For if the "carnal mind is enmity against God" (Rom. viii. 7), it is impossible for us to speak of the day and hour of the coming of Christ without exciting the prejudices of those who love not the appearing of our Lord. But the faithful watchman upon the walls of Zion who, with Paul can say, "I have not shunned to declare unto you all the counsel of God," could not say less concerning definite time than we have; for preferring to know nothing concerning the matter ourselves, we have only set in order and exhibited to view that which is found in God's sacred volume. If it be true that we cannot know aught about the second coming of Christ, why are those who teach this doctrine reduced to the necessity of perverting the word of God by quoting as Scriptural that which is not in the

Bible. Their one universal, and about the only, argument that they pretend to offer is this: "Of that day and hour no man shall know: no, not the angels in heaven, nor even Christ himself." To such we have often said: Show us this in the Bible, and we will destroy every thing we have written on the subject. But why is it that even those who profess to take the Bible as the word of their counsel, are so ready to receive that which is not found there, and so much disposed to reject that which is? If, crucifying our nature, we could become as little children, having no clashing preferments or desires of our own, as much as to receive the express language of Christ, we are taught to believe that the Father will make known to his children not only the day, but the very hour, at which Christ will "appear the second time without sin unto salvation;" for after our Lord had given those signs by which we may know his appearing is near, "even at the door," he informed his disciples that he himself would not reveal the exact day and hour, but that his father would. Let us give his own words: "But of that day and that hour no man maketh known; not even the angels who are in heaven; neither the Son, but the Father." (Mark xiii. 32.) We have here followed Macknight's translation; for King James's translation contradicts the express words of Peter, who declared that Christ knew "all things." (John xxi. 17.) If it be true, "in him dwelleth all the fullness of the godhead bodily" (Col. ii. 9), he must have known the day and hour. To show the correctness of Macknight's translation, we ask who would ever think of translating Numbers xvi. 5 thus: "To-morrow the Lord will know who are his;" and since with one consent, at that place, all translate the same word, "the Lord will show," or "the Lord will make known," why not translate it in Mark in a similar manner? Where the Apostle Paul uses the same word, Macknight renders it "make known,"—thus: "I determined to make known nothing among you but Jesus Christ and him crucified." (1 Cor. ii. 2.) If, when Paul uses the same word, all understand him to mean "make known," why not understand the word, when used by Mark, to have the same meaning? But, it is said, if we render it "make known," it declares that the Father will make known both the day and the hour of the second coming of Christ: and they ask, Where is this made known? The book of Daniel being "closed up and sealed," they were unable to see when the Father had revealed the day and hour; hence, instead of "maketh known," they used the word, "knoweth." As this denies the divinity of Christ, some try to smooth it over by saying, "while he as God knew it, he as man knew it not." But since it is absurd to say that he knew, and yet did not know it, others conclude that this text was not in the original, and that the expression, "neither the Son," must have been added by some author after the apostolic age; in proof of which they tell us it is not "found in the parallel places in the other evangelists." We reply: As Luke and John have entirely omitted what we find in ver. 32, there is no parallel passage except that of Matthew xxiv. 36; and though we do not there find the express words, "neither the Son," yet Matthew uses the expression, "but my Father only," which is equivalent to the expression, "neither the Son, "for the word, "only," excludes the Son; hence, if we are willing to admit that Peter spoke that which was strictly true when he said, "Lord, thou knowest all things" (John xxi. 17), we must admit that Macknight has given a correct translation of this text. According to it, the Father must make known the day and hour at which our Lord will "appear the second time." Since neither the angels of heaven, nor the Son himself is to do this, he could not have meant that the day and hour would not be made known until his coming; for when he comes, the day and hour must then be made known, both by the appearing of himself and the holy angels. We must, therefore, go back to that dispensation in which the Father spoke to man before he sent his Son into the world (Heb. i. 2), and see if indeed He has made known the day and hour; for though it was not for the disciples at that time to know "the times or the seasons which the Father hath put in his own power," "ye shall receive power" to understand "after that the Holy Ghost is come upon you" (Acts i. 8); for "ye, brethren, are not in darkness that that day should overtake you as a thief." (1 Thess. v. 4.) Mark the expression,—not "year," but "day." By reference to the law as given at Mount Sinai in Arabia, when the Father spoke to Moses, we find: "Then shalt thou cause the trumpet of the jubilee to sound: on the tenth day of the seventh month in the day of atonement shall ye make the trumpet sound throughout all your land" (Lev. xxv. 9), which we are taught was "a figure for the time then present," "a shadow of good things to come." In the shadow, the trump did on the same day "sound throughout all" the land; hence, if the type properly represent the antitype, "the great trumpet" must sound throughout all the earth on the 10th of the seventh month. And if at one time this world's great jubilee will be proclaimed throughout all the land, the trump must not begin to sound until the 10th of the seventh month shall have enveloped the whole earth, which will be at the time of the going down of the sun at Jerusalem on Saturday evening. As the Jews began their day "at evening when the sun did set," this hour is at the end of the Jewish sabbath, and commences with the beginning of "the Lord's day." The Lord's day following the seventh day of the week, it was called the eighth day; and Barnabas, who was a companion and fellow-preacher with Paul, says, "the eighth day, —that is, the beginning of the other world. For which cause we observe the eighth day with gladness, in which Jesus rose from the dead." (Barn. xiii. 9.) At A.D. 533, we remarked that the 1335 days commenced about the end of the 10th of the seventh month, on the eve of St. Cyprian. As "the churches were already adorned and illuminated for the festival," the hour seems to have been at about sunset; hence, the 1335 days end at the same hour at which the 10th of the seventh month will have encircled the whole earth, or at which it will in all parts of the world be the 10th of the seventh month. The Lord "hath appointed a day in the which he will judge the world;" and if he "will do nothing, but he revealeth his secrets unto his servants the prophets" (Amos iii. 7), his people will "see the day approaching."

Suppose with those who turn a deaf ear to every thing which is uncongenial to their own carnal nature, we could admit that we are to know nothing about the time of the second coming of Christ; then they who have refused to obey Christ in searching "the Scriptures" are wiser or nearer the truth than those who have both day and night made the Bible their untiring and prayerful study; and Paul must have been mistaken in saying, "All Scripture is given by inspiration of God, and is profitable;" for the prophetic dates of the Bible, so far from being profitable, are only to bewilder and plunge the most zealous seeker for truth into the grossest error. Paul must also have written an untruth when he said: "But ye, brethren, are not in darkness that that day should overtake you as a thief;" for they would be in as gross darkness concerning the time as those on whom we "know perfectly that the day of the Lord so cometh as a thief in the night." (1 Thess. v. 2.) If we are not to "see the day approaching," then the time to assemble ourselves together "so much the more" (Heb. x. 25) can never come; hence, this much at least of inspiration is in vain. If we are unable to know when the time "is near, even at the door," we are unable to obey Christ; for he has positively commanded us "to know." (Matt. xxiv. 33.) If those who have received the Spirit of Christ, have it not in their "power" to know "the times and the seasons" of the restoration of the kingdom of

Israel," then the word of Christ has failed; for he said, "Ye shall receive power after that the Holy Ghost is come upon you." (Acts i. 8.) If the year of jubilee does not point out the time of the great jubilee, then Paul must have been mistaken in supposing this was "a shadow of good things to come;" for without definite time there was no jubilee. If the wise are unable to understand what was meant by "a time, times and a half " as used in Daniel xii. 7, then the word of God is untrue; for he has declared that they "shall understand." If, on the condition that "thou shalt not watch" the signs of the times and unfolding prophetic dates, Christ "will come upon thee as a thief, and thou shalt not know what hour he will come" (Rev. iii. 3), does it not follow that on the condition that we do watch we shall "know what hour he will come?" And if he to whom the Lord will "come in a day when he looketh not for him, and in an hour that he is not aware of," being cut asunder, shall have "his portion with the hypocrites," in "weeping and gnashing of teeth" (Matt. xxiv. 51), does it not become us to give heed to the admonition of Christ: "Watch, therefore; for ye know neither the day nor the hour wherein the Son of man cometh?" (Matt. xxv. 13.)

A.D. 1868. EZEKIEL'S SEVEN-YEARS WAR.—Ezekiel's war with Gog is the same with that of Rev. xix. 19, and Daniel's "time of trouble such as never was since there was a nation even to that same time." (Dan. xii. 1.) This war is to "be in the latter day," after Israel returns home (Ezek. xxxviii. 11, 16), which is at the time of the second coming of Christ. (Rom. xi. 26: Dan. vii. 27.) "The Jerusalem Targum" on Numbers xi. 26 says that "Eldad and Medad" "both prophesied together and said:" "In the very end of time, Gog or Magog and their army shall come up against Jerusalem, and they shall fall by the hand of the King Messiah; and for seven whole years shall the children of Israel light their fires with the wood of their warlike engines; and they shall not go to the wood, nor cut down any tree." This is in harmony with Rev. xix. 21: "The remnant were slain with the sword of him that sat upon the horse," whose "name is called the word of God." (Rev. xix. 13.) According to a Jewish tradition, "In the time when God shall execute vengeance for the people of Israel, he shall feed all the beasts of the earth for twelve months with their flesh and all the fowls for seven years." As Ezekiel's war is with Gog, it cannot begin until the rise of that people called Gog. At present, no people on earth are known by this name. From Rev. xx. 8, we learn that Gog is a term applied to no particular nation, but to all "which are in the four quarters of the earth," —that is, to all who are not recognized as the children of God after the second coming of Christ. It is evident, therefore, that the war with Gog will not begin until after the second coming of Christ. Though the warfare is between Gog and Israel, it is said: "Every man's sword shall be against his brother." What can this mean but that Gog and Israel are brethren according to the flesh. At the time of this war, "the mountains shall be thrown down" (Ezek. xxxviii. 20); and the time the "mountains were not found" (Rev. xvi. 21) was after the coming of Christ.

All the prophetic dates from the time of the Babylonish captivity to the second coming of Christ are according to the year-day system; but those which do not begin until after his coming are literal, which is evident from Rev. xx. 5; and it is unreasonable to suppose the battle with Gog will continue 2555 years; and more so to suppose that they will be 207 years "burying of them;" hence, we understand seven literal years (Ezek. xxxix. 9), which beginning after the coming of Christ in A.D. 1868, will end in 1875. From Revelation xix., it is evident that this war is to be during the interval between the second coming of Christ and the beginning of the great Sabbath of rest. The saints are to "be caught up" "in the clouds to meet the Lord in the air" in A.D. 1868, but will not until 1875 enter "the holy city, New Jerusalem;" for though the saints are delivered before the beginning of "the seven last plagues," which answers to Ezekiel's Seven-years War, "no man was able to enter into the temple" "of God" till the seven plagues of the seven angels were fulfilled." (Rev. xv. 9.)

A.D. 1868. THE FEAST OF INGATHERING.—"The feast of ingathering which is in the end of the year when thou hast gathered in thy labors out of the field" (Ex. xxiii. 16) was a shadow of that feast of joy in which "thou shalt rejoice" (Deut. xvi. 14) with Christ, or "eat and drink" with him at his "table" (Luke xxii. 30), after the ingathering of souls at the end of this world. (Matt. xiii. 30.) It commenced on "the fifteenth day of the seventh month," and continued "seven days." (Lev. xxiii. 39.) As that which is shadowed forth cannot be the same with the shadow, in the antitype each day must be a year; and seven years, reckoning from the 15th of the seventh month, A.D. 1868, end on the 15th of the seventh month, A.D. 1875. "On the first day shall be a sabbath." (Lev. xxiii. 39.) The first day answers to A.D. 1868, which is both a sabbatical year and the year of jubilee. "And on the eighth day shall be a sabbath." The eighth day synchronizes with A.D. 1875, which is a sabbatical year, and the beginning of the great sabbath of rest.

A.D. 1868. THE FEAST OF TABERNACLES foreshadowed that in which the people of God, having been delivered from the "time of trouble such as never was" (Dan. xii. 1), will dwell as it were in tabernacles, or in what is called "the cities of Israel" (Ezek. xxxix. 9) until the end of Ezekiel's Seven-years War, at which time, "the sanctuary" being cleansed, they will enter "the beloved city" (Rev. xx. 9), "the New Jerusalem" (Rev. xxi. 2), "whose builder and maker is God." (Heb. xi. 10.) "On the first day shall be a holy convocation." (Lev. xxiii. 35.) The first day in the antitype answers to A.D. 1868, during which there must be "a holy convocation,"—that is, God will call the holy assembly of Israel." "For the trumpet shall sound and the dead shall be raised. (1 Cor. xv. 52.) "Then we which are alive and remain shall be caught up together with them in the clouds to meet the Lord in the air." (1 Thess. iv. 17.) "On the eighth day shall be a holy convocation unto you." (Lev. xxiii. 36.) The eight day answers to A.D. 1875, at which time, "the sanctuary" being "cleansed," there will be a holy assembly of the saints at "the holy city, New Jerusalem," which cometh "down from God out of heaven prepared as a bride adorned for her husband." (Rev. xxi. 2.) Those who are not ready at the second coming of Christ to "go up from year to year," for seven "years to keep the feast of tabernacles," "upon them shall be no rain" of grace (Zech. xiv. 16, 17); hence, in the terror of the soul, they will cry unto the "mountains and rocks, Fall on us, and hide us from the face of him that sitteth on the throne, and from the wrath of the Lamb." (Rev. vi. 16.)

A.D. 1868. "HOLY CONVOCATIONS TO BE PROCLAIMED IN THEIR SEASON."—That "shadow of heavenly things," as thrown back into the Mosaic dispensation, being "the law" (Heb. x. 1), and not the manner in which the Jews observed it in noticing those "patterns of things in the heavens" (Heb. ix. 23), we must pay strict attention to the express language of the law, regardless of the manner in which the Jews observed it. The Jews, for instance, observed the feast of Pentecost on the 6th of the third month, which, if we regard, we can never find the antitype; but if we adhere strictly to the language of the law, which was, that "the feast of harvest" be observed on the fiftieth day "from the morrow after the sabbath" (Lev. xxiii. 15), we find a most sublime antitype, in strict harmony with every portion of the law. The high-priest entered the most holy on the 10th of the seventh month, which if we regard we will be unable to find the antitype; but if we notice the express language of the law, the difficulty is removed; for at first there was nothing definite as to the time he was to enter, more than this: "That he come not at all times into the holy place within the vail" (Lev. xvi. 2); hence, in the antitype, "He entered in once into the holy place." (Heb. ix. 12.) But while there was at first no law as to the particular day on which the high-priest was to enter the most holy, the time after this was, by a positive law, restricted to "the tenth day of the seventh month" (Lev. xxiii. 27); therefore, if "one jot or one tittle shall in nowise pass from the law till all be fulfilled" (Matt. v. 18), this "shadow of heavenly things" must have a twofold accomplishment: first, without, second, with, regard to definite time; and since that portion of this "shadow of heavenly things" which is without definite time is expressly declared to be that of entering "the holy place," "that he come not at all times into the holy place," it follows that that which remains to be accomplished in definite time is his coming out to bless the people, which was on the day of atonement (Lev. xvi. 17); therefore, He who, without regard to definite time, has entered "into heaven itself now to appear in the presence of God for us" (Heb. ix. 24), will, on the tenth of the seventh month, "appear the second time without sin unto salvation" (Heb. ix. 28),—that is, to "blot out" the "sins" of those who have been "converted" (Acts iii. 19) "and thus turn away ungodliness from Jacob." (Rom. xi. 26.) Concerning the year of jubilee, there was no twofold type: the law here was definite and positive: "On the tenth day of the seventh month," "then," and then only, "shalt thou cause the trumpet of the jubilee to sound throughout all your land," and these holy convocations" "ye shall proclaim in their seasons" (Lev. xxiii. 4); hence, this "shadow of good things to come" can find its antitype nowhere but on the 10th of the seventh month, which must be found in the forty-ninth year of the Jewish cycle; for in no other was the year of jubilee proclaimed.

A.D. 1875. EZEKIEL'S SEVEN MONTHS.—"It shall come to pass in that day that I will give unto Gog a place there of graves in Israel;" "and seven months shall the house of Israel be bearing of them that they may cleanse the land." (Ezek. xxxix. 11, 12.) "For behold the day cometh that shall burn as an oven; and all the proud, yea, all that do wickedly shall be stubble, and the day that cometh shall burn them up, saith the Lord of hosts, that it shall leave them neither root nor branch." (Mal. iv. 1.) "The heavens shall pass away with a great noise, and the elements shall melt with fervent heat; the earth also, and the works that are therein 'shall be burnt up." (2 Pet. iii. 10.) Daniel's 2300 days—at the end of which the sanctuary is to be cleansed—did not begin with the month, Abib, the first month of the sacred year, but on the 15th of the month Nisan (Est. iii. 7), which was the embolismic month, as used once in three years; and A.D. 1875 being also a leap year, they cannot reach the second first month, or Abib, but end on the 15th of Nisan; hence, the seven months which are to be spent in cleansing the land, commencing with the end of the 2300 days, on the 15th of Nisan, will end with the feast of tabernacles on the 15th of the seventh month, A.D. 1875, on which day the world being 6000 years old, reckoning from the fall of Adam, the great Millennial Sabbath of rest will begin.

A.D. 1875. THE LORD'S RELEASE.—Among those "patterns of things in the heavens," was this one: "At the end of seven years thou shalt make a release." (Deut. xv. 1.) The word, "every," was not in the original, but supplied by the translator. If we restrict ourselves to the language of the law, this release is not at the end of every seven years, but "at the end of seven years; hence, is properly a prophetic date. As the ten tribes of Israel were taken captive about the 15th of the seventh month, B.C. 681, the seven-years release end about the 15th of the seventh month, A.D. 1875. At which time the type required, saying: "At the end of seven years, let ye go every man his brother, a Hebrew, which hath been sold unto thee" (Jer. xxxiv. 14;) therefore, those who are ready to go up "to worship the King, the Lord of hosts, and to keep the feast of tabernacles," "from year to year," for seven years (Zach. xiv. 16), may at that time expect a release, or they shall return home to "the holy city, New Jerusalem. Moses's seven times, or 2555 years measure the same period during which the children of Israel must remain absent from their kingdom. (Acts i. 6.) This in no way clashes with the fact that the year of jubilee is to be proclaimed seven years before; for while the type required that "the trumpet of the jubilee" should sound "on the tenth day of the seventh month," the Jews, according to the law, had first to keep the feast of tabernacles before they could "return every man unto their possession;" and though the saints will in A.D. 1868 "be caught up in the clouds to meet the Lord in the air," they may yet be considered absent from their home until they enter "the holy city, New Jerusalem" in 1875. "And I, John, saw the holy city, New Jerusalem, come down from God out of heaven prepared as a bride adorned for her husband." "And the city was pure gold like unto clear glass. "The length and the breadth and the height of it are equal;" for "the city lieth four square," being twelve thousand furlongs," or 1500 miles in length, breadth, and height. If, leaving one-half for those golden streets, which are as "transparent glass," we divide the remaining portion of the city into rooms 16 feet square, and the same in height, it would contain 60,643,687,500,000,000 rooms; therefore, our Lord could well say: "In my Father's house are many mansions." If we allow but 25 years to a generation, and could suppose that during each generation there had lived 1,200,600,000 persons, we would have only 288,144,000,000; hence, if a room of the dimensions we have given were assigned to every individual who has lived on this earth, there would yet remain in our Father's house—the New Jerusalem, the glorious city of our God—more than 60,643,399,356,000,000 rooms* unoccupied.

A.D. 1875. THE WORLD SIX THOUSAND YEARS OLD.—The ancient Jews had a tradition that the world would last but 6000 years. The learned Gregory of Oxford gives us their argument, as follows:—"Because God was six days about the creation, and a thousand years with him are but as one day (Ps. xc. 4), therefore, after six days, that is, after 6000 years' duration of the world, there shall be a seventh day, or millenary sabbath of rest." In our Bible the same doctrine is taught: "They lived and reigned with Christ a thousand years." (Rev. xx. 4.) Paul, in allusion to this great Sabbath of rest, says: "There remaineth therefore a rest" (a keeping of a sabbath) "to the people of God." (Heb. iv. 9.) "For he spake in a certain place of the seventh day in this wise. And God did rest the seventh day from all his works." Our attention is here called to the words of Moses: "God ended his works which he had made, and he rested on the seventh day from all his works." (Gen. ii. 2.) The apostle thus proves this to be typical of that rest which remaineth "to the people of God:" "And in this place again if they shall enter into my rest;" "seeing, therefore, it remaineth that some must enter therein, and they to whom it was first preached entered not in because of unbelief." Paul proves that this rest is yet future, thus: "For if Jesus" (Joshua) "had given them rest, then would he not afterwards have spoken of another day." (Heb. iv. 4–8.) In an epistle to the Colossians, he again teaches the same doctrine: "The sabbath" is "a shadow of things to come." (Col. ii. 17.) And if the sabbath which remaineth

---

* That is 60 quadrillions, 643 trillions, 399 billions, 356 millions.

"to the people of God" is a period of a thousand years, those six days, which were in the type followed by the sabbath, must each foreshadow a period of equal duration; for the type must represent the antitype. Barnabas, Paul's companion and fellow-preacher, taught this same doctrine, thus: "God made in six days the works of his hands, and he finished them on the seventh day, and he rested on the seventh day and sanctified it. Consider, my children, what that signifies: he finished them in six days. The meaning of it is this: that in six thousand years the Lord God will bring all things to an end. For with him one day is a thousand years, as himself testifieth, saying, Behold, this day shall be a thousand years: therefore, children, in six days, that is, in six thousand years, shall all things be accomplished." (Bar. xiii. 3–5.) It is said: "All the early Christian fathers expected the advent at the termination of 6000 years from the creation." And we will here ask, if God's object in the six days' creation was not to give a figure of the 6000 years' interval between creation and the great Sabbath of rest, and thus teach the time of the end, why did he employ just six days in creation. Could he not have spoken all into existence at once, as well as in six days? Why is it mentioned, "he rested on the seventh day" (Gen. ii. 2), if not to point out the time of "rest" which "remaineth . . to the people of God." Are we to suppose that God was weary and required rest? But we are not left to conjecture; for Isaiah expressly mentions that the Lord hath declared "the end from the beginning." (Isa. xlvi. 10.) [See p. 60.]

A.D. 1875. THE SABBATH OF REST.—"There remaineth a rest (a keeping of the sabbath) to the people of God" (Heb. iv. 9); "and they lived and reigned with Christ a thousand years" Justin Martyr, born A.D. 89, says: "A certain man among us whose name is John, being one of the twelve apostles of Christ, in the revelation which was shown him prophesied that those who believe in our Christ shall fulfill a thousand years at Jerusalem;" "that Christ shall reign personally on earth;" and that "all who were accounted orthodox so believed." This our Lord also taught: "Blessed are the meek; for they shall inherit the earth." (Matt. v. 5.) John says: "We shall reign on the earth." (Rev. v. 10.) "Tertullian, about A.D. 180, says: "It was a custom for Christians to pray that they might have part in the first resurrection;" for "Blessed and holy is he that hath part in the first resurrection. On such the second death hath no power; but they shall be priests of God and of Christ, and shall reign with him a thousand years." (Rev. xx. 6.) It is said that "the opinion that Christ was to come and reign a thousand years among men had met with no opposition before the middle of the third century." The great Sabbath, during which the Christians shall "live and reign with Christ a thousand years," commencing A.D. 1875, ends A.D. 2875. At which time "the rest of the dead"—those who have no part in the first resurrection—must be raised "to shame and everlasting contempt." (Dan. xii. 2.)

CONCLUDING REMARKS.

SINCE we do not claim a new revelation, but merely aim to exhibit the sacred truths of our Bible,—that book which has been perused for the last eighteen hundred years,—it may now be asked: If these things be true, why were they not discovered before? We reply: Suppose it were claimed for a volume that it had been written by a certain author, would we not endeavor to ascertain the correctness of the assertion by comparing it with other productions of the same writer, and, if found unlike them, would we not doubt its authenticity? In every department of nature, there is a law of continual progression. If the author of the book of nature be also the author of our Bible, its contents should be subjected to the same law, and its truths continually unfolding. The Bible has been gradually revealing to man the sacred counsels of God; and that spark—"the seed of the woman shall bruise the serpent's head"—which at first was almost too obscure to be noticed has increased in brilliancy through the prophetic age, as the "light that shineth more and more unto the perfect day." (Prov. iv. 18.) The prophets had declared the sufferings of Christ, and he had informed his disciples that he must "be killed, and be raised again the third day;" "yet they knew not the Scriptures, that he must rise again from the dead." But when the proper time for them to know had come, "then opened he their understanding, that they might understand the Scriptures" (Luke xxiv. 45); hence, this has now become so clear that those who know not the way of our God are astonished at what they call the apostle's ignorance. So it is with the book of Daniel. In time past its meaning was unknown; but the truths therein revealed are now so evident that we are filled with awe at their discovery being reserved for the present day. Again: our Lord commanded his apostles to "Go into all the world and preach the gospel to every creature;" yet they were unable, until about seven years afterward, to understand they were to minister to others besides the Jews. And so, too, with the second coming of Christ: it was not for the Christians at that day "to know the times and the seasons which the Father had put in his own power;" but they had the promise that they should in due time: "Ye shall receive power after that the Holy Ghost is come upon you." (Acts i. 8.)

The vision of Daniel was gradually developed. At first it had only been seen by the Babylonish king, and then lost in forgetfulness; but now to the wise men of Babylon its understanding became a matter of life and death. The people of God then gave themselves to prayer, and at length to one the vision was revealed. But it was yet obscure, being only an image representing the kingdoms of the earth, and showing to the people of God that at the end of all earthly dominions the Lord would set up his kingdom. After this the vision was again revealed, when Daniel saw different beasts typifying those earthly powers which were to rule over the Israel of God, accompanied with one prophetic date, yet nothing definite as to the time of the end. But in another vision he saw not only the same powers, but was informed what kingdoms they represented, and received a clear prophetic date measuring the whole length of the vision. After this, in yet another vision, he receives an unbroken prophetic history extending to the coming of Christ, accompanied with dates pointing out the exact time of "the resurrection of the just." This vision has been disclosed to man according to that law of gradual progression in which it was delivered to Daniel; hence, Paul could well say: "But ye, brethren," being obedient to the precepts of Christ in watching the signs of the times and the unfolding prophetic writings, "are not in darkness that that day should overtake you as a thief." Why? "For ye are all the children of light." (1 Thess. v. 5.) Ye have in your possession that book which, being the "path of the just, is as a shining light that shineth more and more unto the perfect day" (Prov. iv. 18), making known to you the time of the coming of Christ. (Dan. xii. 12.)

Brethren,—ye who make so light of our pretensions to know any thing concerning the time of the coming of Christ, saying, "Where is the promise of his coming? for since the fathers fell asleep, all things continue as they were from the beginning of the creation,"—are you aware that He whom you profess to love and obey has given us a positive commandment, both to watch out for, and know the time of, his coming. Having given those signs by which we may know it is near, he admonishes us to "watch." And why? "for ye know not what hour your Lord doth come;" but "when ye shall see all these things" which Christ has given as a sign of his coming, then he commands us to "know that it is near, even at the doors." (Matt. xxiv. 33.) Now, whom shall we obey: those who are so wise as to pretend to know without investigation that we can know nothing about the matter, or him who has a right to command, saying, "Take heed to yourselves lest that day come upon you unawares" (Luke xxi. 34)? It is said, so far from our knowing any thing about the time, the Bible teaches that Christ himself did not know it. It is true that in King James's translation we read: "But of that day and that hour knoweth no man; no, not the angels which are in heaven, nor the Son, but the Father." To which we answer: Will those who offer this objection deny the divinity of Christ?—as much as to say, He who is now seated on the right hand of the throne of God in heaven does not know when he will return the second time to our earth. And if this language teaches that we can know nothing about the time, does it not also teach that Christ our God can know nothing about it? But the New Testament was written not in English by King James's translators, but in Greek by inspired authors; and we have already mentioned that Macknight translates this place, "maketh known,"—the correctness of which is evident from the words of Peter: "Lord, thou knowest all things." (John xxi. 17.) The word of Christ, saying, "God giveth not the Spirit by measure unto him" (John iii. 34), also testifies to the correctness of Macknight's translation; for if that day and hour was unknown to him, then the spirit was given by measure. Paul declares that "in him dwelleth all the fullness of the godhead bodily;" hence, equal with the Father, in all knowledge. Those who "by good words and fair speeches deceive the hearts of the simple," say while Christ as the Son of God knew all things, he as the Son of man knew not the time of his second coming; but if the reader will turn to Mark xiii. 32, it will be seen that the Father, whom in this place, he was alluding to himself as the Son of, was not the husband of Mary, but the God of heaven; hence, their reasoning, if of any weight, all falls into the opposite scale. But even if he had said, "the Son of man," how absurd to say that he knew it, and yet knew it not. We must therefore follow Macknight's translation: "But of that day and hour no man maketh known, not even the angels who are in heaven; neither the Son, but the Father." This text declares that the Father will make known both the day and hour; which being so revolting to that carnal nature, which is "enmity against God," accounts for our translators having rendered it, "knoweth," instead of "maketh known." Our Lord here teaches that while neither men, angels, nor the Son, shall reveal the day and hour of the coming of Christ, the Father will.

There are four books containing the law of God the Father, as delivered in person to his people and recorded by Moses; and there are four containing the words of Christ the Son, as delivered in person to his disciples, and recorded by Matthew, Mark, Luke, and John. The remainder consists of the writings of men as moved by the Holy Spirit. And since neither man nor the Son himself is to make known the day nor the hour of the coming of Christ, we must look for it in the law as delivered by the Father to Moses; and though it was "not for" the first Christians "to know the times or the seasons which the Father hath put in his own power," it is declared, "ye shall receive power after that the Holy Ghost is come upon you" (Acts i. 8); for "the wise shall understand:" "Ye, brethren, are not in darkness that that day should overtake you as a thief." For though God compels none to believe against their will, those who are willing to receive the truth may "see the day approaching." (Heb. x. 25.) But, alas! "My people are destroyed for lack of knowledge" (Hos. iv. 6); their "shepherds cannot understand: they are all looking to their own way, every one for his gain from his quarter" (Isa. lvi. 11): and "how can ye believe, which receive honor one of another, and seek not the honor that cometh from God only?" (John v. 44.) Wo unto you who are at ease in Zion, crying, "Peace! peace! when there is no peace." Since you admit you know not the time, why not take the admonition of Christ: "Watch, therefore: for ye know not what hour your Lord doth come"? Why not believe his word when he says: "If therefore, thou shalt not watch, I will come on thee as a thief, and thou shalt not know what hour I will come upon thee?" Have you, who are shielding yourselves from the coming wrath under the consolation that you know not the time, examined the awful doom of that servant to whom his Lord shall come "in an hour that he is not aware of"? Hear the word of Christ: "If that evil servant shall say in his heart, My Lord delayeth his coming, and shall begin to smite his fellow-servants, and to eat and drink with the drunken, the Lord of that servant shall come in a day when he looketh not for him, and in an hour that he is not aware of, and shall cut him asunder, and appoint him his portion with the hypocrites: there shall be weeping and gnashing of teeth." (Matt. xxiv. 45–51.)

Boast not that you do not sip the intoxicating draught:— "They are drunken, but not with wine; they stagger, but not with strong drink. For the Lord hath poured out upon you the spirit of deep sleep, and hath closed your eyes: the prophets and your rulers, the seers hath he covered. And the vision of all is become unto you as the words of a book that is sealed, which men deliver to one that is learned, saying, Read this, I pray thee; and he saith I cannot; for it is sealed." (Isa. xxix. 9–11.)

Are you, who so much despise the prophetic dates which point out definite time, aware that you are rejecting the time of the second coming of Christ in the same way that the Jews deny Jesus to be the Christ? When they were compelled either to reject the dates which pointed out the time of the coming of their Messiah, or admit that Jesus is the Christ, they pronounced a curse upon all who meddled with prophetic dates, saying, "May their soul be confounded who compute the times;" on which Dr. Clark remarks: "They were fully aware that the time foretold by the prophets must be long since fulfilled, and that their obstinacy must be confounded by their own history and the chronology of their own scriptures; therefore they have pronounced an anathema on those who shall attempt to examine by chronological computations the prophecies that predict his coming. Who can conceive a state of wilful blindness or obstinacy superior to this?" We may reply: In those who reject prophetic dates which are much clearer than those rejected by the Jews, we discover a blindness greater than that which Paul declares had come upon that people; for in rejecting their Messiah, the Jews had only to close their eyes to three clear prophetic dates. Will those who reject the definite time of the second coming of Christ, refuse to see a much clearer light, or more than four times three prophetic dates?

Under that typical dispensation, all who acted the more noble part, in that they "searched the scriptures daily to see whether these things were so," entered into rest through faith in Christ; but those who trusted to the benighted wisdom of man, saying, "Have any of the rulers believed on him?" perished because they knew not the time of their visitation. (Luke xix. 44.)

In the days of Noah, all that were saved knew the very day: "Yet seven days and I will cause it to rain upon the earth forty days and forty nights" (Gen. vii. 4); but those who would not believe the preaching of Noah, were lost "for lack of knowledge:" and "as the days of Noah were, so shall also the coming of the Son of man be." (Matt. xxiv. 37.) In the parable of the good man we are admonished to know not only the day, but the very hour: "If the good man of the house had known in what watch the thief would come, he would have watched, and would not have suffered his house to be broken up." In allusion to this, we are admonished: "Be ye also ready;" that is, in the same manner in which the good man should have been by knowing in what "watch the thief would come." The reason urged as to why we should "watch" the signs of the times and unfolding prophetic dates, in order to know the time is: "for in such an hour as ye think not the Son of man cometh." (Matt. xxiv. 44.) And, true to the letter it is, all who refuse to listen to the admonition, "Search the scriptures," and also the precept of Christ, "Watch, for ye know not when the time is" "*think not*" of his coming during this generation in which Christ has declared that he will come; for they say there must be at least the interval of a thousand years; making the word of Christ strictly true: "In such an hour as ye think not the Son of man cometh." These words are also verified in the case of those who by faith "see the day approaching;" for we now see that the coming of Christ will be at a time which we thought he would not come, until we saw it mirrored forth in the word of God, who commands us, saying, "Call no man your *father* upon the earth;" but "Search the scriptures;" "and what I say unto you, I say unto all, Watch," "lest coming suddenly, he find you sleeping" (Mark xiii. 36, 37) "Watch ye, therefore, and pray always that ye may be accounted worthy to escape all those things that shall come to pass and to stand before the Son of man." (Luke xxi. 36.)

And now, brethren, since you and I must soon appear before the judgment-seat of Christ, let us remember—Oh, forget it not—the carnal mind, so much of which yet remains in our nature, being "enmity against God," he who has *not* that living faith which enables him to "deny himself and take up his cross and follow Christ," even to the hating as it were of "his own life" (Luke xiv. 26), cannot be so regardless of popular opinion, as to throw himself a living sacrifice into the hands of Christ and resolve, with Paul, to say, "I am pure from the blood of all men, for I have not shunned to declare unto you all the counsel of God." Since it requires faith almost transcending any thing human, to proclaim a doctrine which is so much despised, in that it cuts asunder every tie that binds to earth, and the truthfulness of which is so soon to be tested. We know that those whose faith is a mere assent to the religion of their fathers, cannot preach the glad tidings of the glorious coming and kingdom of our blessed Lord and Saviour Jesus Christ; yet may we not hope that they will have charity enough to bear with one to whom "a dispensation of the gospel is committed?" "for necessity is laid upon me;" "yea, wo is unto me if I preach not" this gospel: "for I neither received it of man, neither was I taught it but by the word of Jesus Christ." (Gal. i. 12.) Therefore, silence on my part would be to deny our Lord; for that same word of inspiration which enables me to receive Jesus of Nazareth, the Son of Mary, that meek and lowly Nazarene, as my Lord and my God, taught me to believe in the coming and reign of Christ.

Should you, whom the Lord has set as "watchmen unto the house of Israel," feel the solemn and awful responsibility resting upon us to sound the alarm "and warn the people" (Ezek. xxxiii. 3), "think it not strange concerning the fiery trials which are to try you as though some strange thing had happened unto you, but rejoice inasmuch as ye are partakers of Christ's sufferings" (1 Pet. iv. 12); for the doctrine of the second coming of our blessed Lord and Saviour is not more unpopular than that *entire submission* to Christ as preached in the apostolic age. An assent to the religion of the day, in which one may live, always was and always will be popular; but since "the carnal mind is enmity against God," it is impossible that the religion of Jesus can ever become popular in this sin-polluted world. Since He, whose servants we profess to be, was rejected of men, we must expect to share the same fate (John xv. 20); yet, regardless of the opinion of men, we should not shun to declare "all of the council of God."

DIAGRAM OF HOSEA'S TWO DAYS.

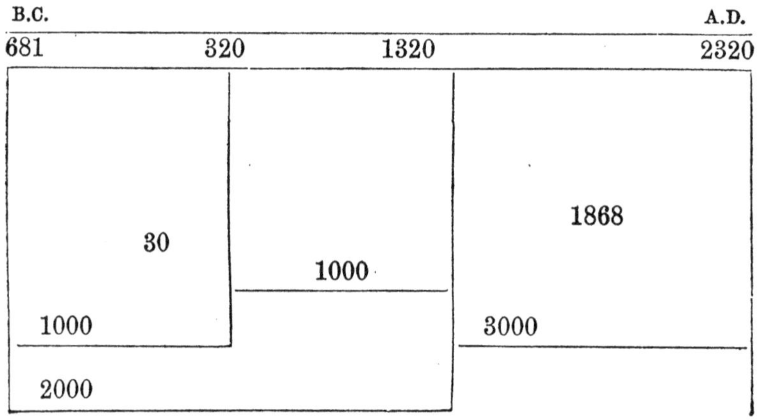

B.C. A.D.

681 320 1320 2320

30

1000

1868

1000

3000

2000

EXPLANATION OF DIAGRAM.

B.C. 681 is the time the kingdom of Israel was destroyed (p. 78), and 2000 is the two days of Hosea. (p. 82.)

A.D. 1320 is the end of Hosea's two days; and line 3000 shows that the third day ends A.D. 2320.

A.D. 1868 is the time at which in the third day the Lord "will raise us up, and we shall live in his sight." (Hos. vi. 2.)

A.D. 30 is the time our Saviour was casting out devils in Hosea's first day. (Luke xiii. 32.)

A.D. 320 is the end of Hosea's first day; and line 1000 is the morrow or second day, ending A.D. 1320; and 1868 the time at which Christ will be perfected in the third day. (Luke xiii. 32.)

DIAGRAM OF THE LAST GENERATION.

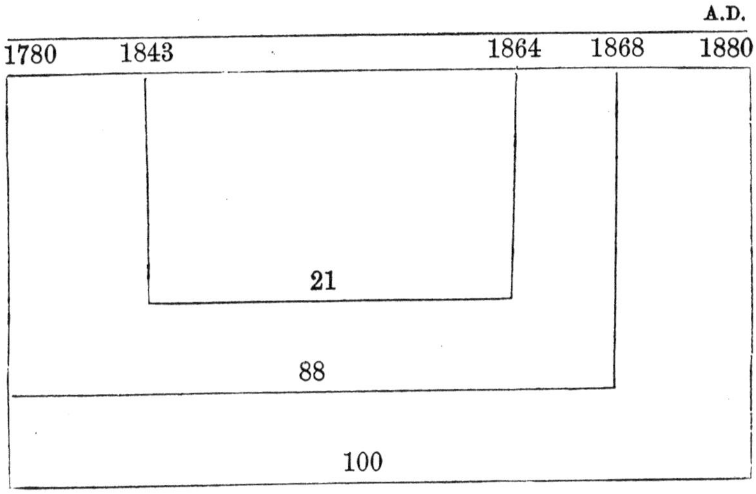

A.D.

1780 1843 1864 1868 1880

21

88

100

EXPLANATION OF DIAGRAM.

A.D. 1780 is the time of the darkening of the sun (p. 24); and line 100 shows that this generation, beginning with the darkening of the sun, ends A.D. 1880. (See p. 27.)

A.D. 1868, being the year of jubilee in which Christ must come, shows that it will be within the limits of this generation, beginning with 1780.

A.D. 1843 is the time the "midnight cry" was proclaimed; and line 21 is the twenty-one years during which the people of God must continue in mourning. (See p. 209.)

A.D. 1864 is the time at which those who have continued twenty-one years in perusing "the little book" (Rev. x. 9), and in prayer to God shall have an "understanding of the vision." (Dan. x. 1, 2.)

DIAGRAM OF DANIEL'S VISION.

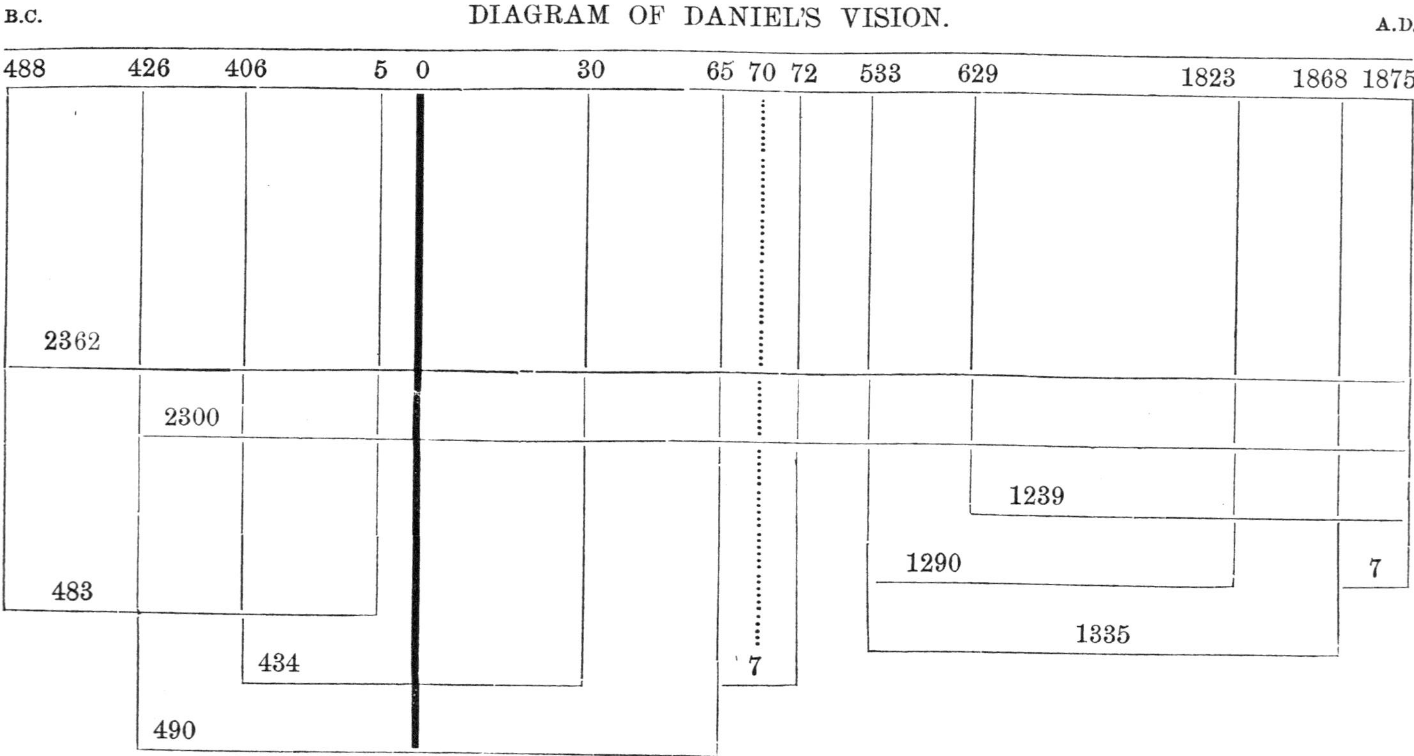

EXPLANATION OF DIAGRAM.

B.C. 488 is the time of the going forth of "the commandment to restore and to build Jerusalem" (see p. 121); from which line 483 reaches "unto the Messiah, the Prince" (Dan. ix. 25), who was "born King of the Jews" in the fifth year before the Christian era. (See B.C. 5 and p. 58.) Line 2362 is Daniel's "time, times, and a half," extending from B.C. 488 to A.D. 1875. (See p. 122.)

B.C. 426 is the time at which the Persian power commenced pushing for the slaughter of Daniel's people (See p. 167); and line 2300 commencing with the beginning of the vision, ends A.D. 1875. (See B.C. 426.) Line 490 is the 70 weeks which, being cut off of the 2300 days, end in A.D. 65. (See p. 168.)

B.C. 406 is the time of the completion of the wall (see B.C. 406); and line 434 is the period after which the Messiah was cut off. (Dan. ix. 26.)

0 is the Christian era. All to the left of which is before, and all to the right after, the Christian era.

A.D. 30 is the year of the crucifixion. (p. 193.)

A.D. 65 is the beginning of the war at Jerusalem; and line 7 is the "one week" during which the covenant was confirmed (A.D. 72).

A.D. 70 is the time at which "the sacrifice and oblation" ceased "in the midst of the week." (A.D. 70.)

A.D. 72 is the end of the war at Jerusalem, and end of the one-week covenant. (See A.D. 72.)

A.D. 533 is the time at which "the abomination that maketh desolate" was set up (see A.D. 533); and line 1290 is the length of time until the end of which the wise shall be unable to understand what was meant by the expression, "a time, times, and a half" (Dan. xii. 7); and line 1335 reaches to 1868, at which time Daniel will stand in his lot. (Dan. xii. 12.)

A.D. 629 is the time at which Mohammed commenced tramping the holy city under foot (see A.D. 629); and line 1239 is John's 42 months, ending 1868. (p. 208,)

A.D. 1823 is the end of the 1290 days; hence, the beginning of the time of the end, during which "the wise shall understand."

A.D. 1868 is the beginning of that great jubilee in which all prophetic dates center; and 7 is Ezekiel's Seven-years war, or the "time of trouble such as never was since there was a nation even to that same time." (p. 214.)

A.D. 1875 is the time at which the sanctuary will be cleansed and the beginning of the great Sabbath of rest. (p. 217.)

DIAGRAM OF TYPES AND SHADOWS.

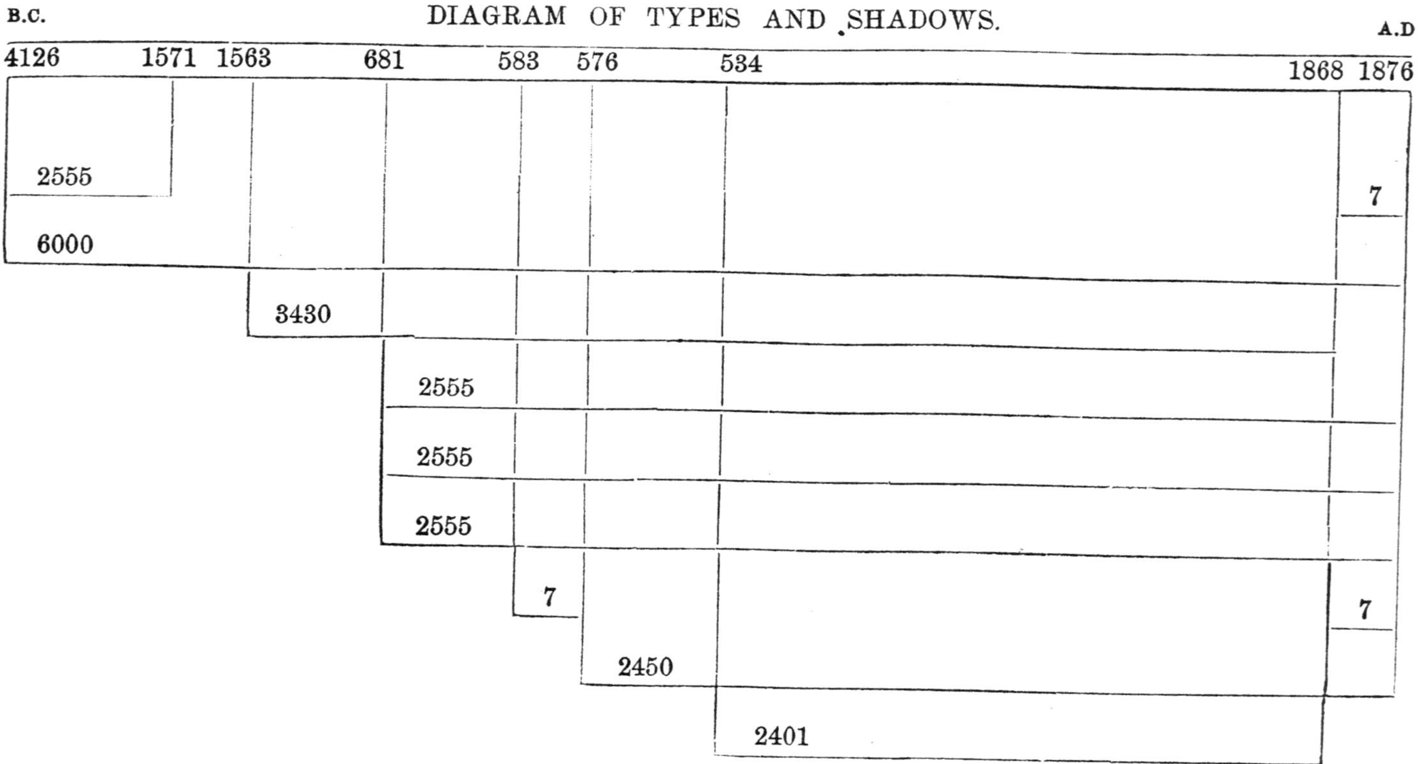

EXPLANATION OF DIAGRAM.

B.C. 4126 is the beginning of creation; and line 6000 shows that the world will be 6000 years old, A.D. 1875. (p. 59.)

B.C. 1571 is the time Israel entered the promised land after seven times' chastisement (p. 63); and line 2555 also represents the first seven-years service of Christ for his Church. (p. 64.)

B.C. 1563 is the first jubilee (p. 65); and line 3430 shows that the seventieth jubilee will end A.D. 1868. (p. 67.)

B.C. 681 is the time the ten tribes of Israel were taken captive (p. 78); and line 2555 shows that Moses's seven times end in A.D. 1875. (p. 79.) The second line of 2555 is the year of release (p. 81); the third is the antitype of Jacob's seven years (p. 64.)

B.C. 583 is the great jubilee passover (p. 86); and line 7 shows that the antitype of the seven days of unleavened bread ends B.C. 576. (p. 88.)

B.C. 576 is the sabbatical year as shadowed forth by the seventh day of unleavened bread; and line 2450 is the great Sabbath of sabbaths, including the fiftieth jubilee (p. 92), as shadowed forth by the seven sabbaths including the fiftieth day. (Lev. xxiii. 16.)

B.C. 534 is the time of the jubilee "sabbath of rest unto the land;" and line 2401 is the sabbath of sabbaths, ending in the jubilee sabbath of 1868.

A.D. 1868 is the forty-ninth year of the Jewish cycle; hence, the year of jubilee and line 7 shows that the antitype of the feast of tabernacles (p. 216) and ingathering (p. 215) end A.D. 1875.

LIST OF ECLIPSES OF THE SUN AND MOON

BY WHICH THE CORRECTNESS OF OUR CHRONOLOGY IS ESTABLISHED.

S, for sun ; M, for moon.

B.C. 755	S	July 16, morn., 7h. 5m., total, in Samaria, the end of Jeroboam's 41 years. Amos viii. 9.
" 682	M	Aug. 3, aft., 7h. 35m., dig. 11½, at Babylon, first year of Mardok Empadus. *Ptolemy.*
" 681	M	Jan. 28, morn., 3h. 49m., total, at Babylon, second year of Mardok Empadus. *Ptolemy.*
" 681	M	July 22, aft., 7h. 42m., total, at Babylon, second year of Mardok Empadus. *Ptolemy.*
" 671	M	Jan. 7, aft., 5h. 50m., total, at Babylon. *Ferguson.*
" 591	M	March 22, aft., 8h. 47m., total, at Babylon, fifth year of Nabopolassar. *Ptolemy.*
" 549	S	June 19, morn., 10h. 9m., lat. 35, long. 40, total, during a battle between the Medes and Lydians. *Herod.*
" 549	S	June 19, morn., 9h. 30m., total, at Jerusalem ; a sign of the ruin of the city. Jer. xv. 9.
" 503	S	June 21, aft., 4h. 18m., total at Larissa, in Media, when Cyrus took the city. *Xenophon.*
" 503	S	June 21, aft., 4h. 18m., total, at Rages, when Cyrus began to overthrow the eastern world. Isa. xiii. 10.
" 479	M	March 14, morn., 5h. 32m., total, at Babylon, the seventh year of Cambyses. *Ptolemy.*
" 479	M	Sept. 7, aft., 9h. 15m., total, at Babylon, "followed by the death of Cambyses." *Ferguson.*
" 475	M	June 26, aft., 8h. 13m., total, at Babylon in "the twentieth year of Darius Hystaspes." *Hales.*
" 465	M	June 6, morn., 0h. 25m., total, at Athens. The battle of Marathon. *Struyk.*
" 464	M	Nov. 19, morn., 0h. 35m., 9¼ dig., at Babylon, "the thirty-first year of Darius Hystaspes." *Hales.*
" 457	S	Dec. 16, morn., 9h. 15m., total, at Celænæ, when Xerxes left to invade Greece. *Herodotus.*
" 455	S	May 31, morn., 9h. 30m., 7½ dig., at the isthmus in Greece, the second year of the Persian War. *Herod.*
" 455	S	May 31, morn., 11h., total, in Asia.

B.C. 431 S Aug. 3, aft., 5h. 54m., 11 dig., at Athens, "first year of the Peloponnesian War." *Thucydides.*

" 424 S March 21, morn., 7h. 51m., 11 dig., at Athens, the eighth year of the war. *Thucydides.*

" 413 M Aug. 27, aft., 11h. 51m., $10\frac{1}{2}$ dig., at Athens, the nine teenth year of the war. *Thucydides.*

" 406 M April 15, aft., 10h. 40m., total, at Athens, the thirty sixth year of the war. *Xenophon.*

" 404 S Sept. 3, morn., 10h. 1m., $7\frac{1}{3}$ dig., at Athens, the last year of the war. *Xenophon.*

" 394 S Aug. 14, morn., 9h. 0m., $11\frac{1}{8}$ dig., in Bœatia,—"th form of the crescent of the moon." *Xenophon.*

" 331 M Sept. 20, aft., 9h. 0m., total, "eleven days before the battle of Arbela." *Plutarch.*

" 218 M Sept. 1, aft., 6h. 30m., total, "the third year of the 140th Olympiad." *Polybius.*

" 201 M Sept. 22, aft., 7h. 5m., $10\frac{3}{4}$ digits, at Alexandria, beginning 25m. after 5; moon rose at six; "eclipse began about half an hour before she rose." *Ptolemy.*

" 200 M March 20, morn., 1h. 22m., total, Athens.

" 200 M Sept. 12, morn., 3h. 0m., total, Athens, first year of the Macedonian War. *Ptolemy.*

" 188 S July 17, morn., 7h. 3m., total, at Rome; "a fearful plague;" "prayer offered up three days to avert the evil." *Livy.*

" 174 M May 1, morn., 2h. 54m., 5 digits, at Athens, "the seventh year of Ptolemy Philometer." *Ptolemy.*

" 168 M June 21, aft., 8h. 0m., total. "End of the Macedonian War." *Livy.*

" 31 S August 20, aft., 6h. 30m., $11\frac{1}{4}$ dig., at Rome. "Great eclipse." *Struyk.*

" 4 M March 13, morn., 2h. 29m., 3 dig., at Jerusalem, before the death of Herod. *Josephus.*

A.D. 14 M Sept. 27, morn., 3h. 32m., total, at Rome, 1 month and 8 days after the death of Augustus Cæsar. *Tacitus.*

" 69 M Oct. 18, aft., 11h. 25m., 9 dig., at Rome, "the year be fore the destruction of Jerusalem." *Tacitus.*

" 95 S May 22, morn., 4h. 44m., $2\frac{3}{4}$ digits, at Ephesus. Ferguson's tables make no eclipse here.

" 125 M April 5, aft., 9h. 10m., 3 digits. (*Ptole.*) Ferguson's tables only eclipse $\frac{3}{4}$ of a digit, which was too small to be seen.

CHRONOLOGICAL TABLE.

Year of the World.	Year before Christ.	Age.	Methusaleh's age		
1	4126	0		Creation of man..	Gen. i. 27
130	3996	130		Adam's age at the birth of Seth........................	v. 3
235	3891	105		Seth's age at the birth of Enos..........................	v. 6
325	3801	90		Enos's age at the birth of Cainan......................	v. 9
395	3731	70		Cainan's age at the birth of Mahalaleel..............	v. 12
460	3666	65		Mahalaleel's age at the birth of Jared................	v. 15
622	3504	162		Jared's age at the birth of Enoch.......................	v. 18
687	3439	65		Enoch's age at the birth of Methusaleh..............	v. 21
874	3252	187	187	Methusaleh's age at the birth of Lamech.........	v. 25
1056	3070	182	369	Lamech's age at the birth of Noah.....................	v. 28
1656	2470	600	969	Noah's age at the beginning of the Flood.........	vii. 6
1657	2469	1		The Flood...	viii. 13
1659	2467	2		Shem begat Arphaxad two years after the Flood.	xi. 10
1694	2432	35		Arphaxad's age at the birth of Salah.................	xi. 12
1724	2402	30		Salah's age at the birth of Eber........................	xi. 14
1758	2368	34		Eber's age at the birth of Peleg........................	xi. 16
1788	2338	30		Peleg's age at the birth of Reu..........................	xi. 18
1820	2306	32		Reu's age at the birth of Serug.........................	xi. 20
1850	2276	30		Serug's age at the birth of Nahor......................	xi. 22
1879	2247	29		Nahor's age at the birth of Terah.....................	xi. 24
2084	2042	205		Terah's age at his death.....................................	xi. 32
2085	2041	1		Abraham went to Canaan....................................	Acts vii. 4
2515	1611	430		The sojourning of the Hebrews.........................	Ex. xii. 40

Year of the World.	Year before Christ.	Cycle of Seven Years.	Cycle of Forty-nine years.	Interval.	Interval.			
2515	1611	1	1	1			Israel in the wilderness 40 years....	Josh. v. 6
2516	1610	2	2	2			The second passover observed.........	Num. ix. 3
2517	1609	3	3	3	1		Caleb's 45 years commences.........	Josh. xiv.10
2521	1605	7	7	7	5		First sabbatical year.....................	Ex. xxi. 2
2554	1572	5	40	40	38		Death of Moses..........................	Deut.xxxiv.7
2555	1571	6	41	1	39		Joshua's 25 years........................	p. 67
2556	1570	7	42	2	40		Sabbatical year..........	p. 65
2561	1565	5	47	7	45		End of Caleb's 45 years.	
2562	1564	6	48	8	1		Division of the land.......................	Josh. xiv. 5
2563	1563	7	49	9			First year of jubilee......................	Josh. xxii. 4
2579	1547	2	16	25			Joshua's death.	
2580	1546	3	17	1			Anarchy 18 years..........................	p. 68
2597	1529	6	34	18			End of anarchy.	
2598	1528	7	35	1	1		Servitude 8, and Judges 450 years...	p. 68
2605	1521	7	42	8	8		End of 8 years servitude.	
2606	1520	1	43	9	1		Rest 40 years.................................	Judg. iii. 11
2612	1514	7	49	15	7		The second jubilee.	
2645	1481	5	33	48	40		End of 40 years rest.	
2646	1480	6	34	49	1		Second servitude, 18 years............	iii. 14
2661	1465	7	49	64	16		Third jubilee.	
2663	1463	2	2	66	18		End of second servitude.	
2664	1462	3	3	67	1	1	Rest 80 years with which the Era of Ehud begins.............	p. 69, 71
2743	1383	5	33	146	80	80		
2744	1382	6	34	147	81	1	Third servitude 20 years........	Judg. iv. 3
2763	1363	4	4	166	100	20	End of third servitude.	
2764	1362	5	5	167	101	1	Rest 40 years..........................	v. 31
2803	1323	2	44	206	140	40	End of 40 years rest.	
2804	1322	3	45	207	141	1	Fourth servitude, 7 years.......	vi. 1
2808	1318	7	49	211	145	5	Year of jubilee.	

Year of the World.	Year before Christ.	Cycle of Seven Years.	Cycle of Forty-nine Years.	Judges.	Era of Ehud.	Interval.		
2810	1316	2	2	213	147	7	End of fourth servitude.	
2811	1315	3	3	214	148	1	Rest under Gideon 40 years....	Judg. viii. 28
2850	1276	7	42	253	187	40	Sabbatical year.	
2851	1275	1	43	254	188	1	Abimelech reigned 3 years......	ix. 22
2853	1273	3	45	256	190	3	End of Abimelech's reign.	
2854	1272	4	46	257	191	1	Tola judged Israel 23 years......	x. 2
2876	1250	5	19	279	213	23	End of Tola's judgeship.	
2877	1249	6	20	280	214	1	Jair judged Israel 22 years.......	x. 3
2898	1228	6	41	301	235	22	End of Jair's judgeship.	
2899	1227	7	42	302	236	1	Fifth servitude 18 years.........	x. 8
2906	1220	7	49	309	243	8	Year of jubilee.	
2916	1210	3	10	319	253	18	End of fifth servitude.	
2917	1209	4	11	320	254	1	Jephthah judged Israel 6 years	xii. 7
2922	1204	2	16	325	259	6	End of Jephthah's judgeship.	
2923	1203	4	17	326	260	1	Ibzan judged Israel 7 years.....	xii. 9
2929	1197	2	23	332	266	7	End of Ibzan's judgeship.	
2930	1196	3	24	333	267	1	Elon judged Israel 10 years....	xii. 11
2939	1187	5	33	342	276	10	End of Elon's judgeship.	
2940	1186	6	34	353	277	1	Abdon judged Israel 8 years...	xii. 14
2947	1179	6	41	350	284	8	End of Abdon's judgeship.	
2948	1178	7	42	351	285	1	Sixth servitude 40 years........	xiii. 1
2987	1139	4	32	390	324	40	End of sixth servitude.	
2988	1138	5	33	391	325	1	Eli judged Israel 40 years.......	1 Sam. iv. 18
3027	1099	2	23	430	364	40	End of Eli's judgeship.	
3028	1098	3	24	431	365	1	Seventh servitude 20 years......	vii. 2
3047	1079	1	43	450	384	20	End of Paul's 450 years..........	See B.C. 1078
3048	1078	2	44		385	1	Samuel judged 12 years...*Jose.*	b.vi.c.xiii.s.5
3059	1067	6	7		396	12	End of Samuel's judgeship.	
3060	1066	7	7		397	1	Saul reigned 40 years....	Acts xiii. 21

Year of the World.	Year before Christ.	Cycle of Seven Years.	Cycle of Forty-nine Years.	Kingdom of Israel.	Era of Ehud.	Kingdom of Judah.		
3099	1027	4	46	40	436		End of Saul's reign.	
3100	1026	5	47	1	437		David reigned 40 years..........	2 Sam. v. 4
3101	1025	6	48	2	438		{ Saul's son reigned 2 years to	2 Sam. ii. 10
3102	1024	7	49	3	439		{ The jubilee........	See B.C. 1024
3139	987	2	37	40	476		End of David's reign.	
3140	986	3	38	1	477		Solomon reigned 40 years.......	1 Kings ii. 42
3143	983	6	41	4	480		Solomon began to build the temple in the 480th year of	
3144	982	7	42	5			the era of Ehud................	p. 69
3150	976	6	48	11				
3151	975	7	49	12			The House dedicated in the 7th month in the year of jubilee	p. 72
3179	947	7	28	40			End of Solomon's reign.	
3180	946	1	29	1		1	{ Jeroboam reigned 22 years..	1 Kings xiv. 20
3181	945	2	30	2		2	{ Rehoboam reigned 17 years.	xiv. 21
3196	930	3	45	17		17	End of Rehoboam's reign.	
3197	929	4	46	*18		1	Abigam reigned 3 years.........	xv. 1, 2
3199	927	6	48	*20		3	End of Abigam's reign.	
3200	926	7	49	21		1	Asa reigned 41 years...............	xv. 9, 10
3201	925	1	50	22	1	*2	Nadab reigned 2 years..........	xv. 25
3202	924	2	2	2		*3	End of Nadab's reign.	
3203	923	3	3	1		4	Baasha reigned 24 years.........	xv. 33
3214	912	7	14	12		15	Sabbatical year..................	2 Chron. xv. 10
3225	901	4	25	23	1	*26	Elah reigned 2 years..............	1 Kings xvi. 8
3226	900	5	26	24	2	*27	End of the reign of Elah.	
3227	899	6	27	1	1	28	Tibni and Omri reigned 3 years	xvi. 21
3229	897	1	29	3	3	30	Tibni died...........................	xvi. 22
3230	896	2	30	1		*31	Omri reigned 12 years............	xvi. 23
3235	891	7	35	6	1	*36	Baasha reigned 1 year.........	2 Chron. xvi. 1
3237	889	2	37	8	1	*38	Ahab reigned 22 years..........	1 Kings xvi. 29
3240	886	5	40	11	*4	41	End of the reign of Asa.	

Year of the World.	Year before Christ.	Cycle of Seven Years.	Cycle of Forty-nine years.	Kingdom of Israel.	Interval.	Kingdom of Judah.			
3241	885	6	41	12	5	1		Jehoshaphat reigned 25 y'rs.	1 Kings xxii. 42
3242	884	7	42	6		2		Sabbatical year..................	See p. 73
3257	869	1	8	21	1	*17	1	Ahaziah reigned 2 years....	1 Kings xxii. 51
3258	868	2	9	22	2	*18	*2	Jehoram reigned 2 years.....	2 Kings i. 17
3259	867	3	10	1		19		Jehoram reigned 12 years...	iii. 1
3263	863	7	14	5		23	1	Jehoram reigned 8 years.....	viii. 16, 17
3265	861	2	16	7		25	3	End of Jehoshaphat's reign.	
3269	857	6	20	*11		7	1	Ahaziah reigned 1 year.......	viii. 26; ix. 29
3270	856	7	21	*12		8		End of Jehoram's reign.	
3271	855	1	22	1		1		{ Jehu reigned 28 years......	x. 36
3272	854	2	23	2		2		{ Athaliah reigned 6 years.	xi. 3
3276	850	6	27	6		6		Athaliah slain....................	xi. 16
3277	849	7	28	*7		1		{ Sabbatical year.............. { Jehoash reigned 40 years.	xi. 4, 5 xii. 1
3298	828	7	49	28		22		Year of jubilee.	
3299	827	1	50	1		*23		Jehoahaz reigned 17 years...	xiii. 1
3313	813	1	15	15		*37		Jehoash associated with his father.	
3314	812	2	16	16	1	38		Jehoash reigned 16 years....	xiii. 10
3315	811	3	17	17	*2	39		End of Jehoahaz's reign.	
3316	810	4	18	3		40	1	Amaziah reigned 29 years...	xiv. 1, 2
3329	797	3	31	16		14		End of Jehoash's reign.	
3330	796	4	32	1		*15		Jeroboam reigned 41 years..	xiv. 23
3344	782	4	46	15		29		End of Amaziah's reign.	
3345	781	5	47	16		1		Amaziah fled to Lachish, and there remained 12 years..	2 Chron. xxv. 27
3356	770	2	9	27		12		Death of Amaziah.	
3357	769	3	10	*28		1		Azariah reigned 52 years...	2 Kings xv. 1, 2
3370	756	2	23	41		14		End of Jeroboam's 41st year.	
3374	755	3	24	1		15		Eclipse of the sun.............	Amos viii. 9
3393	733	4	46	22		37		Jeroboam's death...............	See p. 77
3394	732	5	47	6m.		38		Zachariah reigned 6 months.	2 Kings xv. 8

Year of the World.	Year before Christ.	Cycle of Seven Years.	Cycle of Forty-nine Years.	Kingdom of Israel.	Kingdom of Judah.		Kingdom of Babylon.	Kingdom of Media.		
3395	731	6	48	1mo.	*39				Shallum reigned 1 month.............	2 Kings xv. 13
3396	730	7	49	1	40				Menahem reigned 10 years............	xv. 17
3405	721	2	9	10	49				End of Menahem's reign.	
3406	720	3	10	1	*50				Pekahiah reigned 2 years.............	xv. 23
3407	719	4	11	2	51				End of Pekahiah's reign.	
3408	718	5	12	1	*52				Pekah reigned 20 years.....	xv. 27
3409	717	6	13	*2	1				Jotham reigned 16 years................	xv. 33
3424	702	7	28	*17	16				Ahaz associated with his father.	
3425	701	1	29	18	1	17			Ahaz reigned 16 years.............	xvi. 1, 2
3427	699	3	31	20	3	19			End of Pekah's reign.	
3428	698	4	32	1	4	*20			Hoshea began to reign in the 20th year of Jotham...........	xv. 30
3436	690	5	40	9	*12				Hoshea's 9th year commenced.	xvii. 1
3437	689	6	41	1	13				Hoshea reigned 9 years more...	xviii. 10
3439	687	1	43	*3	15				Hezekiah associated with his father.	
3440	686	2	44	4	16				Hezekiah reigned 29 years	xviii. 1, 2
3443	683	5	47	7	4	1			The 3 years war began.....	xviii. 10
3444	682	6	48	8	5		1		Merodach reigned 12 y'rs.	*Ptolemy*
3445	681	7	49	9	6		2		End of the Kingdom of Israel in the jubilee.	
3446	680	1	50		7		3		The seven times begin.....	Lev. xxvi. 28
3452	674	7	7		13		9		Sabbatical year.......	Isa. xxxvii. 30
3455	671	3	10		16		12		End of Merodach's reign..................	Isa. xxxix. 1
3456	670	4	11		17		1		Archian 5 years.......	*Ptolemy*
3460	666	1	15		21		5	1	Media 6 years.........	p. 84
3461	665	2	16		22		1	2	Interregnum 1 year..	p. 85
3462	664	3	17		23		1	3	Belibus 3 years.......	*Ptolemy*
3464	662	5	19		25		3	5	End of Belibus's reign.	
3465	661	6	20		26		1	6	Apronadius 6 years..	*Ptolemy*
3466	660	7	21		27		2	1	Deioces 53 years......	*Herodotus*
3468	658	2	23		29		4	3	End of Hezekiah's reign.	

Year of the World.	Year before Christ.	Cycle of Seven Years.	Cycle of Forty-nine years.	Kingdom of Judah.	Kingdom of Babylon.	Kingdom of Media.			
3469	657	3	24	1	5	4		Manasseh reigned 55 years...2 Chron.xxxiii.1	
3470	656	4	25	2	6	5		Death of Apronadius.	
3471	655	5	26	3	1	6		Regibelus reigned 1 year.........	*Ptolemy*
3472	654	6	27	4	1	7		Mesessemordak reigned 4 years..	*Ptolemy*
3475	651	2	30	7	4	10		End of Mesessemordak's reign.	
3476	650	3	31	8	1	11		Esarhaddon reigned 13 years....	*Ptolemy*
3488	638	1	43	20	13	23		End of Esarhaddon's reign.	
3489	637	2	44	21	1	24		Saosduchin reigned 20 years.....	*Ptolemy*
3508	618	7	14	40	20	43		End of Saosduchin's reign.	
3509	617	1	15	41	1	44		Chyniladon reigned 24 years....	*Ptolemy*
3518	608	3	24	50	10	53		End of Deioces's reign.	
3519	607	4	25	51	11	1		Phraortes reigned 22 years.......	*Herodotus*
3523	603	1	29	55	15	5		End of Manasseh's reign.	
3524	602	2	30	1	16	6		Amon reigned 2 years........2 Chron. xxxiii. 21	
3525	601	3	31	2	17	7		End of Amon's reign.	
3526	600	4	32	1	18	8		Josiah reigned 31 years............	xxxiv. 1
3530	596	1	36	5	22	12		End of Chyniladon's reign.	
3531	595	2	37	6	1	13		Nabopolassar reigned 29 years...	*Berosus*
3539	587	3	45	14	9	21	1	Jeremiah's 23 years.........	Jer. xxv. 3
3540	586	4	46	15	10	22	2	End of Phraortes's reign..	
3541	585	5	47	16	11	1	3	Cyaxares reigned 40 years.	*Herodotus*
3543	583	7	49	19	14	4	6	The great jubilee passover	See p. 86
		1	50					The holy convocation.......	Lev. xxiii. 7
		2	2					2d day of unleavened bread	Lev. xxiii. 6
		3	3					3d " " "	
		4	4					4th " " "	
		5	5					5th " " "	
		6	6					6th " " "	
		7	7					7th day "holyconvocation"	xxiii. 8
3551	575	1	8	26	21	11	13	"The morrow after the sabbath"	xxiii. 15
3556	570	6	13	31	26	16	18	Death of Josiah..........2 Chron. xxxv. 24	
3557	569	7	14	3m.	27	17	19	Jehoahaz reigned 3 months	xxxvi. 2

Year of the World.	Year before Christ.	Cycle of Seven Years.	Cycle of Forty-nine Years.	Kingdom of Judah.	Kingdom of Babylon.	Kingdom of Media.			
3558	568	1	15	1	28	18	20	Jehoiakim reigned 11 years..	2 Ch.xxxvi.5
3559	567	2	16	2	29	19	21	End of Nabopolassar's reign.	
3560	566	3	17	3	1	20	22	Interregnum 1 year..........	*Berosus*
3561	565	4	18	*4	1	21	23	Nebuchadnezzar 43 years....	*Ptolemy*
3565	561	1	22	*8	5	25		{ In the 8th of Jehoiakim...	See p. 98
3566	560	2	23	9	6	26	1	{ The 70 y'rs service began	Jer. xxv. 11
3568	558	*4	25	11	8	28	3	Jehoiachin 3mo.and 10 days	2 Ch.xxxvi.9
3569	557	5	26	1	9	29	4	{ Zedekiah reigned 11 years { The 70 yr's captivitybegan	xxxvi.11 p. 103
3973	553	2	30	5	13	33	8	The 30th year..........See p. 108,	Ezek. i. 1
3578	548	7	35	10	18	38	13	Sabbatical year........	See p. 110
3579	547	1	36	11	19	39	14	End of the kingdom of Judah	p. 113
3580	546	2	37		20	40	15	End of Cyaxares's reign.....	p. 109
3581	545	3	38		21	1	16	Astyages reigned 35 years...	*Herodotus*
3592	534	7	49		32	12	27	Year of jubilee......	See p. 114
3603	523	4	11		43	23	38	End of Nebuchadnezzar's reign.	
3604	522	5	12		1	24	39	Evil-merodach 18 years.....	*Josephus*
3613	513	7	21		10	33	48	Evil-merodach's exile...... .	See p. 118
3614	512	1	22	1	1	34	49	Neriglissar reigned 4 years.	*Berosus*
3615	511	2	23	2	2	35	50	End of Astyages' reign.	
3616	510	3	24	3	3	1	51	Cyrus reigned 29 years.......	*Herodotus*
3617	509	4	25	4	4	2	52	End of Neriglissar's reign.	
3618	508	5	26	5	9m.	3	53	Labosordacus 9 months......	*Berosus*
3619	507	6	27	6	1	4	54	Belshazzar reigned 17 years	*Berosus*
3620	506	7	28	7	2	5	55	The 7th year of Evil-merodach's exile.........	See p. 119
3621	505	1	29	18	3	6	56	Death of Evil-merodach.	
3635	491	1	43		17	20	70	End of the kingdom of Babylon........	p. 119
3536	490	2	44		1	21		68 Darius reigned 2 years..	p. 120
3637	489	3	45		2	22		69 End of Darius's reign.	
3638	488	4	46			23		70 End of 70 y'rs captivity.	p. 121

Year of the World.	Year before Christ.	Cycle of Seven Years.	Cycle of Forty-nine Years.	Kingdom of Persia.			Mourning.	Indignation.		
3638	488	4	46	23	1		00	59	Ezra's first of Cyrus and	Ezra i. 1.
3639	487	5	47	24	2		58	60	Beginning of Daniel's 69 w'ks.	See p. 121
3641	485	7	49	26	4	1	60	62	Cambyses associated with	
3642	484	1	50	27	5	2	61	63	his father, and reigned 7 y'rs	p. 148
3644	482	3	3	29	7	4	63	65	End of Cyrus's reign.	
3645	481	4	4			5	64	66	Cambyses invadeth Egypt.....	p. 150
3647	479	6	6			7	66	68	Death of Cambyses.............	p. 151
3648	478	7	7	1	17		67	69	The reign of Darius............	p. 151
3649	477	1	8	2	18		68	70	End of 70 years indignation	p. 154
3650	476	2	9	3	19		69		in the 2d year of Darius	Zach. i. 12
3651	475	3	10	4	20		70		End of 70 years mourning...	See p. 154
3653	473	5	12	6	22				The temple finished............	Ezra vi. 15
3661	465	6	20	14	30		1		The battle of Marathon.......	See p. 154
3662	464	7	21	15	31	1	2		Eclipse of the moon...........	p. 155
3665	461	3	24	18	34	4	5	1	Xerxes associated with his father.............................	p. 155
3667	459	5	26	20	36		7	3	Death of Darius.	

OLYMPIC GAMES.

The Olympic games, like that of the Sabbatical year, is an important cycle in establishing the correct chronology; for example, the year Xerxes invaded Greece (see p. 156), and after passing the 105th Olympiad, or B.C. 360, the number of the Olympiad alluded to by historians may be considered reliable: hence, becomes an important era. But when we go beyond B.C. 360, they are of no worth in chronology, save that of a cycle of four years without any regard either to the number of the Olympiad, or the person recorded as victor in a given one; for Plutarch informs us that the "register of the Olympiades was first published by Hippias about the 105th Olympiad, which was done from no certain materials." (*Isaac Newton's Chronology*, p. 47.) Hence, B.C. 360 may be considered the epoch of the beginning of the Olympiads; and as we would have nothing in our Tables of Chronology that cannot be considered reliable, we—omitting the number—have only given the cycle down to the 105th Olympiad, with which we commence to record the number.

Year of the World.	Year before Christ.	Cycle of Seven Years.	Cycle of Forty-nine years.	Olympic Games.	Kingdom of Persia.				
3668	458	6	27	3	1	8		Xerxes reigned 21 years............	*Ptolemy*
3669	457	7	28	4	2	9		Eclipse of the sun....................	See p. 155
3670	456	1	29	1	3	10		Xerxes invaded Greece in the 10th after the battle of Marathon...	See p. 155
3671	455	2	30	2	4			Eclipse of the sun....................	p. 156
3680	446	4	39	3	13	1		Artaxerxes associated with his father, and reigned 41 years...	*Ptolemy*
3688	438	5	47	3	21	9		End of Xerxes's reign.	
3689	437	6	48	4	1	10		The reign of Artaxerxes	See p. 157
3695	431	5	5	2	7	16		Ezra went up to Jerusalem.........	Ezra vii. 8
3700	426	3	10	3	12	21		Beginning of Daniel's 2300 days	p. 160
3703	423	6	13	2	15	24	1	Darius associated with his father, and reigned 19 years	*Ptolemy*
3708	418	4	18	3	20	29	6	Nehemiah began the wall......	See p. 178
5720	406	2	30	3	32	41	18	Daniel's 62 weeks commenced	p. 179
3721	405	3	31	4			19	End of reign of Dariu sNothus.	
3722	404	4	32	1	1			Artaxerxes reigned 46 years	*Ptolemy*
3766	360	6	27	105	45			The 105th Olympiad............	See p. 244
3767	359	7	28	2	46			End of Artaxerxes's reign.	
3768	358	1	29	3	1			Ochus reigned 21 years.........	*Ptolemy*
3788	338	7	49	3	21			End of the reign of Ochus.	
3789	337	1	50	4	1			Arogus reigned 2 years.........	*Ptolemy*
3790	336	2	2	111	2			End of Arogus's reign.	
3791	335	3	3	2	1			Darius reigned 4 years..........	*Ptolemy*
3794	332	6	6	112	4			End of the kingdom of Persia.	
3795	531	7	7	2		1		Alexander reigned 8 years.....	*Ptolemy*
3802	324	7	14	114		8		End of the reign of Alexander	
3803	323	1	15	2		1		Philip reigned 7 years..........	*Ptolemy*
3809	317	7	21	4		7		End of the reign of Philip.	
3810	316	1	22	116		1		Alexander reigned 12 years....	*Ptolemy*
3814	312	5	26	117		5	1	Era of the Seleucidæ...........	See p. 179
3821	305	5	33	4		12	8	End of Alexander's reign.	

Year of the World.	Year before Christ.	Cycle of Seven Years.	Cycle of Forty-nine Years.	Olympic Games.	Era of the Selencidæ.					
3822	304	6	34	119	9	1			The Ptolemys reigned 224 years	*Ptolemy*
2963	163	7	28	2	150	142			Sabbatical year........................	See p. 179
3991	135	7	7	2	178	170			Sabbatical year........................	p. 179
4045	81	5	12	4	232	224			End of the reign of the Ptolemys	
4046	80	6	13	175	233	1			Dionysius reigned 29 years......	*Ptolemy*
4074	50	6	41	182	261	29			End of Dionysius's reign	
4075	51	7	42	2	262	1			Cleopatra reigned 22 years........	*Ptolemy*
4085	41	3	3	*4	270	11			The 4th year of the 184th Olympiad..................................	See p. 180
4086	40	4	4	185	273	12	1		Herod reigned 37 years.......	p. 179
4089	37	7	7	4	276	15	4	1	Herod reigned 24 years.. Sabbatical year..............	p. 180 p. 179
4095	31	6	13	2	282	21	10	7	End of Cleopatra's reign	
4096	30	7	14	3	283	1	11	8	Augustus reigned 43 y'rs	*Ptolemy*
4121	5	4	39	4	308	26	36	33	End of Daniel's 69 weeks	p. 180
4122	4	5	40	194	309	27	37	34	Death of Herod..............	p. 180
4125	1	1	43	4	312	30			The year B.C. 1.	
4126	1	2	44	195		31			The year A.D. 1.	
4133	8	2	2	4		38			Christ 12 years old........	Luke ii. 42
4137	12	6	6	4		42	1		Tiberius associated with Augustus.	
4138	13	7	7	198		43	2		End of Augustus's reign.	
4139	14	1	8	2		1	3		Tiberius reigned 22 years.	*Ptolemy*
4151	26	6	20	2		13	15		Tiberius's 15th year ends August 28.	
4154	29	2	23	202	434	16	18		End of Daniel's 62 weeks	See p. 198
4155	30	3	24	2		17	19		Crucifixion	p. 194
4160	35	1	29			22	24		End of Tiberius's reign.	
4261	36	2	30			1			Caius reigned 4 years.....	*Ptolemy*
4164	39	5	33			4			End of Caius's reign.	
4165	40	6	34			1			Claudius reigned 14 years	*Ptolemy*
4178	53	5	47			14			End of the reign of Claudius.	
4179	54	6	48			1			Nero reigned 14 years...	*Ptolemy*

Year of the World.	Year after Christ.	Cycle of Seven Years.	Cycle of Forty-nine Years.	Kingdom of Rome.			
4190	65	3	10	12	490	End of Daniel's 70 weeks..............	See p. 199
4191	66	4	11	13	1	The 1 week covenant.....................	Dan. ix. 27
4192	67	5	12	14	2	End of the reign of Nero.	
4193	68	6	13	1	3	Galba and others reigned 1 y'r. *Jose.* b. iv. c. ix. s. 2	
4194	69	7	14	1	4	Vespasian reigned 10 years..........	*Ptolemy*
4195	70	1	15	2	5	Sacrifice ceased in the midst of the week......................................	See p. 200
8196	71	2	16	3	6	The sixth year of the war.	
4197	72	3	17	4	7	End of the 1 week covenant..........	p. 201
4658	533	2	37	1	1	Beginning of the 1335 and 1290 days	p. 206
4663	538	7	42	5	5	Beginning of Daniel's "times and the dividing of time"..............	p. 207
4754	629	7	35	96	96	John's 42 months begin...............	p. 208
5905	1780	3	10	1247	1247	The sun darkened........................	p. 24
5944	1819	7	49	1286	1286	The year of jubilee.	
5948	1823	4	4	1290	1290	End of Daniel's 1290 days............	p. 208
5958	1833	7	14	1300		The falling of the stars................	p. 26
5968	1843	3	24	1310		The midnight cry........................	Matt. xxv. 6
5969	1844	4	25	1311	1	The Church in "mourning three full weeks"......................................	Dan. x. 2
5989	1864	3	45	1331	21	The wise have an "understanding of the vision"...........................	p. 209
5993	1868	7	49	1335		End of Daniel's 1335 days in	
5993	1868	7	49			The great Jubilee of jubilees.	
5994	1869	1	50		1	The feast of ingathering............	p. 215
5995	1870	2	2		2	And feast of tabernacles...........	p. 216
5996	1871	3	3		3	The 3d year of Ezekiel's 7 years war..	p. 213
3997	1872	4	4		4	The 4th year of the judgment.......	Dan. vii. 26
5998	1873	5	5		5	The 5th year of the 7 last plagues	Rev. xxi. 9
5999	1874	6	6		6	The 6th year of "trouble such as never was"................................	Dan. xii. 1
6000	1875	7	7	2300		End of the 2300 days and Moses's seven times with the beginning of the great sabbath of rest.	

INDEX.

APPENDIX.

UPON THE IDENTIFICATION OF LOUIS NAPOLEON AS THE COMING ANTICHRIST, OR MAN OF SIN.*

THE increasing number of writers who maintain that the present Emperor of France is to be shortly manifested in the character of the last personal Antichrist, or individual man of sin, entitles this question to at least some measure of attention in any modern work on prophecy.

Among the earliest advocates of the prophetical interpretation upon which this belief is grounded, were Purves, J. H. Frere, and the Rev. Edward Irving, of the Presbyterian Church, and the Revs. G. S. Faber and H. Gauntlett of the Church of England. About the year 1818 to 1821, they all proclaimed, either in their writings or in their discourses, which were afterwards published, that another French Emperor, like the first Napoleon, would arise a few years before 1864–68, and become the infidel Antichrist, or commander-in-chief of the armies of the world that are foretold in Rev. xiii. and xix., Ezek. xxxix., Zech. xiv., &c., to be gathered together by unclean spirits into a place, called in the Hebrew tongue, Armageddon, and there make war with the Lamb, and to be crushed in the wine press of divine wrath, at his descent upon Mount Olivet, preparatorily to the ushering in of the Millennium. Frere and Irving arrived at this conclusion from Rev. xvii. where the seven heads of the beast or Roman Empire are explained to be seven kings (or dynasties); five are fallen, and one (the sixth) is, and the other (the seventh) is not yet come; and when he cometh, he must continue a short space; and the beast that was and is not, even he is the eighth, and is of the seven, and goeth into perdition.

The sixth head, or form of government, of which it was here said by the angel, in A.D. 97, "one is," has been admitted, by the generality of

* By the request of a friend, we give this a place here, for though it exhibits a shade of difference as to opinion on some things, from that of the author of the "Sealed Book of Daniel Opened," it was written by a true believer in the soon appearing and kingdom of Christ. If it be asked how could we who rejecting the views of those who wrote before the time of the end, give this a place which claims as authority the opinion of those who wrote before that time, we answer, this article is concerning that which was not sealed (Rev. xxii. 10). But we were disclosing that which was "closed up and sealed till the time of the end" (Dan. xii. 9).

expositors, to be without doubt the Roman emperorship, then existing under Domitian as its representative; and the five previous heads, which had then fallen or passed away, are usually reckoned to have been the kings, consuls, tribunes, decemvirs, and dictators. After Domitian, there was an unbroken chain or series of Roman Emperors, residing either in the Eastern or Western Roman Empire, until A.D. 1806, when the last of them, Francis, Emperor of Germany, being defeated at Austerlitz, resigned the title and authority of Roman Emperor, of which the German emperors had for many years been the crowned representatives. The seventh head, concerning which it was said, "the other is not yet come, and when he cometh, he must continue a short space," was unquestionably the Napoleon dynasty, which as embodied in Napoleon I, became the head of the chief part of Europe, and the Roman earth, immediately after the fall of the sixth head, and continued for a short space, from 1806 to 1815, when it was overthrown at the battle of Waterloo. The beast then became headless, or politically dead or non-existent, so that it could at such time be properly described as "the beast that was and is not;" and this is the crisis in its history which its picture in Rev. xvii prospectively described, for the angel pointing to the scarlet-colored beast exhibited in this chapter says, "The beast that thou sawest *was and is not*, and shall ascend out of the bottomless pit, and go into perdition." It was not, therefore, forever to remain non-existent, as "the beast that was and is not," but was to reascend to life and power, and then speedily go into utter perdition; and at this ascension from the tomb of political death, it was to become, as it were, an eighth head to itself, "the beast that was and is not, even he is the eighth, and is of the seven, and goeth into perdition." Although it arises under an apparently eighth head, yet it is in reality just one of the former seven heads, evidently the seventh head revived. The fact of the beast becoming its own head, obviously is fulfilled by the power to elect their head being vested in the body of the people. The period of the beast's re-existence under this revived seventh or eighth head, prior to its ultimate perdition at Armageddon, is stated in verse 12 to be "one hour" (compare Rev. iii. 10, xiv. 7, xviii. 10), and is further revealed in Rev. xiii. 5, to be forty-two months, that is, in the proper literal day fulfilment, three and a half years. The Roman Empire, which "was" under its seventh head, the Napoleon dynasty, from 1806 to 1815, now (1863) "is not," in other words, is headless, for it is not existing under any political federal head, over all the principal countries within its limits, but it yet shall ascend to political life and unity under its seventh head, or Napoleon dynasty revived for "one hour," or three and a half years, and then it shall entirely perish at Christ's descent at Armageddon.

Louis Napoleon is making great and wonderful progress in restoring the Napoleon dynasty in his own person, to the position of headship over Europe, and as soon as he shall have succeeded, like Napoleon I, in inducing the leading sovereigns within the limits of the original Roman

Empire, formally to acknowledge him as their federal head, and themselves as his vassals or vicegerents, the seventh revived, or eighth head will then be completely formed. The Roman Empire will by that time be divided among exactly ten kings or horns (Rev. xvii. 12), five of whom will respectively rule over the northeast African coast, and Alexander's original four horn kingdoms, Greece, Egypt, Syria, and the rest of Turkey; the other five kings dividing among themselves England, France, Spain, and Portugal, Switzerland, Bavaria, and Italy, Southern Austria, and the northwest coast of Africa. These ten crowned horn-kings will receive and exercise their kingly power only for "one hour," or "forty-two months" conjunctively and synchronically with Louis Napoleon; and this will constitute his complete development as the eighth head. A similar prophetic declaration of the rise, overthrow, and resurrection of the Napoleon dynasty is given in Rev. xiii. as well as Rev. xvii. Just before the final literal day, forty-two months or three and a half years of the universal massacre of saints, and worship of the beast's last head, the apostle beholds the beast or Roman Empire arise, with its ten horn-kings crowned; and he specially notices that "one of its heads (obviously its seventh head), had been wounded to death, and its deadly wound was healed, and all the world wondered after the beast;" crying out in their amazement, "who is like unto the beast? who is able to make war with him?" and therefore "power was given unto him," to continue forty and two months; "and he makes war with the saints, and overcomes them, and power was given him over all kindreds, and tongues, and nations; and all that dwell upon the earth shall worship him," except the righteous. These words in Rev. xiii, graphically describe the future history of the Roman Empire, under the rulership of the person who shall fully revive the short-lived, sword-slain seventh head, or Napoleon dynasty, which was wounded to death by the sword of military violence at Waterloo in 1815, but which is rapidly being healed of its deadly wound by Louis Napoleon.

More than twenty expositors have maintained the strong probability, if not absolute certainty, of Louis Napoleon being the future personal infidel Antichrist, or last head of the Roman Empire. Among them may be enumerated the following clergymen of the Church of England: the Revs. G. S. Faber, Dr. Keith, E. Nangle, editor of the "Achill Herald," Maynell Whittemore, W. Morehead, J. S. Jackson, R. A. Purdon, author of the able monthly publication, "The Last Vials," J. Brodie, R. Polwhele; also Major Phillips, A. Rees, E. Taunton, A. Porter, H. Verner, Paul Foskett, T. Stephen, J. Frere, E. Irving, Revs. Dr. Seiss, the eloquent author of "The Last Times," R. Beale, author of the English work, "Armageddon" (at Macintosh's, London), R. C. Shimeall, and M. Baxter.*

* Note by the Editor. Books recommended, "The Destined Monarch of the World," by Rev. M. Baxter, of the Church of England, is the most comprehensive, and by far the most able work that has been written on the subject. All the prophetic Scriptures

Scarcely anything can be more remarkable than the above mentioned predictions of Frere, Faber, Gauntlett, and Irving made in 1818–22 as to the certainty of the Napoleonic power being re-established over Europe, a few years before 1864–8, since it was the slain seventh head, which was foreshown to be resuscitated as an eighth head, and then to perish at Armageddon. The reason why they expected the rise and overthrow of this seventh-eighth head about or soon after 1864–8, was because the various chronological dates were understood by them as by more than a hundred other expositors, to terminate about that epoch.

There are other important points of identity between Louis Napoleon and the future last Antichrist, such as his name *Napoleon* or *Apollyon* evidently being the predicted name of the Antichrist, and also the number 666 being contained in his name *Louis*, in its proper Latin form *Ludovicus* (Rev. ix. 11, xiii. 18), and in his other name *Napoleon*, in the dative of its original Greek form *Ναπολεοντι*, and the Greeks always inscribed the names of their deities upon their worshippers or altars or temples in the dative case, as in Acts xvii. 23. Again, his possession of the city of Rome as a Roman head (Rev. xvii. 7–11), his great military strength (Rev. xiii. 6), his support of the scarlet harlot or Romish hierarchy by his bayonets in Rome (Rev. xvii.), his growing supremacy over the future ten horn-kingdoms, are all noteworthy characteristics of the predicted Antichrist.

In the work on Louis Napoleon by the Rev. M. Baxter, all the points are treated upon at some length, and numerous extracts are adduced from various writers.

www.ingramcontent.com/pod-product-compliance
Lightning Source LLC
LaVergne TN
LVHW010254110826
845151LV00004B/1468

* 9 7 8 1 4 2 5 5 2 2 3 8 4 *